New Rhetorics for Contemporary Legal Discourse

New Rhetorics for Contemporary Legal Discourse

Edited by Angela Condello

EDINBURGH
University Press

Edinburgh University Press is one of the leading university presses in the UK. We publish academic books and journals in our selected subject areas across the humanities and social sciences, combining cutting-edge scholarship with high editorial and production values to produce academic works of lasting importance. For more information visit our website: edinburghuniversitypress.com

© editorial matter and organisation Angela Condello, 2020, 2022
© the chapters their several authors, 2020, 2022

Edinburgh University Press Ltd
The Tun – Holyrood Road
12 (2f) Jackson's Entry
Edinburgh EH8 8PJ

First published in hardback by Edinburgh University Press 2020

Typeset in 10/12 Goudy Old Style by
IDSUK (DataConnection) Ltd

A CIP record for this book is available from the British Library

ISBN 978 1 4744 5056 0 (hardback)
ISBN 978 1 4744 5057 7 (paperback)
ISBN 978 1 4744 5058 4 (webready PDF)
ISBN 978 1 4744 5059 1 (epub)

The right of the contributors to be identified as authors of this work has been asserted in accordance with the Copyright, Designs and Patents Act 1988 and the Copyright and Related Rights Regulations 2003 (SI No. 2498).

Contents

List of Contributors — vi

Introduction: New Rhetoric's Tattered Examples — 1
Peter Goodrich

1. Exemplarity and the Resonance of Reasoning — 9
   Mark Antaki
2. In and 'Out of Joint', In and Out of the Norm: On Rhetoric and Law — 28
   Angela Condello
3. From the Norms–Facts Dichotomy to the System–Problem Connection in the Judicial Realisation of Law: Logical Deduction v. Analogical Judgment in Adjudication — 37
   Ana Margarida Simões Gaudêncio
4. Multiculturalism and Criminal Law: Between the Universal and the Particular — 50
   Leandro Santos Da Guarda
5. Cognitive Populism: A Semiotic Reading of the Dialectics Type/Token — 66
   Massimo Leone
6. Exemplarity as Concreteness, or the Challenge of Institutionalising a Productive Circle between Past and Present, Old and New — 83
   José Manuel Aroso Linhares
7. What is Happening to the Norm? Gender as Paradigm of a Deformalised Neo-legal Positivism — 101
   Silvia Niccolai
8. Hypothetically Speaking: How to Argue about Meaning — 119
   Karen Petroski
9. Showing by Fiction: Audience of Extra-legal References in Judicial Decisions — 139
   Terezie Smejkalová
10. Law as a System of *Topoi*: Sources of Arguments v. Sources of Law — 156
    Anita Soboleva

Index — 171

Contributors

Mark Antaki, Associate Professor, Faculty of Law, McGill University (mark.antaki@mcgill.ca)

Angela Condello, Assistant Professor of Legal Philosophy, University of Messina, Law Department; Adjunct Professor and Jean Monnet Module Holder, University of Torino (acondello@unime.it)

Ana Margarida Simões Gaudêncio, Assistant Professor of Legal Theory and Philosophy of Law (Faculty of Law), University of Coimbra Institute for Legal Research (UCILeR), University of Coimbra (anagaude@fd.uc.pt)

Leandro Santos Da Guarda, Federal Attorney at the Brazilian Attorney General's Office, PhD in Legal Studies from Roma Tre University (leandro.guarda@agu.gov.br)

Peter Goodrich hobbles temporalities and accentuates diagrammatic spaces between New York (Cardozo Law School), London (Birkbeck College) and Abu Dhabi (New York University).

Massimo Leone, Professor of Semiotics, University of Turin and Shanghai University (massimo.leone@unito.it)

José Manuel Aroso Linhares, Full Professor of Legal Theory and Philosophy of Law (Faculty of Law), University of Coimbra Institute for Legal Research (UCILeR), University of Coimbra (linhares@fd.uc.pt)

Silvia Niccolai, Professor of Constitutional Law, University of Cagliari (niccolai@unica.it)

Karen Petroski, Professor of Law, Saint Louis University (karen.petroski@slu.edu)

Terezie Smejkalová, Assistant Professor of Legal Theory, Masaryk University (terezie.smejkalova@law.muni.cz)

Anita Soboleva, Associate Professor of the Department of Legal Theory and History of Law, National Research University – Higher School of Economics (asoboleva@hse.ru)

Introduction

New Rhetoric's Tattered Examples

Peter Goodrich

> To thee I send this written ambassage,
> To witness duty, not to show my wit
> (. . .)
> Till whatsoever star that guides my moving
> Points on me graciously with fair aspect
> And puts apparel on my tatter'd loving,
> To show me worthy of thy sweet respect.
>
> Shakespeare, Sonnet 26

There has been no shortage of new rhetorics in the modern era and in the present volume another morphosis, the contemporary novelties of persuasion, is tracked anew. There is something of a genre, a rhetoric of the *novum*, that accompanies the proliferation of new media and causes disruption and disturbance in the supposed stasis, the permanence, publicity and authority of law. A genealogy of new rhetorics would thus take account of a variety of different contexts of oratorical renovation and their disciplinary proponents and limitations. The most notable instances were the late Enlightenment, associated particularly with Scottish philosophical elaborations, Nietzsche's lectures on eloquence and then the better-known or at least more jurisprudentially recognised Belgian *nouvelle rhétorique* promulgated as a *logique juridique* by Chaïm Perelman.[1] It is in relation primarily to the latter that the current upsurge takes its place as something of an inversion of the earlier juridification of the rhetorical in favour now of a recognition of the inevitable and critically contested persuasiveness of law. As belief in the inexorable logic of law, the authority of the legal norm and validity of juristic examples dims and wanes, it is no longer rhetoric that draws on law but rather the jurists who need to legitimate judgment through mustering the categories and borrowing the performative techniques of a discipline of persuasion that had previously been viewed as not simply impertinent to the gravitas of justice but actively misleading if inserted into the logic of law. The much maligned flowers of rhetoric are now the seeds of survival of an embattled normative form.

---

[1] Most notably in Perelman (1976). For a broad contemporary overview, see MacDonald (2017).

The context of the current work, its novelty, lies primarily in the recognition and attempt to come to terms with the new media of legal dissemination, the anarchy of multiplications, the exigencies of a novel episteme and techne. Advanced algorithms of execution, proliferating platforms, and the mobile optimisation of bytes and nibbles, screenshots, gifs, tweets, emojis, emoticons and more unleash the law from its earlier methodological norm, *scrutamini scripturas*, and its archival and disciplinary restraint, its biblically endorsed and exegetically composed transmission of *exemplum* and norm. Law is in transition in the forms of its transmission, changing gender, performance, sex, identification, level, platform and place. The new rhetoric is necessarily gauged to the immediate, plural in forms, aligned or equiparated to disruption and, as adverted already, engaged not simply in the disturbance of prior forms, hierarchies and modes of promulgation but also in upending and inverting the priority of law over rhetoric to recognise both the prevalence and the pre-eminence of the discipline and methods of persuasion as the vital source of the survival of law. Rhetoric becomes the carapace that protects and the skin that joins an antiquated legality to the novel forums and disparate relays of contemporary, exponentially connected public spheres.

1. IMMEDIACY AND PLURALITY

For roughly a millennium and a half, law has existed in the stable and relatively unchanging form of written collections, the *Corpus Iuris Civilis*, of course, in its trinitarian Roman form, and latterly under the rubric *secundum* in many US jurisdictions where formality is prized as much as anything else as a bulwark against the perception of law's novelty. In the paradoxically unwritten law of England and its dominions, it is nonetheless, since the early modern era, since the *Reports* and *Institutes* of Sir Edward Coke – the great fabricator and chef of English jurisprudence – the various breviaries and latterly the official transcriptions and collations of decided cases, nonetheless a matter simply of a different set of authoritative collections, separate collects, other modes of supposedly permanent inscription, of print, vellum, leather and library. Hermeneutics has thus had priority over rhetoric, understood as orality, and so the linear over the ambulatory, schemata over performance and event.

Hermeneutics as a textual discipline requires critical distance and takes time, scrutiny of the text and interpretation of what were classically the four levels of exegetical analysis as applied in legal elaborations.[2] The text was the marker of stability, the expression of publicity and harbinger of priority, tradition and authority. The text, the books of the law, was in early *emblemata* becomes an image of permanence, of a legality that did not change – captured in depictions of immortality, *vivitur ingenio*, or more commonly in the maxim *verba volant scripta manent*.

---

[2] On critique in its contemporary senses, see Felski (2018). The best account of the levels of exegetical analysis is to be found in de Lubac (1998).

The archive was monumental and solid, guarded, sacral in aura and subject to rites and ceremonies of access and distribution. The tomes were tombs, coffins of knowledge, housed and restrained, curated and unbending. The aura of the text, the atmosphere of library and archive, the wound of inscription all signify a temporal plenitude, an anachronic coherence and stability preserved in a language that earlier lawyers viewed as a geometry untainted by and impervious to quotidian use and political change. The medium of legality was in significant part the message of law in the permanent form of print and portrait, bar and throne, thresholds, columns and costumes. Law did not die in large measure because of the *longue durée* of its architectural and scriptural forms, the media of its transmission and the centrifugal force of its manifestations.

The virtual, etymologically from *vis* – power and force – presents another modality and distinct medium of legal relay that exceeds both the form and the temporality of prior law. What was previously the seamless web of Anglican common law, for instance, is now the exponentially connected worldwide web, a plethora of sites and platforms, vehicles and screens that is transforming constantly, dissipating and reforming at accelerated pace. The key feature of the new media – mobile, social, stochastic and staccato – lies in immediacy, an ever present *perpetuum mobile*, an endless and unlimited dance of new forms, and diversities of site that can be accessed from any place at any time without delay. The hyper is linked to limitless relays, site after site, a world of webs that trap, engross, distract, diffract and diffuse. And law too is caught up in that play of immediacy and mobility, the ever present now of the *novum*, the theatre of 24-hour news, the mediatic dominions of constant entertainment, and an unavoidable politicisation that comes with publicity, that travels along with hashtags and handles, tweets and tweeps.

The rhetoric of immediacy is one of semiotic diffuseness in which the constraints of legality are bent to the needs of competition for attention, shark aesthetics, impact and effect within a crowded videosphere or online public realm. Speed displaces the exegetical and hermeneutic principles of textualism with the desiderata of policy and the protocols of instantaneous relay. The juristic text, the judgment, the applications of codes are no longer informed by the detailed grammatological procedures of exegetical form which dictated black letter procedures of printing a completed text, review and then signature and authorisation. Now the plurality of platforms and of mediatic modes, from microblogging, to the multiple sites via which law circulates, decisions are reported, legislation relayed and administrative actions divined and diffracted necessarily diffuse and reformulate the juridical according to the *sensus communis* of instantaneous virtual audiences in rapidly evaporating and constantly metamorphosing sites. The new rhetoric of law takes on an unrestrained form, by virtue and virtuality of multiplicity, because of the instantaneous quality of relay and commentary, by dint of diffusion via bytes, fragments, précis, addenda, replete with frequent typographical errors, inaccuracies, extrinsic opinations or medium-dictated orientations.

The immediate implies presence, law paradoxically without mediation, without delay, nothing interposing between judgment and reportage: the rule is visible, seen, expressed directly on screen, either in the space of its initial deliberation or as the linguistic manifestation of partial promulgations, bits and bytes from judgments, fragments of decision, soundscapes, clips, pictures that disseminate in plural and political form. It is thus because of the multiplicity of sites of relay and the plural character of enunciations and visibilities that a degree of diffusion and dissipation of law into the media, the political, the evanescence of policy, blog and tweet becomes a reality, however much the tribunals and the guardians of records might wish to claim otherwise. In transformation, in pluralism, also lies opportunity, the possibilities of morphosis and change, radicalisation both described and promoted.

The tattered love of which the epigraphical sonnet speaks, the tottering affections, the need for new apparel, reflect both a spirit of change and a loss of direction, dissipation in its dual sense of lust and loss. Specifically multiplication, pluralisation, diffusion of media and relays signal a comparable diffraction of the rule which in this volume is tracked in terms of the dissipating and mutable modes of exemplification and exemplarity of law. What was a hierarchy and unity, a set series of *exempla*, meaning authorised and serially distributed precedents, authorised norms, code sections, within a common frame has pluralised epistemically, coming unloosed from the limited distribution and closed confines of established juridical collections. The tottering examples, destabilised by critique, tattered by indifference and then more dramatically by the market, the old exemplifications of rule, have given way to new openings, multiple *exempla* in a virtual environment of instantaneous and immediatised fragmentary mobile transmissions. The combined effect of virtuality, plurality and an immediatised demand for instantaneity is that *exempla* are diluted, that the juridical figures of authority and the juristic sites of certainty are diffused. Not only does the example lose some of its status but its survival is shortened, the lifespan of the specific instance, the exemplification of the norm, in the political domain of the videosphere is brief and generally of low cathartic value. Law totters between domains and epistemes, moving between politics and literature, swaying amongst companion fields of economics, sociology and psychology without any longer a clear and resounding autonomy or exemplification of its own. The example is tattered, law's apparel less pleasing or lacking the distinction and distinctiveness of yore.

2. SEMIOTIC DISRUPTIONS

Where policy and ideology increasingly play the role of law, subordinating doctrine to political expediency and media pressures, rhetoric becomes the primary medium of legality. The disruption of prior forms and norms creates an opening which the current essays exploit to advantage in tracking the dilutions of legality at the same time as pursuing the semionautical and new rhetorical possibilities of an augmented reality and insistent materiality that change the face – literally the aspect and appearance – of law, its exemplary instances and modes of presence. The question to be posed is that of the opportunities unleashed, the political and juridical potential, epistemic and ontological of the new forms of the law to come, the juridical continuing but with the exemplary in tatters, examples torn and proliferating, tottering between disciplines and open to persuasion, seeking new apparel, unleashing desires of their own.

The semiotic disruption of legality adumbrated in terms of the sea change in technologies of transmission cannot but open law to novel influences. In addition to immediacy and plurality, connotative in large part of an anarchy, an instability that causes law to totter, its funding reduced, its legitimacy increasingly questioned, there is now the opportunity of the new technical modalities, and the increase in modes of signification, in differences of sign systems. The most evident, which is to say visible, is the visual character both of legal presence, the intrusion of the camera into the courtroom, of video links to prisons, Skyped witnesses, and also the use of pictures in the relay not only of the theatre of law but equally of doctrine and decision. The novelties of law online alter, literally render other, the rhetoric by means of which relay occurs. The audience, those that watch, are manifold and different, the topics and the media of transmission have changed and this impacts both the modality and the quality of reasoning, the character of its expression, the figures and tropes, defences and lures that the anxiety of the occasion of judgment provokes and the desire for acceptance propels. The semiotic dance begins.

It was Cornelia Vismann who some time ago pointed out that cameras in court, the now pervasive phenomenon of being watched, the surveillance of the internet, of email, search engine use, online social media, as well as of phone, pad, and computer cameras bring the world into the courtroom.[3] The lives of judges, the interiority of jurist and institution, of decisions in process of being made, as theatre and performance, now emerges on screen, is flung onto the diverse relays and platforms of the internet, is there to be seen, reviewed, commented on, blogged about, challenged and contested. The previously monastic life of the lawyer, *forma vitae* is now much more apparently and directly linked to *regula vitae*, and the *conversati fratrum*, the way of life of officials, as Antaki elaborates, is exposed to view as the source of rule.[4] What is indicated is the commonality of lawful life, the collective form of the *regulae*, the relationship between practice – habit – and law.[5] The judge as an example becomes increasingly visible and the interiority of law, doctrine and decision are opened to scrutiny in their multiplicity and diversity of

---

[3] Vismann (2003). For further discussion of the technological transparency of courtroom and law-makers, see Delage et al. (2019).

[4] Agamben (2013), discussed by Mark Antaki in this volume.

[5] Transcription of the way of life of the community is the first rulebook and Agamben goes on to comment that '[t]hey are not hagiographies, even though they are frequently mixed together with the life of the founding saint or Father to such a degree that they present themselves as recording it in the form of an *exemplum* or *forma vitae*'.

sites. The court is online, officials are in email contact, trials often arranged now over the internet with the judicial presence an appearance on screen in prison or immigration detention centre. Wikipedia, to begin with the most basic, has entries on the personnel, Facebook and other sites log and track, bloggers and hashtag movements review and critique behaviours, reasons and judgments.

The visibility of lives, the exposure and surveillance of the grounds and reasonings of decisions necessarily impacts the formulation of law. Open now to review from above and below, laterally publicised, recorded and reported, officially and unofficially excoriated in immediatised forms what was true of the legislature, that the politics of lawmaking was open to unlimited debate and censure is now true also of the laws that are made. Formally distinct, and historically protected by an esoteric rhetoric and technical argot, cloaked in Latin or vernacular archaisms, the trend now is towards a necessary encounter, literal and figurative, verbal and visual, between law and its other, the social. Thus, and the US is probably the most advanced, which is to say least restrained, jurisdiction, a wild diversity of genres and styles of judgment emerge and the political, the economic, the lobbyist and corporation are increasingly visible in the manner and promulgation of judgment. Law is to be found in all the wrong places, nascent, emergent, disrupting according to the site and frame, the rhetoric and the semiotic circumstances of its expression as a form of life.[6] The winds of policy, forces external to doctrine increasingly determine outcomes. The formulation of decision, the *formulae* as were, is ever more often in terms of the economic advantage, the social benefit, the market provenance or political expediency of the outcome dictated by the facts of the case and the nature of the dispute or infraction, as events infer.[7]

From a semiotic perspective, in the mode of new rhetoric as a critical tool for analysis of the expression of rule, example, justification and outcome, being able to see more of the context, of the character of the judge, of the nature and circumstances of argument, of the events that triggered the *agon* of trial or of intervention and the parties impacted, allows for an expanded analysis. The decisions are not simply rendered more visible but the effect of exposure, the visibility of legal action, from dashcam to chestcam to postings of passerby videos, all bring the world into the courts and other forums of legal action and propel the officials, judges, advocates, litigants, clerks, to take account of an exponentially increasing and multiplied audience. Narrative justifications now incorporate increasing numbers of maps, diagrams, photographs, real time Google images, CCTV, hyperlinks and screenshots, and these need their literary figures of accompaniment. The life of the law becomes paradoxically common again in the sense of being visible and evidently shared amongst officials and relayed around the globe. The world then has to provide the legitimations of

---

[6] The expression comes from Constable et al. (2019). The most theoretically expansive collection is Philipopoulous-Mihalopoulos (2018).
[7] For more on this theme, see Desaults-Stein and C. Tomlins (2019).

judgment, an image that shows the size of the vehicle, the site of the crash, the mask that was worn, the occasion of the shooting, all emergent so as to provide a reality effect in judgment and are then accompanied by poetic asides, literary quotations, markers as much of appeal as of syllogism or *ratio scripta*.

An alternative manner of formulating the last point adumbrated would be to reference a new sense of demonstrative reasoning. To demonstrate is to show – *monstro* means to point, depict, designate, and also to inform, instruct and teach. For the future semiotician, the new rhetoric engages with the novel multiplicity of the legal text, the multi-media character of law's circulation and the diversity of relays both internal and external to judgment. To show is to look, to bring the gaze of rhetoric to bear upon the new visibilities of doctrine and decision and this means looking to the interiorities of the form of life that produces law, the rules – acceptations, figures, images – that hitherto passed unnoticed or coded exegetically but which now can be seen in the practice of the courts and officialdom, in the insertions and other emblems of judgment, in the collective morphosis that transparency of institutional location and visibility of enunciation introduce.

Recognition of commonality, demonstration of the inner workings of purportedly authorless decisions, analysis of objects and events depicted in doctrinal texts or accompanying fragments and bytes of reported legal actions allow for a radical re-figuration of legality. Where the *exempla* were previously secreted, hidden and guarded from any focused public purview, the opposite now obtains and a crescendo of visibilities allows for the elaboration of rhetorical novelties and the rise of an oratorically informed jurisprudence. Where law had subordinated rhetoric to legality, and oratory to juristic rules of restraint – the auditor should not be bent – rhetoric now increasingly governs law and subordinates juristic decisions, official actions, the practices of doctrine and rule to the criteria of rhetorical effect. Law has to engage and persuade using the media of its social environment and the political figures – the *exempla* – of rapidly changing, policy-driven discourses of legitimation. The tattered example, the tottering law, needs new apparel and that is precisely the role of the new rhetoric, the purpose of the essays that follow, as adumbrated here.

Bibliography

Agamben, G. (2013), *The Highest Poverty: Monastic Rules and Form of Life* (trans. A. Kotsko), Stanford, CA: Stanford University Press.
Constable, M., L. Volpp and B. Wagner (eds) (2019), *Looking for Law in all the Wrong Places*, New York: Fordham University Press.
Delage, C., P. Goodrich and M. Wan (2019), 'Introduction: West of Everything', in C. Delage, P. Goodrich and M. Wan (eds), *Law and New Media*, Edinburgh: Edinburgh University Press.
Desaults-Stein, J. and C. Tomlins (eds) (2019), *Searching for Contemporary Legal Thought*, Cambridge: Cambridge University Press.
Felski, R. (2018), *The Limits of Critique*, Chicago: University of Chicago Press.

Lubac, H. de (1998), *Medieval Exegesis* (trans. M. Sebanc), vol. 1, Grand Rapids, MI: Wm. B. Eerdmans Publishing Co. and Edinburgh: T. & T. Clark.
MacDonald, M. (ed.) (2017), *The Oxford Handbook of Rhetorical Studies*, New York: Oxford University Press.
Perelman, C. (1976), *Logique juridique: Nouvelle rhétorique*, Paris: Dalloz.
Philipopoulous-Mihalopoulos, A. (ed.) (2018), *Routledge Handbook of Law and Theory* (2018), Abingdon: Routledge.
Vismann, C. (2003), 'Tele-Tribunals: Anatomy of a Medium', 10 *Grey Room*, 5–21.

Chapter 1

Exemplarity and the Resonance of Reasoning

Mark Antaki*

1. WHAT DOES THE TURN TO EXEMPLARITY EXEMPLIFY?

In recent years, we have witnessed a scholarly turn to exemplarity (see, e.g. Gelley 1995; Ferrara 2008; Lowrie and Lüdemann 2015), including more specifically in the study of law (see, e.g., Del Mar 2013; Toracca 2017; Condello 2017a and b). This turn has contributed to enriching reflection on the universal (or, as sometimes put, general) and singular (or, as sometimes put, particular) and their relation. As Lowrie and Lüdemann write:

> [w]hether it comes as paradeigma or paradigm, as exemplum, exemplar, or mere instance, as Exempel or Beispiel, as (role) model or precedent, exemplarity mediates between the particular and the general, between a singularity and some larger cognitive framework by way of empirical observation and illustration, imagination and narrative. (2015: 1)

In law, the universal seems to take the shape of rules or norms and the singular that of facts. As Angela Condello puts it, '[t]here is no exemplarity without contradiction, without threshold, and without a gap separating facts and norms – a gap to be filled with a process of embodiment between . . . facts and norms' (2017a: 9). As she also writes, '[t]he exemplary cases stand on the threshold between the bodies of rules and the world we inhabit: because it is from the world we inhabit that they emerge, but they get promoted to the level of the system of rules. Exemplarity thus mediates between the grammar of norms and the grammar of life' (2017a: 9).

As I reflect on the turn to exemplarity, I am tempted to ask what the turn to exemplarity exemplifies. If the turn to exemplarity is a reminder of the inescapability of exemplification in human life and judgment, including in the practice of law, what does attending to this inescapability reveal? If the turn also suggests that (at least some) practices of exemplification are to be self-consciously cultivated,

---

* I would like to thank the participants of the International Roundtable for the Semiotics of Law workshop on 'Singularity, Generality, and Exemplarity in Legal Discourse' for their helpful comments. I would like to thank Amy Preston-Samson for her research assistance. I would like to acknowledge the support of the Maître Guy Fortin et Maître Suzanne E Forest Research Assistantship in Legal Philosophy.

what might this cultivation entail and achieve? To what are practices of exemplification and, to perhaps coin a phrase, 'cultures of exemplification' alternatives (I think, for example, of scholarship regarding a shift from a 'culture of authority' to a 'culture of justification' in the South African context; Mureinik 1994) and what might they have to offer us for reflection, inspiration, even imitation? A simple but determined emphasis on jurists' recourse to examples, broadly understood, and on the indispensability and significance of the work of examples might be of momentous import. The unruliness of examples (see the title of Gelley 1995) may be bound up with the unruliness of rights, judgment and law themselves (e.g. Meyer 2000; Nonet 1995). Indeed, what if law does not reside in rules only, or at all – but, in addition, or rather, in examples (Antaki 2014b: 299)?

The turn to exemplarity may call into question nothing less than contemporary tendencies towards rationalism in law (on proportionality's rationalism, see Antaki 2014b) and may even point towards Wittgenstein's affirmation that 'ethics and aesthetics are one and the same' (Wittgenstein 1958, aphorism 23). Indeed, the turn invites us to consider the question of sensible judgment (see Antaki 2019), i.e. of how sensible judgments, that is, those that accord with common sense or make sense or make good sense, depend on human sensibility, thus making primordial the inter-related questions of discursive and perceptive felicity (see, e.g., Frank 2005: 97) in legal reasoning and reason-giving.

A simple emphasis on examples might, as the title to this volume suggests, (re)turn us to law as a rhetorical practice – in the most radical sense of rhetoric (see, e.g., Smith 1998). For instance, James Boyd White suggests that law is best understood as a species of 'constitutive rhetoric,' i.e. 'the ways we constitute ourselves as individuals, as communities, and as cultures, whenever we speak' (White 1985: 690). Indeed, '[i]f one is to talk about justice in the law,' writes White, 'it must be in the light of' the 'reality' that 'law is not a set of rules at all, but a form of life' (White 2012: 1). The inseparability of *logos* from *ethos* and *pathos* in the 'original argument' of rhetoric (Smith 1998: 7) brings us to how, as I have suggested elsewhere, '[r]hetoric belongs to and exemplifies the "basic state" of human beings. Being-in-the-world means to be with others, to be attuned by way of one's mood and to be concerned with what is to be done' (Antaki 2014a: 71 turning to Heidegger 1962: 155, 172).

The turn to exemplarity brings to the fore the resonance (and consonance and dissonance) that always already comes along with – even underlies and sustains – the seeing or sensing and saying of law, legal reasoning and reason-giving. This chapter is a tentative and exploratory foray into how exemplarity can be understood as a confrontation with rationalism in the name of resonance.

2. ARENDT'S EXAMPLES AND THE SHARING OF A WORLD

Hannah Arendt stands out as an important initiator of this turn to exemplarity (and her work has been picked up by various others, especially in political theory; see, e.g., Zerilli 2005; Ferrara 2008). Exemplarity's confrontation with rationalism is evident in Hannah Arendt's reading of Kant's *Critique of Judgment* in her search for his (unwritten) political philosophy (1982). If the *Critique of Pure Reason* concerns (human beings as) rational beings, Arendt says, it is in the *Critique of Judgment* that Kant treats human beings as beings who share a world, i.e. who experience singulars (or particulars) and make sense of their experiences and those singulars (particulars) together. Indeed, as she writes in 'The Crisis of Culture', '[j]udging is one, if not the most, important activity in which this sharing-the-world-with-others comes to pass' (1968: 221). In Kant's *Critique of Judgment*, Arendt finds an account of judging that emphasises human plurality (and temporality) and makes possible a form of sharing that is not 'compelled' by 'reason'. With regard to judgments, such as 'This is beautiful' or 'This is wrong', Arendt writes, 'one can only "woo" or "court" the agreement of everyone else' (1982: 72).

The impossibility of severing justification from persuasion in practical, human matters, the impossibility of pure intellectual arm-twisting, is important not only to Arendt the political theorist who emphasises that 'men, not Man, live on the earth and inhabit the world' (1958: 7) but also to those, like White, who argue that law is best understood as a form of (constitutive) rhetoric (putting to one side Kant's expelling of rhetoric; see Arendt 1968: 135). The impossibility of pure intellectual arm-twisting invites us to attend to what I have called above resonance, including what Smith calls 'the ultimate origins of argument in the ground and soil of voice' (1998: 305). As Smith writes, 'logos, namely reasoned argument in speech, originates . . . in a primarily acoustical experience where the principle of sufficient reason, nihil est sine ratione, and the logical "laws" of non-contradiction and self identity propping it up have yet to obtain' (1998: 302; see also Antaki 2014a; on voice, see Cavarero 2005).

Arendt's finding centres on what Kant calls 'reflexive judgments'. With reflexive judgments, the universal or general is not given in advance. And so, as opposed to 'determinant judgments' that 'subsume the particular under a general rule' which is given in advance, reflexive judgments '"derive" the rule from the particular' (Arendt 1982: 83). 'A particular contains in itself, or is supposed to contain, a concept or a general rule' (1982: 84). Exemplarity, suggests Arendt, is Kant's most promising answer to what makes reflexive judgments valid (1982: 76). In 'judgments that are not cognitions', an 'exemplar is and remains a particular that in its very particularity reveals the generality that otherwise could not be defined. Courage is *like* Achilles. Etc.' (1982: 77). Thus, a judgment of someone's courage can be made 'without any derivation from general rules' (1982: 84) by way of Achilles – whom a Greek 'would have in the depths of one's mind'. 'The judgment,' says Arendt, 'has exemplary validity to the extent that the example is rightly chosen' (1982: 84). It is worth dwelling on how the so-called unavailability of a 'universal' makes the 'singular' the privileged and only path to a 'universal' – which can be lived and shared but cannot be defined and cannot be said directly, and certainly not 'propositionally' (Constable 1994: 85).

At stake in 'rightly' or 'justly'[1] choosing examples is the world or, one might say, the uni-verse, the (lived) unity of a plurality of singulars. As Arendt reads Kant, 'the activity of judging . . . is inherently social, because our aesthetic judgments make reference to a common or shared world, to what appears in public to all judging subjects . . . In matters of "taste" I never judge only for myself' (Arendt 1982: 119). Rightly choosing and sharing an example involves both perceptive and discursive felicity as the right or felicitous example is not necessarily given in advance (see Frank 2005). Accordingly, the right choosing of an example at once draws on a shared world and helps re(constitute it), perhaps – if not always – with a twist, a difference. Examples contribute to reasoning to the extent that, and in the way in which, they resonate in and with a world.[2]

Arendt's turn to Kant raises a host of interesting questions regarding what we might call practices and cultures of exemplification. I think of two related ones here, one more closely aligned with memory and the inheritance of a past (practices of exemplification?), and the other with the phenomenon of authority (cultures of exemplification?). According to Arendt, someone – a man like Achilles or Jesus – can be exemplary to those who 'know' him 'either as his contemporaries or as the heirs to this particular historical tradition' (Arendt 1982: 84–5). If imagination is key to her account because something, or to be more specific someone, not present is made present (e.g. 1982: 83; on the turn to imagination in legal theory, see Antaki 2012), so too then is memory. But there are different ways to remember and to inherit a past. For instance, Plato can fruitfully be read as reworking the likes of Homer and Hesiod, thereby proposing Socrates as a new hero, succeeding or complementing Achilles or Odysseus, or replacing Achilles with Odysseus, and possibly remodelling courage (see, e.g., O'Connor 2007; Deneen 2003).

What is more, Arendt's references to the 'depths of one's mind' (1982: 84; and also the 'back of our minds') raises the question of how aware we are of the exemplars that we hold – and that have a hold on us: if we are aware of some of what is in the 'depths' or 'back' of our minds, we are certainly not aware of all that is there. Not all readers of Plato will be equally aware of Homer and of Plato's reworking of Homer, or of the ways in which Plato's resonance draws from Homer's, so Homer may be in the depths of our minds without our knowing it. Similarly, many who live in 'a secular age' (Taylor 2007) will not be aware of the theological and Christian character of their inheritance. If we 'are strangers to ourselves' (Kristeva 1991), might this be because our exemplars can be – or often are – strangers to us as well? If, as Gadamer writes, 'It [what tradition says] is always part of us, a model or exemplar' (1995: 282) attending to practices of exemplification raises the question of the 'presence of the past', of its resonance,

---

[1] I am thinking of French here and *le mot juste*.
[2] While the above quotes from Arendt emphasise exemplars and not, for instance, hypothetical examples, the degree and the way in which hypotheticals resonate may themselves be a question of their reference to and reconstitution of a shared world – and, moreover, the resonance of these hypotheticals may itself be more than incidentally indebted to non-hypothetical historical examples or exemplars.

including how a disavowed or hazy or forgotten past may guide, influence or haunt us. Practices of exemplification, then, draw on a past wilfully and selectively but also in ways that may escape their participants.

If practices of exemplification are inescapable and raise the question of how to inherit a past, we might find the more or less self-conscious cultivation of these practices in what we can call cultures of exemplification. These might be closely tied to the phenomenon of authority, which Arendt opposes to both coercion and persuasion (1968: 93) and links to Rome, and the 'augmentation' (1968: 122) of a 'foundation' (1968: 98). As Arendt writes, for the Romans, 'under all circumstances ancestors represent the example of greatness for each successive generation, that they are the *maiores,* the greater ones, by definition' (1968: 119) and 'the Romans conceived of history as a storehouse of examples taken from actual political behavior, demonstrating what tradition, the authority of the ancestors, demanded from each generation and what the past had accumulated for the benefit of the present' (1968: 64–5). For Arendt, authority, which, as we have seen, is bound up with the cultivation of practices of exemplification, 'gave the world the permanence and durability which most human beings need precisely because they are mortals – the most unstable and futile beings we know of. Its loss is tantamount to the loss of the groundwork of the world' (1968: 95). In Rome, Arendt writes, 'the function of authority was political, and it consisted in giving advice, while in the American republic the function of authority is legal and it consists in interpretation' (1963: 200).

Tradition, which helps make the past present through memory, and authority, which helps solidify the world, turn out to be a big part of what I have called practices and cultures of exemplification. Tradition and authority sustain exemplification and nourish it, allowing exemplification to sustain and nourish both our access to the past and the solidity of the world. What I find striking is the way in which political theorists and others have turned to exemplification precisely as part of an answer to the problem of the loss of tradition and the loss of authority, i.e. the loss of 'the thread which safely guided us through the vast realms of the past' (Arendt 1968: 94) and the 'loss of worldly permanence and reliability' (1968: 95). Is it paradoxical, aporetic even, that exemplification emerges as an answer to the loss of those things that sustain and nourish it? For Arendt, it must be said, tradition and authority are not synonymous with the past and the world: the loss of tradition does not destroy the past, nor does that of authority destroy the world. However, because the loss of tradition and that of authority threaten the past and the world, human beings may become even more responsible for these. This may mean an even greater responsibility 'to *choose* one's examples and one's company' (1968: 113, my emphasis).

3. AGAMBEN'S PARADIGMS AND THE SPEAKING OF LAW

Arendt's concerns in turning to Kant, e.g. the question of how to share a world, as well as the question of the sayability of rules, of universals, of law, are also to be found at the forefront of Giorgio Agamben's discussion of 'paradigm' and of his own philosophical 'method', or way (2009). Referring to Foucault's 'panopticon', he writes that 'the panopticon functions as a paradigm in the strict sense: it is a singular object that, standing equally for all others of the same class, defines the intelligibility of the group of which it is a part and which, at the same time, it constitutes' (2009: 18). Agamben here appears to be working on the same level as Arendt, on the level of a movement from one singular to another, from this (courageous) man to Achilles, and vice versa. There is no genuine access to the class and to courage itself – if one can even speak this way – but for the, or a, singular object. Referring to Aristotle, Agamben writes, 'while induction proceeds from the particular to the universal and deduction from the universal to the particular, the paradigm is defined by a third and paradoxical type of movement, which goes from the particular to the particular' (2009: 18–19). Indeed, 'joining Aristotle's observations with those of Kant', Agamben says, 'a paradigm entails a movement that goes from singularity to singularity and, without ever leaving singularity, transforms every singular case into an *exemplar* of a general rule that can never be stated a priori' (2009: 22).

The implications of the methodological turn towards the paradigm and the 'analogical logic of the example' (Agamben 2009: 18) are significant. The turn towards the paradigm 'calls into question the dichotomous opposition between the particular and the universal' (2009: 19). Agamben asks, with Kant in mind, 'if the rule is missing or cannot be formulated, from where will the example draw its probative value?' (2009: 21). He answers

> The aporia may be resolved only if we understand that a paradigm implies the *total abandonment* of the particular-general couple as the model of logical inference. The rule (*if it is still possible to speak of rules here*) is not a generality preexisting the singular cases and applicable to them, nor is it something resulting from the exhaustive enumeration of specific cases. Instead, it is the exhibition alone of the paradigmatic case that constitutes a rule, which as such cannot be applied or stated. (2009: 21, my emphasis)

It may well be that the methodological turn towards the paradigm invites – if not enjoins – one to call into question the very oppositions and grammars that exemplarity is said to bridge or mediate, such as those of fact and norm, world and rule, life and norm (to use the language of Condello 2017a: 9). Immediately after confronting Kant's aporia, Agamben recalls the history of monastic orders in order to call into question the very opposition of life and rule. He recalls that:

> [i]n the most ancient testimonies, *regula* simply means *conversati fratrum*, the monks' way of life in a given monastery. It is often identified with the founder's way of living envisaged as *forma vitae* – that is, as an example to be followed. And the founder's life is in turn the sequel to the life of Jesus as narrated in the Gospels. With the gradual development of the monastic orders, and the Roman Curia's growing need to exercise control over them, the term *regula* increasingly assumed the meaning of a written text, preserved in the monastery, which had to be read by the person who, having embraced the monastic life, consented to subject himself to the prescriptions and prohibitions contained therein. However, at least until Saint Benedict, the rule

does not indicate a general norm but the living community (*koinos bios, cenobio*) that results from an example and in which the life of each monk tends at the limit to become paradigmatic – that is, to constitute itself as *forma vitae*. (2009: 21–2; see further Agamben 2013)

Agamben's replacement of 'the empire of the rule' with that 'of the paradigm' (Agamben 2009: 11) does not dispense with 'the rule' but revisits, if not challenges, its gap with life. This methodological turn, then, resonates with White's claim that 'law is not a set of rules at all, but a form of life' (White 2012: 1). However, it invites us to read White's claim and the language of 'rule' differently. If 'examples' are 'unruly' (Gelley 1995), can it be that some are – and must be – rules themselves? Example and paradigm, then, both raise the questions of whether and how law resides in rules, of what a rule is or can be, and of whether and how rules and law are sayable.

At least with regard to the word 'paradigm', these questions may be much closer to us than we think. If, as Arendt explains in her *Lectures on Kant's Political Philosophy*, 'example' comes from Latin *eximere*, 'to single out some particular' (1982: 77), 'paradigm', as is also well known, comes from the Greek *paradeiknumi*, which means 'to exhibit side by side, to show' (Liddell and Scott 1889), and *paradeigma*, which means 'a pattern or model of the things to be executed . . . an example' (1889: 596). Indeed, *para* says 'besides' and *deiknumi* says 'to bring to light, to display . . . to show' (1889: 176).

And there is even more to *deiknumi*. *Deiknumi* is related to *dikê*, which we imperfectly translate as 'justice', as well as *dikasterion* ('court of justice') and *dikastês* ('judge' or 'juror'). Moreover, *deiknumi* is not merely 'to show' but 'to point out by words, to tell, explain, teach' (Liddell and Scott 1889: 176). From *deiknumi*, we get the Latin *dicere*, which is also the root of the French 'dire' and the English 'diction'. If *dike* and *deiknumi* are eminently juris-dictional words and make the word 'juris-diction' itself feel repetitive – because *jus* or law is always already in 'diction' – *para-deiknumi* may raise the question of whether all speaking of law is impossible, inescapably 'besides the point' so to speak. The displacement of the 'empire of the rule' by that of the 'paradigm' (Agamben 2009: 11) suggests that every *deiknumi* is a *paradeiknumi*. The logic of analogy makes one think of Roland Barthes on the kind of reading or the kind of book that leads to better thoughts because it is the fruit of the practice of being with someone one loves while thinking of something else (Barthes 1975: 24). As Barthes writes:

> To be with the one I love and to think of something else: this is how I have my best ideas, how I best invent what is necessary to my work. Likewise for the text: it produces, in me the best pleasure if it manages to make itself heard indirectly; if, reading it, I am led to look up – often, to listen to something else.

4. FACTS AND LAW IN THE COMMON LAW

The questions of whether and how law is sayable in the form of rules, and of whether and how examples are essential to the saying of law, resonate enormously with the common law tradition. As Peter Goodrich reminds us, 'the example is the defining feature of the jurisdiction' and is 'emblematic of the specific tradition of infinite particulars (2015: 140). 'Memory is . . . the compilation of examples' (2015: 142). Even more strikingly, he writes: 'At common law the rule exists only in its examples' (2017: 409). Law may be unsayable in the common law except by way of singulars (particulars). The law always comes with facts, with *these* facts. The, or a, 'universal' cannot *be* or *be said* 'on its own'.

In my own learning and teaching of the common law, the inseparability of law and fact became more vivid for me as I came to be struck by the centrality – and sequence – of the terms 'interpretation' and 'application' in how many people spoke about law. Law is basically the interpretation and, then, the application of rules. Interpreting a rule and then applying it is what it is to 'do' law. What could be more obvious?

A first step in thinking through these terms and their sequence may be to consider Hans-Georg Gadamer's work on the 'exemplary significance of legal hermeneutics' (1995: 320) and the way in which a rule cannot be understood apart from its application: 'application does not means first understanding a given universal in itself and then afterwards applying it to a concrete case, it is the very understanding of the universal – the text – itself' (1995: 341). But this step is only a first one because it may allow one to continue to take for granted the 'givenness' of law as written rules that *can* be stated (recall Agamben 2009: 21) along the lines of a statute (however impoverished one's understanding of statutes; for a rich understanding, see Manderson 1995). As Forray and Pimont put it, written law makes 'interpretation' *the* key legal operation (*'L'interprétation s'impose comme l'opération indispensable et complémentaire au droit écrit'* 2017: 33; see also Vismann 2008 on the media-technological conditions of interpretation).

In the common law, before one can even speak of a 'rule' being 'interpreted', the rule in question must be found and articulated, in large measure by compiling and considering historical exemplars and examples. Only then may the rule or 'universal' be stated, if it is to be stated at all, however tentatively or provisionally. As A. W. B. Simpson points out:

> The common lawyer sees the law as starting from decisions in tricky cases . . .; law consists of the principles according to which these cases have and ought to be determined, and these principles are thought to have no uniquely correct verbal form. The common law is not a text, and there is a sense in which, because it is always on the move from case to case, you never quite know from case to case what it is. (1988: 73)

He further explains:

> . . . in the case of judicial decisions, unlike statutes, authority is not attributed to the actual text of the judicial opinion. Although judicial decisions, recorded in the law reports, are used as sources of statements by judges as to what the law is, their status as authorities is thought to depend ultimately more on what was done than what was said. (1988: 73)

As a result, every judge can and probably must, in principle, rearticulate the law after an exercise of memory. Every judgment can and must, in principle, recompose the law, re-undertake all the preparatory work that makes possible the articulation, however tentative or imperfect, of a rule. Rather than a posited law, one may even speak of the common law as a 'com-posed' law (Antaki and Popovici 2019: 237), a law com-posed both by individual judges at a given point in time and also by the collaborative effort, through time, of different judges faced with different singulars. It may even be that the composition of the law lies less in the statement of a rule and more in the re-collection of a history of singular cases, a set of singular cases that, together, may contribute to constituting a legal world, a 'form of life' (White 2012: 1), *regula* (Agamben 2009: 21). Indeed, it may turn out that the 'preparatory' work of finding and articulating the law is not simply preparatory but *is* the work.

Throughout all of this, the question persists whether law can be said in the form of a 'rule'. The turn to the example, to the paradigm suggest that we not put too much stock in any 'verbal form', to return to Simpson's words (1988: 73). This reticence is not too controversial as we have known for a long time that every verbal statement of a rule will be under- or over- inclusive. The more difficult question, it seems to me, is whether, and the extent to which, the turn to exemplarity calls on us to give up on the sayable (and timeless?) rule as a kind of 'regulative ideal'. Should one practise and cultivate the objectification of 'rules' and their separation from 'life' (recall the language evoked in Condello 2017a)? (How) should common lawyers be invested in the separation of law from fact? (On the potential impossibility of speaking facts without law, see Scheppele 1990; see also Gordon 1984.)

In the common law, practices of exemplification may be threatened by pedagogical, scholarly and professional trends that do away with the memory exercise of compiling historical examples, thus making the past less present, harder to access. One such trend may be the editing of commercial casebooks in such a way as to 'pre-digest' a line of cases for students by either skipping (or summarising) the previous cases and then jumping to the part of the case in question that reads as 'rule' and 'application'. Indeed, the editing of casebooks in this way is made even easier when judicial opinions themselves are structured and presented with headings such as 'rule' (or 'the law') and 'application' (see, e.g., the Supreme Court of Canada's *Bow Valley Husky* 1997 and compare it with earlier House of Lords judicial opinions, such as those in *Hedley Byrne* 1964). With such editing, all or most of the memory exercise of compiling and considering examples is omitted (on one instance of editing, see the last pages of Stern 2011). By editing out the discussion of previous cases, one is left with the facts of the present case but not with the facts of the cases that came before. Because, as Anselm Haverkamp writes, 'an example always emerges as one of many' (2015: 47), such editing threatens the very practice of analogy, made possible by memory, and maybe even an appreciation for 'case law' itself ('all case law and, indeed, all rules of precedent operate through relations of analogy', writes Ando 2015: 114). As law no longer appears to come with facts, the editing of commercial casebooks – and the transformation of judicial opinions themselves – can make it look like, even if such is not or cannot be the case absolutely, the 'empire of the rule' has displaced that of the 'paradigm'.

If the practice of exemplification is undermined by the editing of commercial casebooks in such a way as to make it look like one can truly 'begin' with stated rules, 'rationalizing legal analysis' is, in Roberto Mangabeira Unger's words (1996: 59), the kind of legal thinking that refuses to cultivate exemplification, that refuses the culture of exemplification. Indeed, this kind of legal thinking appears to sever law from facts so much so that it even leaves rules behind! As Unger explains, referring to the 'principle-based and policy-oriented style of purposive legal reasoning' (1996: 59):

> On this account of the aims of legal doctrine, the chief enemy is the surrender of legal analysis to unreflective analogy. Much of lawyers' reasonings in many legal traditions gives a central role to analogical comparison and distinction, clinging to the ground of usage and precedent and refusing to climb up the ladder of abstraction, generalization, and system. The decline of the project of nineteenth-century legal science may leave a vacuum that undisciplined analogy can once again occupy. It cannot, however, occupy that space for long so the argument goes if we are to be clear-sighted in our thinking about law.
>
> If we persist in a practice of analogical judgement we discover that the drawing of analogical comparisons and distinctions relies, at least implicitly, upon judgements of purpose connected to significant human interests. As the factual situations multiply on one side, the effort to articulate and connect these purposes advances on the other side. Under the double pressure of experience and analysis, a loose, unshaped mass of analogies begins to take form. The invoked purposes move toward greater generality of definition. They begin, little by little, to resemble the policy and principle-laden purposes of rationalizing legal doctrine. Through this reciprocal clarification of relevant context and guiding purpose, the law, in Lord Mansfield's phrase, works itself pure: it approaches its desired form as an intelligible and defensible scheme of human association. An unreconstructed practice of analogical judgement turns out, in retrospect, to be the first, confused step toward reasoning from policy and principle. It stands to rationalizing legal analysis as crawling stands to walking. (1996: 59)

At the top of 'the ladder of abstraction' is to be found the 'universal'. Climbing up the ladder of abstraction is reaching for this universal and, at least eventually, doing so without the help of the singular (or 'particular'), i.e. without the practice of analogy and precedent. The belief that that the first few rungs of the ladder can be left behind suggests a diminished willingness or even ability to cultivate analogy and exemplification.

5. AN EXAMPLE: *DONOGHUE* v. *STEVENSON*, THE DUTY OF CARE AND NEGLIGENCE

Former Chief Justice of Canada Beverley McLachlin echoes Unger's account of 'rationalizing legal analysis' in her writing about negligence and the duty of care:

Universalism seeks the broad, general principles underlying the imposition of responsibility and the corresponding rights of recovery. It seeks to rationalize both the disparate branches of the law and the doctrine within those branches. Principle is prime; broad considerations of policy are foremost. Where principle and policy require, sweeping changes are permissible. The law is open and flexible, and rule systems and principles overlap. Old arbitrary lines of demarcation . . . crumble. (2000: 22–3)

The 'polar opposite' of 'universalism', of rationalizing legal analysis, is, C. J. McLachlin writes, 'formalism', which 'places great emphasis on rules, precedent and categories' (2000: 22). In her account, as I understand it, 'rules, precedent and categories' remain lower down the ladder of abstraction precisely because they are fact-bound ways of saying law. We can illustrate this, as McLachlin herself does, with reference to the evolution of negligence and the duty of care and, more specifically, the significance and legacy of *Donoghue v. Stevenson* (1932), the famous case about the snail in the bottle of ginger beer that has become a leading case in negligence law, even playing a discursively foundational role (see, e.g., Foucault 1984).

Prior to *Donoghue*, 'negligence liability was defined primarily by reference to established categories, such as innkeepers, common carriers, and surgeons' (Chamberlain 2010: 98). Indeed, the narrow holding of *Donoghue* was articulated in such 'categorial' terms. In Lord Atkin's words:

> a manufacturer of products, which he sells in such a form as to show that he intends them to reach the ultimate consumer in the form in which they left him with no reasonable possibility of intermediate examination, and with the knowledge that the absence of reasonable care in the preparation or putting up of the products will result in an injury to the consumer's life or property, owes a duty to the consumer to take that reasonable care. (*Donoghue*: 599)

However, the case has come to be known and celebrated for Atkin's famous 'neighbour principle':

> The rule that you are to love your neighbour becomes in law, you must not injure your neighbour; and the lawyer's question, Who is my neighbour? receives a restricted reply. You must take reasonable care to avoid acts or omissions which you can reasonably foresee would be likely to injure your neighbour. Who, then, in law is my neighbour? The answer seems to be – persons who are so closely and directly affected by my act that I ought reasonably to have them in contemplation as being so affected when I am directing my mind to the acts or omissions which are called in question. (*Donoghue* 580)

Rather than simply add another category, 'manufacturer', to the existing ones, the neighbour principle sought to capture, in Atkin's words, the 'general conception of relations giving rise to a duty of care, of which the particular cases found in the books are but instances' (*Donoghue*: 580). For this reason, and with Lord Atkin in mind, C. J. McLachlin writes that 'Donoghue falls squarely in the tradition of universal rationalism and, indeed, it may be seen as the 20th century incarnation of rationalism in the law' (McLachlin 2000: 35). When singulars are 'but instances' – *mere* instances? – of a universal that can be said directly, we may be seeing rationalism at work. After a successful 'assault on the limiting conditions of Lord Atkin's universal principle of negligence' (2000: 179), including the opening up of recovery for pure economic loss, *Donoghue*'s rationalism eventually led to *Anns* (1978), 'a triumph of the universalist approach to tort law' (McLachlin 2000: 180). *Anns* featured a famous two-part test for the finding of a duty of care: a first step asking whether there is 'a sufficient relationship of proximity or neighborhood' and a second step – a 'policy' step – asking whether 'there are any considerations which ought to negative' the *prima facie* duty established in the first step (Lord Wilberforce, in *Anns* at 751–2.[3] While eventually repudiated by the House of Lords (see *Murphy* 1990), *Anns* contributed to further entrenching rationalising legal analysis, 'principle' and 'policy', in the discourse and method of the Supreme Court of Canada.

However, another leading opinion in *Donoghue* that made recovery possible was that of Lord Macmillan. Macmillan, while not at all hostile to the move towards general conceptions (see *Donoghue* 614), did not articulate one himself, as Lord Atkin did, instead famously asserting that '[t]he categories of negligence are never closed' (*Donoghue* 619). Indeed, while Atkin and Macmillan both do the work of remembering previous cases, Atkin – much more than Macmillan – gestures towards a future where this no longer seems necessary to do. While 'categories' are not the same as a singular set of facts, they are to be found lower down the ladder of abstraction and always come with facts. The move up the ladder from several 'rules' involving the likes of 'manufacturers' or 'innkeepers' to *one* 'rule' – or 'principle' – involving 'neighbours', broadly understood, invites an abstraction from the facts and seemingly threatens both the possibility and necessity of analogy.

However, even what may be seen as the '20th century incarnation of rationalism in the law' (McLachlin 2000: 35), draws on resonance in its reasoning. For one thing, despite Atkin's apparent disinterest in the facts of the case before him (Chamberlain 2010: 95: 'Oddly enough, nowhere in Lord Atkin's judgment did he recite the facts of the case before him'), he used 'numerous analogies to hypothetical consumers harmed by poisonous foodstuffs or other household products' (2010: 95). Perhaps more significantly, Atkin's universalism itself depends on the resonance of 'neighbour' and, more precisely, on the exemplary resonance of the Parable of the Good Samaritan. Indeed, Maksymilian Del Mar invites us to think of 'examples as parables', reminding us that 'Para bole is literally, in ancient Greek, to put beside – it is something that helps our thought move from one side (the already familiar, the known, the past) to the unknown (the future)' (2013: 401). Moreover, because Atkin both draws on the Parable and adapts it to the common

---

[3] It is interesting to note that Wilberforce does not use the word 'policy' in his seminal statement of the test.

law, he invites his readers to think analogically about how the duty of care he articulates is both like the duty captured in the Parable (there can be a duty to strangers) and unlike it (there is no duty to rescue in the common law). In other words, he invites one to address the kind and reach of the Parable's exemplarity in and for law. Were one to allow the Parable to resonate *too much*, one might find oneself understanding the duty to rescue as 'the paradigm for the duty of care' and no longer as 'an anomaly or an exclusion' (see Manderson 2006: 93). Moreover, it may be that this excess of resonance is just waiting there, so to speak, to restructure the common law (an untapped exemplarity?).

Lord Atkin's use of the Parable of the Good Samaritan, as well as C. J. McLachlin's interesting, if passing, reference to the 'incarnation of rationalism', also gesture towards the theological context of 'monotheism', a context to which Unger turns in his own critical treatment of the 'scorn for analogy' (1996: 62). Monotheism, he writes, understands

> the relation between God and humankind by analogy to the relations among people. The narrative of revelation deepens the narrative of personal encounter, and affirms the revolutionary transvaluation by which the personal comes to be valued more highly than the impersonal as a source of insight and authority. Analogical reasoning and knowledge of people are constant companions: the interpretation of self-experience and the interpretation of other people's experience provide each other with the analogies that rescue us, if only a little bit, from both solipsism and self-obscurity. The suppression of analogical judgement in legal thought would, if it could be accomplished, result in a radical dehumanization of the law: one method for people, and another for rules. (1996: 62)

So much so, at least for Unger, for the appeal of the 'empire of the rule'. Unger's words also help us to see better how choosing one's examples and choosing one's company, to refer back to Arendt (1968: 113), are inseparable, how *paradeiknumi* may accompany *deiknumi*.

6. THE RESONANCE OF REASONING AND REASON-GIVING

As I have suggested, moving up the ladder of abstraction may involve a shift away from a shared world (in Arendt's language) and a leaving behind of the 'empire of the paradigm' (in Agamben's). In the language of this chapter, the move up the ladder is a move from a reasoning bound up with resonance to a reasoning that can do without – or at least claims it can. As one moves up the ladder of abstraction, the memory exercise of recollection seems increasingly incidental and optional to the work of judgment. 'Principle and policy' supplement (dangerously?) or replace 'rules, precedent and categories'.

Nevertheless, it is important to draw attention to what may be the inescapability of practices of exemplification. After *Donoghue*, judges struggled with the question of the proper use of general conceptions such as the 'neighbour principle'. If the 'neighbour principle' could be stated a priori, however imperfectly, many judges thought it could not be simply applied (recall Agamben 2009: 21). For instance, in *Hedley Byrne* (1964), which opened up recovery for economic loss, Lord Devlin wrote:

> . . . it is not, in my opinion, a sensible application of what Lord Atkin was saying for a Judge to be invited on the facts of any particular case to say whether or not there was 'proximity' between the plaintiff and the defendant. That would be a misuse of a general conception and it is not the way in which English law develops. What Lord Atkin did was to use his general conception to open up a category of cases giving rise to a special duty. It was already clear that the law recognised the existence of such a duty in the category of articles that were dangerous in themselves. (1964: 524)

Devlin also drew attention to the opinions of Lords Thankerton and Macmillan in *Donoghue* as they 'approached the problem fundamentally in the same way, though they left any general conception on which they were acting to be implied' (1964: 525).

Just as the move to principle need not and perhaps cannot do away with categories, such may also be the case with the related move to policy. For instance, the judgments of J. La Forest of the Supreme Court of Canada are characterised both by the prominence of policy talk and reasoning *and* by a desire and willingness to categorise different types of factual scenarios for legal purposes (but from the point of view of policy) rather than simply to confront each new singular set of facts on its own (see, e.g., *CN v. Norsk Pacific Steamship Co.* 1992), so much so that McLachlin described him as exhibiting some formalism just as he participated in the Supreme Court of Canada's universalism.

However, the rise of principle and policy may lead to a diminished sense of the kind of cultivation practices of exemplification require. For instance, judges such as J. La Forest routinely separate 'precedent' from 'policy' both conceptually and in the reasons they give (see *Norsk* again). In the same vein, in *Norberg* (1992), we see C. J. McLachlin fault La Forest for 'offering no basis' for an assertion 'in principle, policy or authority' (1992: 283). Noteworthy here is the separation of 'authority' from reason ('principle and policy'). These kinds of conceptual and discursive separations may easily be seen as inoffensive or trivial or even as triumphs of clear thinking. However, precisely because they may reflect the prominence of a confident 'rationalizing legal analysis', they invite us to ask the question of whether and how different forms of reasoning and reason-giving perform or encourage what we may call a disembedding of reason that suggests we can actually get to and remain at the top of the ladder of abstraction.

In the face, or against the backdrop, of these kinds of conceptual and discursive separations, however, there are those who refuse to leave or abandon reason to the rationalists. With this refusal may come the understanding not only that practices of exemplification are inescapable but also that this inescapability is a *good* thing too, at least for human beings who share a world. For these scholars, it is not so obvious that analogy is *like* crawling and policy and principle *like* walking. The conceit that one can move up the ladder of abstraction and remain there, perhaps even jettisoning the lower rungs, emerges as dehumanising and worldless, a kind of unlearning of both crawling and walking rather than a movement from one to the other. In addition to Unger, other legal scholars call into question the habits of thought that allow one to sever *logos* from *analogy* and raise the former over the latter, to make *paradeiknumi* a lower form of *deiknumi*. These scholars have in common a refusal to reduce practical reason to theoretical reason.

For instance, Linda Meyer seeks to undo law's rationalism by following Heidegger in thinking of human reason as bound up with 'being-in-the-world-with-others' (2010: 26). 'Our fundamental knowledge of each other is a practical, personal, one imbedded in context: it is a 'knowing how' to be with others,' (2010: 29) she writes. Her attempt to reclaim reason from the rationalists involves confronting what she calls 'the kanticism of law' (2010: 11) by, in a way similar to Arendt, inviting jurists and legal theorists to look beyond Kant's *Groundwork* to his *Critique of Judgment*. By doing so she provides a philosophical ground and frame to her claim that the common law resides not in the application of universal rules (2010: 30) but in judgments of fit, which involve 'more perception than deduction' (2010: 31) and are made possible by 'analogical reference to prior categories, holdings, and facts' (2010: 30). 'Justice,' she writes, 'is the "fittingness" of what we do as beings who *are* the kinds of beings who are already with others in a world' (2010: 45). While she continues to use the language of 'rules', these emerge more as practices embedded in, and reflective of, forms of life, ways of getting along. It is not 'rules' that are *given* to us in advance but these ways.

Meyer accordingly reframes justice in aesthetic terms drawn from Kant's *Third Critique*: 'In justice as the unity of the beautiful and the sublime, primal mercy is at play in the *givenness* of the past traditions that guide us, as well as the *givenness* of our immediate, passionate, embodied response and perception of the situation we confront' (2010: 46). Rather than sever 'rules' (the givenness of the past traditions) from 'fact' (the situation we confront), she seeks to articulate their unity:

> We tend to understand the run-of-the-mill case as involving the mere application of a rule, though on attentive examination, *the (beautiful) judgment's unmediated perception of 'fit' or relevance that grounds the application of any rule is seen to be grounded in the same 'given' of singular experience.* (2010: 47)

Scholarly work such as Meyer's helps one identify how rationalist investments themselves make possible the conceit that one can move naturally up the ladder of abstraction from analogical crawling to principle and policy, perhaps by way of 'rules'. Meyer links her account of and case for the common law's reasoning by analogy to a 'Wittgensteinian perspective on language', according to which 'there is no context-free meaning' and for which 'natural language is metaphorical and analogical, not categorical and logical' (2010: 32). Indeed, '[l]anguage naturally links a new present with the past through a Wittgensteinian "family resemblance" of situation to situation'. Propositional language is *not* to natural language as walking is to crawling, hence the inescapability of exemplification, of the lower rungs of the ladder.

For his part, Steven L. Winter moves from 'Wittgenstein's demystifying critique of rationalist categorization' (2001: 71) to work in linguistics, anthropology and cognitive psychology to elucidate a non-rationalist understanding of categories. He suggests that even defenders of analogy unwittingly reduce analogy to 'reasoning from policy or principle' when they 'convert everything to a problem of rationalist categorization expressed in terms of necessary and sufficient conditions' because they 'have no other conception of reason' (2001: 227). Once categories are conceived in rationalist terms, the move up the ladder of abstraction is inexorable, if only one bothers to think. However, in cognitive, as opposed to rationalist, terms, Winter suggests, not all members of a category are equal:

> ... one would expect legal categories to be organized by idealized cognitive models grounded in some experientially meaningful gestalt. These models would produce prototype effects: Some category members – that is, those that most fully embody the characteristic features of the model – would readily be perceived as paradigmatic examples of the category and could be expected to serve as cognitive reference points about the category. (2001: 144)

As a result, not all examples can be exemplars as not all category members resonate in the same way as the prototypical one(s). Indeed, Winter's work on 'sedimented tacit knowledge' (2001: 144) and the importance of prototypes in anchoring categories may help us fruitfully revisit Arendt's references to what lies in the 'back of our minds' and Gadamer's suggestion that what tradition says 'is always part of us, a model or exemplar' (1995: 282). Exemplars attune us and we may not always be aware of them and of how we are attuned.

7. RESONANCE-GIVING

A short word in the guise of a conclusion: when thinking about the practice and culture of exemplification in the common law, one would be remiss to ignore the question of how judicial opinions themselves present themselves, consciously or not, as exemplary. Their 'fitness' as judicial opinions, their 'justice', lies not only in their result but also in their reasoning, i.e. in the resonances they draw on and make possible, in the forms of life and senses of fit they inherit and rework. Perhaps the turn to exemplarity exemplifies a reluctance or refusal to accept instances of rationalising legal analysis as exemplary, to experience their dissonance, but also an openness to appreciating the resonance at work in all reasoning, including rationalism.

Bibliography

Anns v. Merton London Borough Council [1978] AC 728
Bow Valley Husky v. Saint John Shipbuilding [1997] 3 SCR 1210
CN v. Norsk Pacific Steamship Co. [1992] 1 SCR 1021

Donoghue v. Stevenson [1932] AC 56
Hedley Byrne v. Heller [1964] AC 465
Murphy v. Brentwood [1991] AC 398
Norberg v. Wynrib [1992] 2 SCR 226
Agamben, G. (2009), *The Signature of All Things: On Method*, Brooklyn, NY: Zone Books.
Agamben, G. (2013), *The Highest Poverty: Monastic Rules and Forms-of-Life*, Stanford, CA: Stanford University Press.
Ando, C. (2015), '*Exemplum*, Analogy, and Precedent in Roman Law', in M. Lowrie and S. Lüdemann (eds), *Exemplarity and Singularity: Thinking Through Particulars in Philosophy, Literature and Law*, Abingdon: Routledge, 111–22.
Antaki, M. (2012), 'The Turn to Imagination in Legal Theory: The Re-enchantment of the World?', 23 *Law and Critique*, 1–20.
Antaki, M. (2014a), '"No Foundations"?', 11 *No Foundations: Interdisciplinary Journal of Law and Justice*, 61–77.
Antaki, M. (2014b), 'The Rationalism of Proportionality's Culture of Justification', in G. Huscroft, B. W. Miller and G. C. Webber (eds), *Proportionality and the Rule of Law: Rights, Justification, Reasoning*, Cambridge: Cambridge University Press.
Antaki, M. (2019), 'Le tournant sensoriel en droit: vers un droit sensible et sensé?', 34 *Canadian Journal of Law and Society*, 361–70.
Antaki, M. and A. Popovici (2019), 'Barthes et les lieux communs du droit', in J. Guittard and E. Nicolas, *Barthes face à la norme*, Paris: Éditions Mare et Martin.
Arendt, H. (1958), *The Human Condition*, Chicago: University of Chicago Press.
Arendt, H. (1963), *On Revolution*, New York: Penguin.
Arendt, H. (1968), *Between Past and Future: Eight Exercises in Political Thought*, New York: Penguin.
Arendt, H. (1982), *Lectures on Kant's Political Philosophy*, Chicago: University of Chicago Press.
Barthes, R. (1975), *The Pleasure of the Text*, New York: Hill and Wang.
Cavarero, A. (2005), *For More than One Voice: Toward a Philosophy of Vocal Expression*, Stanford, CA: Stanford University Press.
Chamberlain, E. (2010), 'Lord Atkin's Opinion in Donoghue and Stevenson: Perspectives from Biblical Hermeneutics', 4 *Law and Humanities*, 91–114.
Condello, A. (2017a), 'Exemplarity: Story, Time and Gesture of a Threshold', 30 *Law and Literature*, 437–48.
Condello, A. (2017b), 'Exemplarity, Singularity and Generality. Remarks made between Law and Literature', 11 *Polemos*, 459–71.
Constable, M. (1994), *The Law of the Other. The Mixed Jury and Changing Conceptions of Citizenship, Law, and Knowledge*, Chicago: University of Chicago Press.
Del Mar, M. (2013), 'Exemplarity and Narrativity in the Common Law Tradition', 25 *Law and Literature*, 390–427.

Deneen, P. J. (2003), *The Odyssey of Political Theory: The Politics of Departure and Return*, Lanham, MA: Rowman & Littlefield.
Ferrara, A. (2008), *The Force of the Example: Explorations in the Paradigm of Judgment*, New York: Columbia University Press.
Forray, V. and S. Pimont (2017), *Décrire le droit . . . et le transformer: Essai sur la décriture du droit*, Paris: Dalloz.
Foucault, M. (1984), 'What is an Author', in P. Rabinow (ed.), *The Foucault Reader*, New York: Pantheon Books.
Frank, J. (2005), *A Democracy of Distinction. Aristotle and the Work of Politics*, Chicago: University of Chicago Press.
Gadamer, H.-G. (1995) [1960], *Truth and Method*, 2nd rev. edn, New York: Continuum.
Gelley, A. (1995), *Unruly Examples: On the Rhetoric of Exemplarity*, Stanford, CA: Stanford University Press.
Goodrich, P. (2015), 'The Exampleless Example: Of the Infinite Particulars of Early Modern Common Law', in M. Lowrie and S. Lüdemann (eds) (2015), *Exemplarity and Singularity: Thinking Through Particulars in Philosophy, Literature and Law*, Abingdon: Routledge, 140–50.
Goodrich, P. (2017), 'The Example of Undressing: Obnubilations on the Empty Space of the Rule', 30 *Law and Literature* 409–22.
Gordon, R. W. (1984), 'Critical Legal Histories', 36 *Stanford Law Review*, 57–125.
Haverkamp, A. (2015), 'Equivalence Unbalanced – Metaphor, Case, Example', in M. Lowrie and S. Lüdemann (eds), *Exemplarity and Singularity: Thinking Through Particulars in Philosophy, Literature and Law*, Abingdon: Routledge, 46–57.
Heidegger, M. (1962) [1953], *Being and Time*, New York: Harper & Row.
Kristeva, J. (1991), *Strangers to Ourselves*, New York: Columbia University Press.
Liddell, H. G. and R. Scott (1889), *An Intermediate Greek-English Lexicon Founded Upon the Seventh Edition of Liddell and Scott's Greek English Lexicon*, Oxford: Clarendon Press.
Lowrie, M. and S. Lüdemann (eds) (2015), *Exemplarity and Singularity: Thinking Through Particulars in Philosophy, Literature and Law*, Abingdon: Routledge.
Manderson, D. (1995), '*Statuta* v. Acts: Interpretation, Music and Early English Legislation', 7 *Yale Journal of Law and the Humanities*, 317–66.
Manderson, D. (2006), *Proximity, Torts and the Soul of Law*, Montreal: McGill-Queen's University Press.
McLachlin, B. M. (2000), 'Evolution of the Law of Private Obligation: The Influence of Justice La Forest', in R. Johnson, J. P. McEvoy, T. Kuttner and H. W. MacLauchlan (eds), *Gérald V La Forest at the Supreme Court of Canada, 1985–1997*, Winnipeg: Canadian Legal History Project, Faculty of Law, University of Manitoba.
Meyer, L. R. (2000), 'Unruly Rights', 22 *Cardozo Law Review*, 1–50.
Meyer, L. R. (2010), *The Justice of Mercy*, Ann Arbor, MI: University of Michigan Press.

Mureinik E. (1994), 'A Bridge to Where? Introducing the Interim Bill of Rights', 10 *South African Journal on Human Rights*, 31–48.
Nonet, P. (1995), 'Judgment', 48 *Vanderbilt Law Review*, 987–1007.
O'Connor, D. K. (2007), 'Rewriting the Poets in Plato's Characters', in G. R. F. Ferrari (ed.), *The Cambridge Companion to Plato's Republic*, Cambridge: Cambridge University Press.
Scheppele, K. L. (1990), 'Facing Facts in Legal Interpretation', 30 *Representations*, 42–77.
Simpson, A. W. B. (1988), *An Invitation to Law*, Oxford: Blackwell.
Smith, P. C. (1998), *The Hermeneutics of Original Argument. Demonstration, Dialectic, Rhetoric*, Evanston, IL: Northwestern University Press.
Stern, S. (2011), 'Detecting Doctrines: the Case Method and the Detective Story', 23 *Yale Journal of Law and the Humanities*, 339–87.
Taylor, C. (2007), *A Secular Age*, Cambridge, MA: Harvard University Press.
Toracca, T. (2017), 'Towards Exemplarity: When the Particular Matters', 30 *Law & Literature*, 465–77.
Unger, R. M. (1996), *What Should Legal Analysis Become*, London: Verso
Van Rijswick, H. (2012), 'Neighbourly Inuries: Proximity in Tort Law and Virginia Woolf's Theory of Suffering', 20 *Feminist Legal Studies*, 39–60.
Vismann, C. (2008), *Files: Law and Media Technology*, Stanford, CA: Stanford University Press.
White, J. B. (1985), 'Law as Rhetoric, Rhetoric as Law: The Arts of Cultural and Communal Life', 52 *University of Chicago Law Review*, 684–702.
White, J. B. (2012), 'Justice in Tension: An Expression of Law and the Legal Mind', 9 *No Foundations: Interdisciplinary Journal of Law and Justice*, 1–19.
Winter, S. L. (2001), *A Clearing in the Forest: Law, Life, and Mind*, Chicago: University of Chicago Press.
Wittgenstein, L. (1922), *Tractatus Logico-Philosophicus*, New York: Harcourt.
Wittgenstein, L. (1958), *Philosophical Investigations*, Oxford: Basil Blackwell.
Zerilli, L. M. G. (2005), *Feminism and the Abyss of Freedom*, Chicago: University of Chicago Press.

Chapter 2

In and 'Out of Joint', In and Out of the Norm: On Rhetoric and Law

Angela Condello

> And still your fingers on your lips, I pray.
> The time is out of joint. Oh cursed spite,
> That ever I was born to set it right.
> Nay, come, let's go together.
>
> William Shakespeare, *Hamlet*, I, v, 186–90

1. DISJOINTMENTS

In the development of this chapter, I have been largely inspired by an essay entitled 'The Time is Out of Joint', written by Jacques Derrida and concerning (mainly) Hamlet's madness (Derrida 1995: 14). In that essay, Derrida recounts Hamlet's crisis and argues on the deep meaning of the famous sentence uttered by Hamlet – 'The time is out of joint':

> Whether Hamlet played or lived his madness, whether he was able to mimic it only *in order* to think it (in view of thinking it and because already he thought of himself on the basis of madness), the one who said 'The time is out of joint' knew in any case, as nearly as possible, what '*disjoncter*' means. What happens if time is mad? And what if what time gives is first of all the measurelessness of all madness? (1995: 15)

Hamlet is mad with regard to dates, events, causes and consequences. He is mad because all reality before him appears to be disjointed. His present, his memory, his mind are all suffering from traumas, from a symbolic loss – and thus the madness of the character stands to signify 'anachrony, mourning, haunting, oath, survival, and the name – which in that instance as well is the name of the father' (Derrida 1995: 19). The tragedy begins with and develops around an event, an irruption of time, a deadly and ghostly time. And it is around a series of *contretemps* that the plot expands. Hamlet is exhorted to count the days, 'to cut short the time of mourning, to measure it in a measured fashion' (1995: 20).

In trying to bring accident back within a system of pre-established rules (like temporality), law is in itself hamletic. And, by consequence, tragic. What does it mean to be within the juridical joints? What does it mean to go across them, to go beyond the settled thresholds of the law? Both order and disjointment are innate in law. In and out of joint is a movement parallel to that in and out of the joints of a norm. Do the facts of the case fall within that category? If not, why not? What (other, different) classificatory criterion could be used?

In and out of joint, in and out of the norm: in and out of joint is the movement from the case to the norm, or from chaos to order, from contingency to generality. The sentence 'the time is out of joint', in this sense, reflects the idea that the world is out of laws – a sentence which would synthetically refer to the fact that (compared to the normative structure of the law, describing how things ought to be) all reality is potentially out of joint. 'The time is out of joint', in other words, is a phrase that reflects the gap between *Sein* and *Sollen*, between how things are and how they should be. The movement from the case-event to the order of norms concerns both what is possible (i.e. what could happen but will not necessarily happen) and what is necessary (i.e. what is prescribed by a norm). Doubt, reconsideration and hesitation: all these elements stand between Hamlet and the actions he will decide to undertake. Doubt, reconsideration and hesitation lie in the gap between what happens and what could have happened (or what should happen).

It is inside these interstices that rhetoric works, functions, unravels: in the disjointments and anachronisms, in the possibility of the impossible. Another example will help clarify what I mean by this. Surprise and anachronism also burst into the plot of *The Merchant of Venice*, when the feminine wit of Portia overturns the fate of the merchant – there, rhetoric works as the picklock that messes up all argumentation. Interpretation, together with cunning use of language, changes what appeared to be impossible into something possible, at least contingently. In this case, again, it is the singularity of the case that barges into the preceding equilibrium, smashing it and trying to create a new balance between the general order and the singular quest for justice.

2. ROOTS OF AN INTERCONNECTION

Law and rhetoric are thus interconnected, first and foremost, through the case, in the singularity and in its contingent nature. And the hamletic trauma is the perfect paradigm of all disjointment between *Sein* and *Sollen*. The movement of argumentation that brings the eventuality into (and out of) joint, or in and out of norms is the *rhetorike techne*: the art of the orator, of the speaker, of he or she who knows better or tries to know more. The term derives from *rhesis*, 'speech', which in turn derives from *rhema*, 'word, phrase, verb'. Rhetoric originated as a movement in and out of joint, in relation to singular quests for justice. The legal context was indeed crucial for the development of rhetoric in Sicily in the mid-fifth century BCE, especially for the rhetorical innovations of the sophists, and for the critical assessments of rhetoric by Plato and Aristotle (Gagarin 2017: 44, and Barthes 1970: 175).

The relationship between law and rhetoric in ancient Greece was, in fact, intimate: 'law played a leading role in the development of oratory from the earliest times and in the study of rhetoric from its beginnings, traditionally assigned to Corax and Tisias in fifth-century Sicily' (Gagarin 2017: 44). The very birth of rhetoric is linked to law.

According to Roland Barthes, rhetoric originated in trials to defend property rights in the Greek colonies: towards 485 BCE two Sicilian tyrants, Gelon and Hieron, made some deportations, transferring people, and expropriations, in order to populate Syracuse and to re-assign mercenaries to the army. There were consequent uprisings that overthrew the authority of the tyrants, led by people who wanted to re-establish the status quo. There were also innumerable trials, since property rights had fallen into obscurity (Barthes 1970: 175 ff.). These trials were peculiar: they mobilised large popular juries before whom eloquence played a crucial role. According to traditional accounts, rhetoric was invented by Corax and his pupil, Tisias, during the overthrow and the subsequent trials (Gagarin 2017: 43–4). They began to teach the art of rhetoric to those who wanted to win a legal case or to influence public policy. Because of the particular nature of the historical context in which rhetoric emerged, its origin is also linked to the rise of democracy and the defence of rights.

The ability of litigants and their logographers (speechwriters) influenced the nature and outcome of the litigation. From this point onwards, there were continuous discussions on speech and argument, in particular among the sophists, especially, to mention the two most famous, Gorgias and Protagoras. In the Platonic dialogue *Gorgias*, Socrates gets Gorgias to agree that he teaches the craft (*techne*) of rhetoric, which is the 'producer of persuasion', and then gets him to specify that it is the persuasion 'in jury courts and in other crowds . . . about things that are just and unjust' (Plato, *Gorgias* 453a).[1] At any rate, Greek rhetoric, although not uniquely confined to the legal realm, originated in the first instance to serve forensic needs (Gagarin 2017: 46). In the construction of plausible accounts of the facts and in explaining the meaning to be attributed to laws, experts in rhetoric essentially worked like lawyers today. Thus, the technique of the argument, or rhetoric, emerged in this purposeful interaction between language and law, with a specific connection to the defence of particular situations. Rhetoric and law are reciprocally bound in the case, in the singularity: in the movement, in other words, in and out of joint – or in and out of the norm. Rhetoric in Athens contributed to the promotion of democracy and the rule of law. For Plato, though, this link could also represent a problem: in *The Laws*, he describes rhetoric as little more than a tool for persuading an audience, regardless of the truth or the concrete situation or facts of the case.

---

[1] The earliest surviving use of the word *rhetorike* is in Plato's dialogue, *Gorgias*, which appeared about 387 BC. It has been conjectured that Plato coined the word, along with words for other verbal arts, including dialectic (*dialektike*), antilogic (*antilogike*) and eristic (*eristike*). *Rhetorike* means the art or skill of the 'rhetor', or orator. 'Rhetor' or 'orator' originally referred to a politician who put forth motions in public settings such as the courts or the assembly, though eventually it began to mean any public speaker (Gagarin 2017: 33).

In Rome (Leo Enos 2017: 173) legal rhetoric played a crucial, and even more relevant function. It was considered not only a dynamic activity of interpretation and argumentation, but also a source of the law, a way of making the law. As a metalanguage (*dicendo dicere*), rhetoric shapes the way people communicate.

3. AVOIDING THE RÉDUCTION TROPOLOGIQUE: TOWARDS A NEW RHETORIC OF LAW?

This incursion backwards – into the origins of the relationship between law and rhetoric – invites further reflection. Why dig (once more) into this relationship? It was a conversation with Peter Goodrich that inspired these reflections. It began with a common interest in the case, specifically on the relationship between singularity and generality in law, both in common law and civil law. Reasoning and arguing through cases became more frequent in civil law: what used to be different juridical traditions are currently going through a hybridisation. Many changes in legal form and transmission have been generated both by globalisation and by common law's irreversible encounter with the methods of European law. Thinking law through its relationship with rhetoric and in particular in connection with the case leads to an emphasis between singularity, generality and exemplarity which is cross-cultural (since it is a practice common to both civil law and common law systems). When reflecting on the case during a conference we organised in 2017,[2] Peter Goodrich suggested I should dig into the idea of a *new* legal rhetoric, approached from the perspective of the case – by looking, in other words, at the shared traditions of casuistry. Today it seems particularly timely to reflect on how the law is related to language, since forms of communication and information are changing rapidly. Pluralist normative orders today require a new rhetorical approach. The complexification of the informative and communicative systems in the contemporary world is making the event and the singularity more and more crucial.

Against this background, what are the founding principles of the *new* legal rhetoric? Is there something that can really fill the hole that lies at the core of the legal norm? Some have found an answer to this problem in a sort of 'exodus' from the law, especially in the humanities. Faced with the law's incapacity to be 'in the joint', so faced with law's permanent 'disjointment' (see above), lawyers have tried to build new discourses on law – and thus a new rhetoric as well – seeking inspiration in literature, ethics, semiotics and psychoanalysis. This exodus has often produced, instead, a short-circuit, an inaccurate polarisation: on the one hand, rhetoric has gradually become the topic of analytical studies on legal argumentation and has been reduced to a study of the tropes used by lawyers – against Genette's exhortation to avoid the '*réduction tropologique*' of rhetoric, which should not be limited to a classification of figures of speech (Genette 1970:

---

2 See https://labont.it/events/18th-international-roundtable-for-the-semiotics-of-law-2017

160). On the other hand, interdisciplinary studies on law tend to consider law as a social phenomenon parallel to other social phenomena (such as religion). This polarisation has in some sense excluded the possibility of considering each event as the potential force that might overturn the equilibrium of the legal system. The ancient bond between law and rhetoric shows, on the contrary, that rhetoric is the field that inhabits the threshold connecting what is 'in and out of joint', 'in and out of the norm', a threshold on which the balance between legal logic and societal values is permanently (re)defined.

For Roland Barthes, ancient rhetoric was a complex practice, a metalanguage (Barthes 1970: 175) which included different operations:

1. a *technique*, i.e. an *art* in the classical meaning of the term: the art of persuasion, the set of rules used to convince an audience;
2. a *teaching* methodology, which then became widespread and was taught by experts in that art;
3. a *science*, a field of knowledge and observation about the effects of language and a classification of related phenomena;
4. an *ethic*, i.e. a system of rules that converge towards a common task;
5. a *social practice* that teaches one how to handle language in social relations;
6. a *recreational practice*, which developed parallel to the institutional one, made up of rhetorical games, puns, etc.

Understood as such, rhetoric was entirely embedded in society for its 'political' capacity to overturn an established system of norms. It was measured around the specificity of the case; Genette recounts that rhetoric progressively lost this character and became instead a recollection of figures of speech and their potential uses (Genette 1970). In its original use and sense, rhetoric was the art of handling the interconnection between the specificity of the single situation and the general norms and principles. Avoiding the *réduction tropologique* – today – means to bring the focus back to the disjointment, and to the function played by rhetoric in the process of building joints and links between chaos and order, in an hamletic sense.

A new rhetoric of law should thus be focused on the most ancient joints between law and rhetoric and especially on the tension between the contingency of the singular case and the legal order.

4. APOLOGY OF THE CASE

Rhetoric, thus understood, is the study of contingency. Ancient rhetoric in particular was generally opposed to 'any elaboration of knowledge which was dependent upon the use of absolutised categories of reason or necessity. Rhetoric was both radical and to a degree theoretically innocent; it pre-existed the division and separation of the political and the social' (Goodrich 1987: 98). As a linguistic practice, rhetoric was the instrument of resistance, the way towards the proof of the possibility of what seemed impossible. A space of revolution and rebellion, as in ancient Greek colonies.

Every contingency is heretical: it embodies an opinion, a logic at odds with what is generally accepted. Contingency entails possibility. It is like a rubber band building an interaction between authority and confutation: it is polemic. It is the space of existence of rejection and defence of individual requests against a prevailing interest. Goodrich has compared legal rhetoric to theological heresy (Goodrich 1996: 57 ff.), connecting its attitude to that of the reactions against a dominant doctrine and a revealed truth. The study of legal rhetoric, according to this view, is thus among the most 'polemic' fields of legal rhetoric.

From this perspective, focusing on the 'revolutionary' and groundbreaking potential of the singular conditions in the contingent situation (like in *Hamlet* or *The Merchant of Venice*), legal discourse appears to be an 'historically and rhetorically organised product' (Goodrich 1987: ix). Contrary to this point of view, legal theorists have instead

> maintained a superb oblivion to the historical and social features of legal language, and rather than studying the actual development of legal linguistic practice, both spoken and written, have asserted deductive models of law application in which language is the neutral instrument of purposes peculiar to the internal development of legal regulation and legal discipline. (Goodrich 1987: 1)

A new rhetoric of law for the contemporary age should have a different objective, more similar to that of ancient rhetoric: it should be a *critical* rhetoric, or a rhetoric conceived as a methodology of casuistry, aimed at deconstructing the myth of the isolation and independence of the law from other social phenomena. Law tries to build a 'control over meaning' (Goodrich 1987: 1) and expresses the balance of interests for domination. Neither language nor law is neutral, and rhetoric is exactly that polemic device standing and operating in between them.

A new rhetoric of law today should thus retrieve the roots of its ancient origins in order to establish itself, again, as a technique, a practice, a discourse, a science of the contingent. Precisely in the age of the correspondence between information and communication, in fact, the study of the socio-political uses of language can become fundamental (as the recent phenomenon of 'post-truth' testifies). And such study should be, as it was originally, apologetic (Goodrich 1996: 60): standing as the dimension of justification, in and out of joint, in and out of the norm. It should embody, again, the art of the speech in defence, of the insightful remarks on the specificity of the facts of the case: I think this is particularly important at this very moment in which algorithms are starting to be used in the legal science and profession. Understanding rhetoric as apology of casuistry, then: as the space and possibility of well-reasoned replies, of excuses, of what is out of joint (and of its capacity to be brought back into joint, dynamically). Such a gesture would be strongly revolutionary for legal theory, both in common law and civil law systems: by looking at what aspects of rhetorical science have been gradually excluded, we should be able to read once again 'the history of the excluded discipline' and, by doing so, to see 'the terms of its repression'. And, thus, it would be 'possible to reconstruct the rise of the formalist and essentially patriarchal myth of a determinate and univocal language of legal authority' (Goodrich 1987: 88).

As reported by Barthes (1970), Genette (1970) and Gagarin (2017), rhetoric is like a space of interaction between individuals and the community in which they live and operate. In the ancient communities of which Barthes and Gagarin speak, power and authority were more dispersed than today, and thus rhetoric was really used as an instrument, a fluid force, through which power relations were constantly redefined. Those communities were open to the uncertain, the possible, the indeterminate: this made the role of singular cases, and contingency, more important – where there was room for the rhetorical argument, in fact, there was room for the development of a new general rule on the enthymematic basis of the facts of a singular case (Goodrich 1987: 102).

The apology of the singularity brings (new) rhetoric into its original joints, which are those of the probable and not of the certain. Nor are they those of the *nouvelle rhétorique* by Perelman and Tyteca (1958), which according to Goodrich were a 'theory of argumentation and of practical philosophy, the theory of the old rhetoric partially revived, partially rewritten' (Goodrich 1987: 111).

5. CONCLUSION

These remarks have, I hope, proved that the interconnection between law and rhetoric lies in the unique characteristics of the singular situation before a certain joint or form of measure. And it is precisely on measure that I wish to bring, as a conclusion, the line of the discussion. Law constitutes a measure for the unmeasurable: as Derrida would put it, law is deconstructible, but justice is not. Rhetoric is positioned in the tension between law and justice, that is, between the quest for justice and the joints, limits and measures posed by the law. Justice is always the justice of the singular situation: there can be no universal justice inasmuch as there can be no universal life or individuation. Rhetoric, in the search for the available means of persuasion allowed by the circumstances of each singular case, is the terrain of dialogue between justice and law – for this reason it is democratic and has been such since antiquity. Rhetoric, in other words, depicts a certain view of the law: it can be understood as the mere profession of words, or as a means to achieve justice (Sarat 1996: 5). To pair rhetoric with law is

> to invite inquiry about many things at once, about law's literary and linguistic qualities, its interpretive practices and idiosyncrasies, its verbal and written productions, the rules that govern who can speak and in what ways in a legal forum; it is also to invite questions about justice. (Sarat and Kearns 1996: 5)

As revealed in J. B. White's works, law depends on words and, in so doing, it

> avows, or professes, faith in the capacity of language to work in the world. But as a 'profession of words', law does more than avow its faith in language; it creates occupations in which rhetorical facility is claimed and cultivated. Law, thus, provides a set of resources for thought and argument. (Sarat and Kearns 1996: 8)

Rhetoric always reflects a certain conception of the world and participates in the constitution and description of potentially new conceptions. As a matter of fact, in the space of action of the law not all subjects are heard or can talk, and among those who are included, not all are valued equally. As such, rhetoric denies the existence of a fixed system of arguments for legal decision making, while interlacing contingent (possible and impossible) legal worlds.

New and future turns to rhetoric in legal scholarship could constitute a response 'to issues of inclusion and exclusion, as well as to anxiety about the nihilistic indeterminacies of interpretation' (Sarat and Kearns 1996: 16). What must be rediscovered is rhetoric's unsettling force (i.e., its capacity to dis-joint) and force to discern – behind the self-conscious use of tropes and figures of speech – the unconscious structures of institutional reason. A force which is heretical, apologetic, revolutionary: before heterodoxy, in and out of joint, in and out of the norm. Tracing the justifications for each argument, and linking it with a larger system of values, rhetoric constitutes, case by case, the foundation and legitimation of the law within society – portraying a certain apprehension and anxiety of the law for its source and origin. And a certain fear of the void which lies at the core of all norms. It is the practice of discussing once again the value of what has been taken for granted (Goodrich 1996: 73):

> The judges take the role of custodians of a peculiar and antique 'spirit of the law', of the *arcana iuris*, which is to be defended as axiom, maxim, and judicial declaration, against all secular, imperite, or vernacular forms of knowledge. Legal reason, in short, is conjoined with judicial power, tradition with authority, source with truth: it is the great lesson of legal history that the power and authority of reason are one and the same ... The reason of law shares in the two natures of the ecclesiastical and civil polity; it is explicitly a knowledge of things divine and human; it is necessarily a language unto itself ... The first allegory or dissimulation of common law is that of its identity. The origin of common law is an obsessive object of doctrinal description, and the first law of England is variously depicted as being Samothean, Albion, Druidic, Greek, Trojan, and Arthurian.

If it is true, then, that 'law feeds and is fed by the world around it' (Calabresi 1989), it is also true (and crucial) that such reciprocal feeding is never without consequences. If law is like a language, then rhetoric is its psychoanalysis, revealing its foundational drives through arguing, reasoning, acting and looking for the satisfaction of certain needs or desires.

Bibliography

Barthes, R. (1970), 'L'ancienne rhétorique: Aide-mémoire', 16 *Communications*, 172–223.
Calabresi, G. (1989), 'Introductory Letter', 1 *Yale Journal of Law and Humanities*, vii.
Derrida, J. (1995), 'The Time is Out of Joint', in H. Averkamp (ed.), *Deconstruction is/in America*, New York: New York University Press.
Gagarin, M. (2017), *Rhetoric and Law*, in M. J. Macdonald (ed.), *The Oxford Handbook of Rhetorical Studies*, Oxford: Oxford University Press.
Genette, G. (1970), 'La rhétorique restreinte', 16 *Communications*, 158–71.
Goodrich, P. (1987), *Legal Discourse. Studies in Linguistics, Rhetoric and Legal Analysis*, New York: Palgrave.
Goodrich, P. (1996), 'Antirrhesis: Polemical Structures of Common Law Thought', in A. Sarat and T. R. Kearns, *The Rhetoric of Law*, Ann Arbor, MI: University of Michigan Press, 57–102.
Leo Enos, R. (2017), *Rhetoric and Law*, in M. J. Macdonald (ed.), *The Oxford Handbook of Rhetorical Studies*, Oxford: Oxford University Press.
Plato, *Gorgias*.
Plato, *The Laws*.
Sarat, A. and T. R. Kearns (1996), *The Rhetoric of Law*, Ann Arbor, MI: University of Michigan Press.

Chapter 3

From the Norms–Facts Dichotomy to the System–Problem Connection in the Judicial Realisation of Law: Logical Deduction v. Analogical Judgment in Adjudication

Ana Margarida Simões Gaudêncio

1. INTRODUCTION: LEGAL REALITY V. ADJUDICATION(?)

Facing legal reality as a multitude of facts and the legal system as a set of norms in some approaches to judicial decision, as representations or images of the adequate projection of law in reality, traditionally allowed for understanding logical deduction as the ideal rationalisation of adjudication, as a deductive modus operandi entailing the generality and abstraction of norms and the particularity and concreteness of facts. Such understandings of the realisation of law do not only appear in formalistic-positivistic legal thinking inherited from the nineteenth century, but rather still arise in contemporary practical-argumentative and practical-critical perspectives on legal method(s), considering law as a normative order directed to social practice requiring syllogistic reasoning, and presupposing the lack of autonomous normatively constitutive relevance of facts in adjudication.

A critical overcoming of such an understanding of judicial decision, entailing a dialectical connection between the juridical problem and the juridical system, will state adjudication as a judicative realisation of law, and will, therefore, lead to a specific contemplation of the role of norms, and, eventually, of other criteria, such as judicial precedents and dogmatic models. Accordingly, legal thinking will be presented as a kind of reasoning that is essentially material and axiological, though also teleological and – in its expression, though not in its essence – argumentative.

2. THE ROLE OF RULES AND NORMS AND THE RULES–NORMS DICHOTOMY

Rules and norms play specific and distinct roles, expressing different meanings in law. Hence, questioning the role of rules and norms in adjudication presupposes a reflection on the rules–norms dichotomy, mainly because rules may be strictly understood as regulatory instructions to action, based on an agreement, as rules of a game, whether finalistically or formalistically assumed – meaning materially or formally assumed as rules that play a role understood as a practical function in a consequentially, or only formalistically, regulating practice; and norms, as rational enunciations, may be strictly distinguished as general and abstract determinative enunciations to action, comprehending a hypothesis and a consequence. Conversely, it might be immediately questioned which is the ground of the objectivity conferred to rules and/or to norms, that is, their legitimating horizon of reference – consensus to rules, authority-*potestas* to norms – requiring a theoretical and practical distinction between the role of rules and the role of norms in legal reasoning, taking into account the distinction between common law and civil law (Ost 1991: 241–72; Neves 1998: 45–51; Pettit 2002: 275 ff.; Schauer 1991, 2015).

3. LEGAL (IN)DETERMINACY AND LEGAL INTERPRETATION – VAGUENESS AND OPEN TEXTURE: *IN CLARIS NON FIT INTERPRETATIO?* INTERPRETATION AS A CONSTITUTIVE RESOURCE TO THE MEANING OF LAW

In normativistic-positivistic approaches to law and legal thinking, the clearness of legal (juridical) criteria, understood as rules or as norms, when stated by (that is, identified with) the texts which support them, could be generally presented – and has historically been presented – as the justification of the assertion *in claris non fit interpretatio* (Neves 2003). Accordingly, not only in normativistic-positivistic approaches, but also in some other perspectives in which the legal text is meant to be the object of interpretation – considering the core of interpretation to be in its literal meaning – easy cases and hard cases would be clearly distinguished, in many different understandings, mostly by considering the former as being related to clear juridical criteria texts, that is, determinate legal texts, and the latter as being those to which, due to legal indeterminacy and/or the vagueness of legal texts, it would be possible to offer distinct – even opposite – solutions equally justifiable by different legal criteria. Interpretation would, then, be an abstractly accomplished exercise of clarification (Linhares 2017: 25 ff.; Vaquero 2013a).

Beyond normativism(s), adjudication as a practical, concrete realisation of law required the inclusion of interpretation in adjudication, as an operative step towards the realisation of law, and as an essential resource to the constitution of the meaning of law, comprehending integrative moments, which means that the scission between interpretation and integration would have no place, as remembering Radbruch (1925: 129), 'The interpretation is the result of its result'.

In a judicative decision taken as a practical realisation of law there would be no deductive application based on logic normativistic subsumption, or on other strictly procedural mechanisms, rather a specific dialectical relationship between legal system and concrete problem. Such an approach presupposes legal criteria as juridically intentional operators – consequently, a legal norm, as the object of interpretation, should be seen not strictly as a text, as a norm-text, meaning a constitutively textual assertion, but as a specific kind of problem, as a norm-problem, meaning a constitutively practical-intentional assertion. Therefore, this normative intention, and not strictly that constitutive text, would found the object and objective of legal interpretation (Neves 1993, 85 ff., 118–19; Bronze 1993).

4. LEGAL REALITY AND ADJUDICATION: JURIDICALLY RELEVANT FACTS V. JURIDICALLY RELEVANT PROBLEMS (CASES)

Legal reality as the counterpoint (the field of application) of rules (norms) – theoretical-normativistic approaches

In theoretical-normativistic approaches, facts, as the counterface of norms, should be acknowledged as empirical phenomena, confronted with a closed, unidimensional, logically complete system of norms as major premises to which those facts may or may not be subsumable. And norms should be stated as definitions of law, as determinative previsions of legal reality. Legal reality would then be stated as the facts described in the texts of legal norms, meaning the definition of facts in a selection narratively and textually constituted by the text of a norm, as and in the meaning of that textual constitutive substrate (Neves 1998: 59–60).

The norms–facts dichotomy – rules-norms as abstract predefinitions of juridicity

Norms – as textual abstract predefinitions of juridicity – and, in a sense, rules – if they could be understood as signs – whilst structurally stated as norms, would present and figure out juridically relevant facts in their abstract predefinitions of juridicity. This would allow acknowledging norms (and/or rules) as abstract predefinitions of juridicity, as general and abstract logically determinative enunciations of reality whose meaning – including sense and reference (Nöth 1995: 92 ff.) – should be stated in a previous, logical-abstract moment, through interpretation, a hermeneutical moment. And facts, on the opposite side, would then be the empirical correlate of the normative preliminary description of legal relevance as stated in the text of norms (Neves 1995: 305–7).

The deductive modus operandi

For such normativistic proposals – not only in the nineteenth century but nowadays too – rules and principles should be understood as norms, that is, general and abstract normative criteria for action, ordered by the authority of the institutionalised instance to enunciate them, in common law and civil law systems.

In civil law systems, a normativistic intentional dualism would counterpoint the practical character and intention of law – created as and instantiated as a legal norm – and the theoretical, apophantic character and intention of legal thinking – understood as and instantiated as legal positivistic science – which was to consider legal norms as cognoscible objects (Neves 1995: 307–8, 1998: 58). As illustrated by Jhering's proposal, in his quasi-chemical understanding of the legal system as a formal-abstract structure logically constructed through legal (juridical) concepts, the jurisprudence of Concepts (*Begriffsjurisprudenz*) exemplarily showed that meaning of legal thinking, and legal dogmatic, as legal science, to be assumed as an inductive construction of increasingly general and abstract logical formulations, while increasingly both normatively more simple and logically clearer. The juridical bodies (*Körper*) in Jhering would then represent the logical purification of legal data (whether consuetudinary or legal criteria, translated by normative propositions), in order to construct objective law (Jhering 1858; Chiassoni 2016: 590–7). And the pyramidal structure of Puchta would also demonstrate such an inductive/deductive rationale (Larenz 1991: 19 ff.). In such normativistic approaches the legal system was structured as a logically rational concatenation of norms, from which general principles of law and legal concepts would be constructed, conferring a horizontal-coherent rational unity to the system of norms, which is to be clearly distinguished from a vertical-consistent logical rational unity of the system of norms – such as the one stated in Kelsen's proposal (Kelsen 1934; Neves 1998: 55–7). Still in that context, once in the dogmatic-scientific moment the truth of the legal norm was determined – in its correspondence to general principles of law and legal concepts – the application moment would take place, as a technical operation, through subsumption (Neves 1995: 307, 1998: 57–8). In considering adjudication as a theoretical-deductive application, and therefore stressing that paradigm of application, the legal norm would be taken as a major premise to deduction, and so the minor premise would be built through subsumption itself, while considering the fact(s) under analysis as a species of the gender abstractly prescribed in the norm's hypothesis. If it were so, a logical deduction would then determine the application of the legal consequence stated by the norm to the fact(s) in question, without any normatively constitutive contribution of reality to juridicity.

Though differently, in common law systems, criteria inducted from *rationes decidendi*, mostly in formalist approaches – such as the developments of Langdell's proposals (Grey 1983; Posner 1987) – represent a decisive contribution for adjudication as deduction, as well as the consideration of legal dogmatic as legal science (Ibbetson 2003), whilst the dialogue between common law and civil law systems, mostly in the European context, when confronting legal norms, judicial jurisprudence and legal dogmatic in adjudication, and determining a continuously growing '"continentalisation" of English law and "insularisation" of Continental law' (Bronze 1982: 123 ff., 165 ff., 174 ff.), represents a decisive enhancement to the relevance of analogical construction of judicial decisions, considering judicial precedents as juridical criteria to adjudication, mostly throughout the overcoming of the normativistic heritage(s) (Vaquero 2013b).

Legal reality as a global complex of goals and interests – practical-finalistic approaches

Empirically (juridically) relevant facts – the norms–facts dichotomy: rules/norms as instrumental criteria
From practical-finalistic approaches, distinctly considering legal reality as a global complex of goals and interests, as in practical-argumentative finalistic approaches, the norms–facts dichotomy would be stated between instrumental criteria (possibly) structured as norms and empirical practical situations (possibly) perceived

as facts. Therefore, norms, and, in a way, rules – which could perhaps in different ways also be understood as signs – would constitute, from these perspectives, the instrumental definition of juridically relevant facts, meaning that norms (rules) would be acknowledged as tools whose function would have been strategically defined by a finalistic programme, predicted by external determinations – economic, political, sociological, technological or other (Neves 1998: 70 ff., 1999a: 1–39). Within such a finalistic programme, instrumental determinative enunciations of reality would be required, whose meaning – including sense and reference (Nöth 1995: 92 ff.) – should be stated in a previous enunciation of a finalistic programme and be tested and accounted by their practical reflections as effective results or effects. And, correspondingly, facts would then be, generally, the empirical correlate of the determination stated in the normativity of legal description.

The finalistic decision as modus operandi

Overcoming legal positivism embodied in some ways an alternative paradigm of judicial realisation as a practical-finalistic decision – it could be said a paradigm of decision – even mobilising rational theories of decision to shape adjudication as an effective option taken from alternatives considered as means to ends, which would require the external establishment of objectives to law and law as the instrumentally binding assumption of a final programme (Neves 1998: 102–5).

In such an approach, the selection of alternatives and the viability and adequacy of judicial decisions – thus taking the finalistic decision as the modus operandi – would be determined by its consequences, as objectives turned into effects-results. This would mean that law should be pragmatically (as in American Legal Realism and in Law and Economics, for instance) valuated, in function of – and as a function of – the objectives for whose achievement it would be called as an instrument, and, concomitantly, of the effective results obtained through judicial performing in the social stage (Neves 1993: 205 ff.; Gaudêncio 2012: 101).

Legal reality as a specific, intersubjectively practical problem – practical-normative approaches

Legal reality as a juridically relevant problem (case) – the dialectics system/problem: rules/norms as juridical criteria

In normativistic, and, in a way, finalistic approaches, legal reality might be seen as an ensemble of facts (whether natural, social, economic or technological), which would presuppose the existence of prevision – whether in rules (in common law) or in statutes or norms (in civil law) – as a condition for their juridical relevance. But legal reality, not only as the field of law's application, but also, among many other ways, as an autonomous (juridically) relevant reality, might be seen as stating a specific practical problem, requiring an answer from law whilst intentionally relating to the normativity of the legal system. Therefore, distinctively, beyond formalistic and instrumental approaches, regarding law as an autonomous practical-normative intention, considering legal reality as a specifically stated intersubjective practical problem leads to a different understanding of legal reality, starting from each juridically relevant problem (case) and focusing on the dialectics system/problem. Therefore, adjudication may be understood as a judicative decision – beyond a strictly theoretical-deductive application or a strictly practical-finalistic decision – requiring an effectively practical, concrete, rationally dialectical-dialogical realisation of law, to which the whole legal system is convoked.

The judicative decision as modus operandi
Adjudication will be specified as a practical judicative decision, in fact consisting of an analogical judgment, recalling the Aristotelian terms, for comparing the problem stated in concrete by the case *sub judice* and the problem solved in abstract by the juridical criterion, without inductive/deductive movements. And, while mobilising an analogical juridical reasoning, this judicative decision establishes its horizon of reference through the mediation of an autonomous meaning of law, stated in a multidimensional legal system, considering the proposal presented by Neves and Bronze (Neves 1999a: 48–51, 1993; Bronze 2009, 2011/12). Such a construction of adjudication, mostly under the influences of Esser, Kriele, Fikentscher, Kaufmann, Müller and Schapp, asserts the analogical character of legal reasoning – proposing a specific juridical, practical reason – and the relevance of the case – *qua* concrete juridical problem – as the prius in adjudication, not the formal-logical reference, but the materially normative and methodologically operative statement (Bronze 1993, 2009). And this is to be considered through the account of juridical criteria as strata of that juridical system, in which the axiological horizon is stated by another stratus, that of normative principles – understood as foundational warrants, meaning specifically juridical foundational values – which are meant to support the normative adequacy of the concrete judgment of realisation of law as a judicative decision.

Recognising such an image of judicial decision as a judicative decision requires, then, that specific analogical connection between legal problems and the legal system, proposing a possibility to overcome the norms–facts dichotomy through a distinct perspective – that of concrete problems – and establishing a dialogical connection with the legal system. It requires distinguishing, on such a connection, the perspective of the norm and the perspective of the case. In the former, as presented exemplarily by Fikentscher's *Fallnorm*, the nuclear concern is to establish the connection between norm and problem, considering the juridical problem as a practical problem which is regarded and solved by the norm (Fikentscher 1977: 207 ff.; Bronze 1993, 2012). It demands, then, the accommodation of legal reality to the normative coherence of the criteria stated by the constitutively enunciated norm – in its normatively material and formal statements, though constituted in relation with the problem. In the latter, the problem is the effective starting point and core of legal reasoning and adjudication, as proposed, though distinctly, by

Esser, Kriele, Neves and Bronze (Esser 1970; Kriele 1979; Neves 1993: 155 ff.; Bronze 1993, 2012). And so the concrete problem no longer represents the factual correlate of the normative enunciation of a norm, in its textuality, generality and abstractness, but it is decisively the starting point to consider its own juridical relevance towards the intentionality of the criteria and principles offered by the legal system, and to comparatively-analogically analyse the resemblances and the differences between two relata: (1) the intentionality inserted in the concrete problem – as a particular and concretely provided problem-questioning to law, and thus in its problematic intention; and (2) the intentionality inserted in the legal norm – as a general and abstractly provided resolution of a problem, and thus in its problematic intention (Bronze 1994: 139, 1993, 1997, 1998, 2007, 2009, 2012). So the specific role of the decident jurist, in the moment of the normatively intentional articulation constituting the judicative decision, entails the reference to *judicia* (*Judiz*), as a specific skill allowing (and requiring) the jurist – mainly the judge – to previously draw the *sub judice* case and (noetic-noematic) dominate the reflexive *iter* implied (Gröschner 1987; Bronze 2008a: 83–8).

Such an approach, assumed as jurisprudentialist (Neves 1999a: 40 ff., 2012), is axiological-materially and practical-normatively designed to be built on an autonomous reflection on the rational practice which specifically concerns law, and on the specific juridical materials it convokes, with practical implications directly ensuing from the autonomisation of normative principles as foundations, which determine the dialectical (re)construction of the legal system (in and by) itself (Neves 1999b). Considering such a judicative-decisory realisation of law allows for the understanding of adjudication as a singular moment, that of reflection and articulation between system and problem (Neves 1993: 196–205), even between problem – the one considered (in abstract) in the invoked criteria and foundations – and problem – the one presented *in concretum*, in space and time, requiring an answer from law, and which will resist the centrifugal forces present, linking the essential valuations law confers to the reality which requests it. Thus, the specifically juridical time dimension as such congregates an assimilating system of bounded and bounding normative experiences, regarding a practical answer to the concrete problem which may provide a truth *jus dicere* (Bronze 1994: 139, 1993, 1997, 2007, 2009: 63–6, 2012).

Such a perspective on the concrete legal problem is to be methodologically distinguished from a narrative intentionality, undertaking a normative intentionality. It will not therefore establish its foundations and aim in getting a strictly systematically coherent adjudication – thus, not essentially looking for the realisation of the meaning of integrity, as stated by Dworkin (1986: 225–75), for instance, but in getting a normatively adequate adjudication – as an effectively judicative decision. This could be understood as aiming at a practical-normatively adequate resolution to the phenomenological manifestation of legal reality (of juridical concrete problems) in its proper meaning, on the one hand, and practical-normatively adequate to the legal system, meaning dialectically related to a normatively constitutive legal system, on the other hand – and therefore, in a practical-rational and normatively constitutive connection between problem and system. Or, more specifically, as has been said, on a comparison-analogy between problem and problem – between case-*thema* and case-*forum*, thus emphasising the problematic intentionality of legal norms while intentionally resolving in general and abstract a juridical problem, at the moment when legal norms are invoked by the problematic intentionality of concrete problems as concrete interpellations to their normativity (Bronze 1994: 139, 1993, 1997, 2007, 2008b, 2009: 63–6, 2012).

5. THE METHODOLOGICAL ROLE OF ANALOGY IN ADJUDICATION

Analogy in theoretical-deductive application

In theoretical-deductive application, considering the methodological role of analogy in adjudication requires observing that, in normativistic understandings, whether in civil law or in common law systems, law should be stated in legal norms, thus set as the primarily relevant criteria of juridicalness – as constitutive juridical criteria, mostly in the construction of statute law, but also in adjudicating juridical criteria – presupposing law as norm, placed in a logically linked one-dimensional system. Judicial jurisprudence and legal dogmatic would represent, in such approaches, external logical reflective consequences of the logically deductive application of legal norms. This would be a fundamental question in the construction of common law systems, on the assumption of judicial jurisprudence as a source of law.

In common law systems, the binding force of *stare decisis*, representing an effective *auctoritas*, resting on *rationes decidendi*, would constitute practical memories of valuation institutionally binding as criteria to future decisions in analogous cases. At this point, the distinction between interpretation, application and integration would be decisive. The core question would then be to distinguish judicial precedents as concrete decisions on cases – and their eventual normative bindingness – and as normative general and abstract criteria inductively obtained from those decisions. Secondly, the possibility of regarding judicial precedents as criteria would be questioned, meaning the judicial decision as a decision of a former analogous concrete case, or as solely the solution scheme proposed in its *ratio decidendi* (Peczenik 2007: 26 ff.).

In civil law systems, the principle of legality would, though differently, also require a strict distinction between interpretation, application and integration, in order to allow the deductive application of law. Consequently, in civil law systems analogy would be affirmed as a logical operation, required, in certain circumstances, if and when there would be no possibility of subsumption – through syllogism – of the facts under analysis to the interpretative, literally admissible meanings of the legal criteria, even to the point where there would be no connection between the literal selected meanings of legal text (grammar), in association with the meanings admitted by the other intra-textual elements – logic, history, system – and, when allowed, the extra-textual element – teleology – and the empirical factuality in question (Savigny 1840: 216 ff.). Analogy would, then, mean comparing facts – the facts *sub judice*, to which there would be no possibility of subsumption to a legal norm's hypothesis text, since there would be no literal prevision on such a norm text that could signify, in general and abstract, what the fact shows in particular and concrete circumstances. Thus, such a comparison – analogy – would take place in order to state the possibility of the omitted facts and the correspondent omissions, or gaps, identified in the legal text being subsumed to the literal positive relevance of the text of another juridical criterion, that which had stated the analogous fact(s) in its *littera*: such a subsumption would be a result of the so-called *analogia legis*. And, distinctly, when and where *analogia legis* procedures were impossible, meaning when and where there would be no legal norm which could include in its significances the omitted facts, the possibility of subsumption of those omitted facts to the general principle(s) of law in force on the matter could be asserted, and in which the omission could be subsumed: it would be *analogia juris* (Neves 1993: 207 ff., 238 ff.; Bronze 2007).

Analogy in practical-concrete realisation of law

Conversely, when considering the methodological role of analogy in adjudication as a practical-concrete realisation of law, in which analogy is understood as the juridically specific, practical rationale, interpretation in legal adjudication should not be affirmed as a logical and abstract operation accomplished in an autonomous methodical hermeneutical moment, for the meaning of a juridical criterion should then be understood in the moment of and by the mediation of the concrete relevance of the case-problem *sub judice*.

Analogy will, then, translate, using such an approach, a distinct judgment, whilst evoking the Aristotelian construction of analogy (Neves 1993: 240–1; Bronze 2007), a comparison between two particular terms, as relata – without transition from particular to general, and back to particular – and having by *tertium comparationis* the meaning (sense) of legal normativity, and stating the similarities and the differences between those relata in constructing a judicative decision. This way, there would be no intentional distinction between interpretation and application, on the one hand, nor between application and integration, on the other: these would be methodological structures to the constitution of judicative decision, with or without the mediation of a legal norm, and, then, to the normatively constitutive dialectical relation settled between problem – the concrete situation of reality requiring a legal answer – and system – the juridical intentionality and content proclaimed in the legal system (Neves 1993: 238 ff.; Bronze 2007, 2012).

In such a practical realisation of law, the specific analogical relation between the concrete case-problem presented and the constituting legal system will not be a matter of subsumption of facts to the hypothesis of norms. It will require a dialectical-dialogical judgment, through practical legal rationality – materially founded and constituted, and, nonetheless, normatively and argumentatively enunciated (Neves 1993: 155 ff.; Neves 1999a: 48–52; Bronze 2007, 2012). Consequently, the judicative decision can be progressively built within a methodical scheme in which the distinction between question-of-fact and question-of-law is only allowable as an analytical tool. Indeed, the distinction between question-of-fact and question-of-law is not actually at stake in such a construction, meaning that what matters in this judicative decision is the dialectical link, analogically constructed between the concrete case-problem (the case-*thema*) and the legal system as a whole (or the case solved in abstract by the legal norm – the case-*forum* or *exemplum*), in its distinct dimensions, or strata: normative principles, legal norms, precedents, dogmatic and legal reality (Neves 1993: 196–7; Bronze 1993, 1994: 139, 1998: 110–22, 2008b: 335–73; Linhares 2012; Gaudêncio 2012: 95–6).

6. CONCLUSION: BEYOND THE LEGAL REALITY–ADJUDICATION DICHOTOMY – JURIDICALLY RELEVANT PROBLEMS (CASES) AS EXEMPLARY REALISATIONS OF THE MATERIALLY NORMATIVE INTENTIONALITY OF THE LEGAL SYSTEM

Regarding the establishment of a practical-dialectical relationship between legal reality and adjudication, beyond the legal reality–adjudication dichotomy, the methodological exercise in which juridically relevant problems (cases) are settled as exemplary realisations of the materially normative intentionality of the legal system requires outlining a dialectical reconstitution of law through adjudication. In fact, no dichotomy between legal reality and adjudication remains when the juridicalness of legal reality is seen as the correlate of the juridicalness of the legal system. Accordingly, juridically relevant problems (cases) constitute exemplary realisations of the materially normative intentionality of the legal system, pursuing the dialectical reconstitution of law through adjudication, distinctly from both the nineteenth-century legal science and the subsequent formalist legal thinking approaches, and from contemporary discussions on positivism and non-positivism proposals on legal thinking, and also some other post-positivistic approaches. This means, mainly in the latter reference, stating a specifically practical-normatively constructed and axiologically bounded legal system, asserting that the unity of the legal system should be conferred not by the reduction of its constitutive elements to a formal-rational-logical presupposition, but by the dialectically normative-substantial relation of bindingness within its constitutive elements, or strata – normative principles, legal norms, precedents, dogmatic and legal reality (Neves 1999a: 48–51). Such a multidimensional, or multi-layered, legal system consequently requires distinguishing normative principles as foundational axiological principles, from which normative criteria – set in legal norms, precedents and dogmatic – are normatively operative consequences whose decisive task is to accomplish that axiology in relation to intersubjective juridical reality. And so, this requires affirming a teleonomology, meaning a practical-material foundation for law and legal thinking, on the one hand, and a specific teleology, expressed by and integrated through the reflections on the positive and negative frontiers of juridicity, on the other.

Legal thinking assumes, therefore, the representation of the exemplarity of practical-material normative and argumentative rational construction on legal practice and on legal theory. Beyond the norms–facts dichotomy – and its correspondent logical deduction – and also beyond the pragmatic analysis of facts in reality through instrumentally constructed criteria, and its finalistic decision, by establishing the connection system/problem in the judicial realisation of law – and its analogical judgment in adjudication – it plays its decisively critical-dialectical-reflexive role in the projection of law in reality, critically (re)constructing legal normativity within an autonomous analogical-dialogical reflection on what the law substantially is and on what it could or should be.

Bibliography

Bronze, F. J. (1982), 'Continentalização' do direito inglês ou 'insularização' do direito continental?, Coimbra: Coimbra Editora.

Bronze, F. J. (1993), 'Breves considerações sobre o estado actual da questão metodonomológica', LXIX Boletim da Faculdade de Direito da Universidade de Coimbra, 177–99.

Bronze, F. J. (1994), A metodonomologia entre a semelhança e a diferença (reflexão problematizante dos pólos da radical matriz analógica do discurso jurídico), Coimbra: Coimbra Editora.

Bronze, F. J. (1997), 'As margens e o rio (da retórica jurídica à metodonomologia)', LXXIII Boletim da Faculdade de Direito da Universidade de Coimbra, 81–119.

Bronze, F. J. (1998), 'O jurista: pessoa ou andróide?', in A. Varela, D. Freitas do Amaral, J. Miranda and J. J. Gomes Canotilho (eds), Ab uno ad omnes – 75 anos da Coimbra Editora, Coimbra: Coimbra Editora, 73–122.

Bronze, F. J. (2007), 'O problema da analogia iuris (algumas notas)', in R. de Albuquerque and A. Menezes Cordeiro (eds), Estudos em memória do Professor Doutor José Dias Marques, Coimbra: Almedina, 147–62.

Bronze, F. J. (2008a), 'A imaginação no quadro da judicativo-decisória realização do direito (quatro variações sobre o tema)', LXXXIV Boletim da Faculdade de Direito da Universidade de Coimbra, 59–88.

Bronze, F. J. (2008b), 'A metodonomologia (para além da argumentação)', in J. de Figueiredo Dias, J. J. Gomes Canotilho and J. de Faria Costa (eds), Ars Ivdicandi – Estudos em Homenagem ao Prof. Doutor António Castanheira Neves, vol. I – Filosofia, Teoria e Metodologia, Coimbra: Coimbra Editora, 335–73.

Bronze, F. J. (2009), 'Praxis, problema, nomos (um olhar oblíquo sobre a respectiva intersecção)', in M. da Costa Andrade, M. J. Antunes and S. A. de Sousa (eds), Estudos em Homenagem ao Prof. Doutor Jorge de Figueiredo Dias, vol. IV, Coimbra: Coimbra Editora, 37–66.

Bronze, F. J. (2011/12), 'Pj – Jd: A equação metodonomológica (as incógnitas que articula e o modo como se resolve)', *Boletim da Faculdade de Direito da Universidade de Coimbra*, LXXXVII, Tome II (2011), 87–134, and LXXXVIII, Tome I (2012), 13–53.

Chiassoni, P. (2016), 'Rudolf von Jhering', in E. Pattaro and C. Roversi (eds), *Legal Philosophy in the Twentieth Century: The Civil Law World (A Treatise of Legal Philosophy and General Jurisprudence vol. 12)*, Dordrecht: Springer.

Dworkin, R. (1986), *Law's Empire*, Cambridge, MA: Harvard University Press.

Esser, J. (1970), *Vorverständnis und Methodenwahl in der Rechtsfindung. Rationalitätsgrundlagen richterlicher Entscheidungspraxis*, Frankfurt am Main: Äthenaum.

Fikentscher, W. (1977), *Methoden des Rechts in vergleichender Darstellung*, vol. IV, Tübingen: Mohr Siebeck.

Gaudêncio, A. M. (2012), 'From Centrifugal Teleology to Centripetal Axiology(?): (In)adequacy of the Movement of Law to the Velocity of Praxis', LXXXVIII *Boletim da Faculdade de Direito da Universidade de Coimbra*, 91–103.

Grey, T. C. (1983), 'Langdell's Orthodoxy', 45 *University of Pittsburgh Law Review*, 1–53.

Gröschner, R. (1987), 'Judiz – was es ist und wie läßt es sich erlernen?', 19 *Juristen Zeitung*, 903–8.

Ibbetson, D. J. (2003), 'Case-Law and Doctrine: a Historical Perspective on the English Common Law', in R. Schulz and U. Seif (eds), *Richterrecht und Rechtsfortbildung in der Euröpäischen Rechtsgemeinschaft*, Tübingen: Mohr Siebeck, 27–40.

Jhering, R. v. (1858), *Geist des römischen Rechts auf den verschiedenen Stufen seiner Entwicklung*, Leipzig: Breitkopf und Hartel.

Kelsen, H. (1934), *Reine Rechtslehre*, Wien: F. Deuticke.

Kriele, M. (1979), *Recht und praktische Vernunft*, Göttingen: Vandenhoeck und Ruprecht.

Larenz, K. (1991) [1960], *Methodenlehre der Rechtswissenschaft*, 6th edn, Berlin: Springer.

Linhares, J. M. (2012), 'Na "coroa de fumo" da teoria dos princípios: poderá um tratamento dos princípios como normas servir-nos de guia?', in F. Alves Correia, J. E. M. Machado and J. C. Loureiro (eds), *Estudos em Homenagem ao Professor Doutor José Joaquim Gomes Canotilho, vol. III – Direitos e interconstitucionalidade: entre dignidade e cosmopolitismo*, Coimbra: Coimbra Editora, 395–421.

Linhares, J. M. (2017), *O binómio casos fáceis/casos difíceis e a categoria de inteligibilidade sistema jurídico: um contraponto indispensável no mapa do discurso jurídico contemporâneo?*, Coimbra: Coimbra Jurídica, Imprensa da Universidade de Coimbra.

Neves, A. Castanheira (1993), *Metodologia Jurídica. Problemas Fundamentais*, Coimbra: Coimbra Editora.

Neves, A. Castanheira (1995), 'Método jurídico', in A. Castanheira Neves, *Digesta – Escritos acerca do Direito, do pensamento jurídico, da sua metodologia e outros*, vol. II, Coimbra: Coimbra Editora, 283–336.

Neves, A. Castanheira (1998), 'Teoria do Direito.Lições proferidas no ano lectivo de 1998/99', policop., Coimbra: n.p.
Neves, A. Castanheira (1999a), 'Apontamentos complementares de Teoria do Direito – Sumários e textos', policop., Coimbra: n.p.
Neves, A. Castanheira (1999b), 'O problema da autonomia do Direito no actual problema da juridicidade', in J. A. Pinto Ribeiro (ed.), *O Homem e o Tempo. Liber amicorum para Miguel Baptista Pereira*, Porto: Fundação Eng. António de Almeida, 87–114.
Neves, A. Castanheira (2003), *O actual problema metodológico da interpretação jurídica*, Coimbra: Coimbra Editora.
Neves, A. Castanheira (2012), 'O "jurisprudencialismo" – proposta de uma reconstituição crítica do sentido do direito', in N. M. Morgadinho dos Santos Coelho and A. Sá da Silva (eds), *Teoria do Direito. Direito interrogado hoje – o Jurisprudencialismo: uma resposta possível? Estudos em homenagem ao Senhor Doutor António Castanheira Neves*, Salvador: Juspodivm/Faculdade Baiana de Direito, 9–79.
Nöth, W. (1995) [1990], *Handbook of Semiotics*, Bloomington and Indianapolis, IN: Indiana University Press.
Ost, F. (1991), 'Jupiter, Hercule, Hermès: Trois Modèles du Juge', in Pierre Bouretz (ed.), *La force du droit: Panorama des débats contemporains*, Paris: Esprit, 241–72.
Peczenik, A. (2007), *Scienta Juris. Legal Doctrine as Knowledge of Law and as a Source of Law (A Treatise of Legal Philosophy and General Jurisprudence vol. 4)*, Dordrecht: Springer.
Pettit, P. (2002), *Rules, Reasons, and Norms*, Oxford: Oxford University Press.
Posner, R. (1987), 'Legal Formalism, Legal Realism, and the Interpretation of Statutes and the Constitution', 37 *Case Western Reserve Law Review*, 179–217.
Radbruch, G. (1925), *Einführung in der Rechtswissenschaft*, Leipzig: Quelle & Meyer.
Savigny, F. K. von (1840), *System des heutigen Römischen Rechts*, vol. I, Berlin: Veit und Comp.
Schauer, F. (1991), *Playing by the Rules. A Philosophical Examination of Rule-Based Decision Making in Law and in Life*, Oxford: Clarendon Press.
Schauer, F. (2015), *The Force of Law*, Cambridge, MA: Harvard University Press.
Vaquero, Á. Nuñez (2013a), 'Some Realism for Hard Cases', 1 *Theory & Practice of Legislation*, 149–71.
Vaquero, Á. Nuñez (2013b), 'Five Models of Legal Science', 19 *Revus*, 53–81.

Chapter 4

Multiculturalism and Criminal Law: Between the Universal and the Particular

Leandro Santos da Guarda

How may cultural diversity be accommodated in the structure of criminal law? This is not a new question. However, in light of multicultural challenges, the debate concerning cultural diversity has been gaining space in the law, stressing the tension between universalism and particularism in criminal law. The multicultural theory brings to light underlying issues in criminal law and questions the possibilities and limits of a juridical consideration of cultural diversity.

'When in Rome, do as the Romans do' is the expression often recalled to illustrate the prevalent approach regarding the cultural practices of the others in criminal law. The approaches that defy this 'when in Rome' perspective represent an attempt to overcome the inflexibility of modern criminal law, which is linked to the Enlightenment notion of the nation-state and the liberal logic of universal individualism. It is precisely the idea of universalism that is challenged by multiculturalism, which questions to what point universal values are simply a reflexion of the majority culture.

The compromise between particular pretensions derived from the defendant's cultural allegiances and the idea of universal ascription of rules in a liberal democratic state is not a straightforward objective. In cases involving cultural arguments, general rules are confronted by singular elements, especially when the recognition of cultural evidences challenges the fundamental rights of others. In the end, the main question is how to balance punishment and individual justice without weakening the doctrine of liberty, certainty of rights and deterrence, nor, as a consequence, citizens' guarantees.

The goal of this chapter is to explore how the tension between the universal and the particular in criminal law is put into evidence in multicultural societies. I do not intend to give all answers to this problem, but rather to demonstrate the importance for the jurist to acknowledge these fundamental dynamics.

In this context, it is essential to go beyond commonsensical arguments about multiculturalism and culture. We cannot take for granted the idea of cultural identity and the influence of culture on human behaviour. For this purpose, the study of anthropology and political theory is the way to overcome outdated ideas that are still present in analyses about multiculturalism and cultural defence.

Indeed, the essentialist views of cultural identity that permeate these analyses are derived from misunderstandings of the role of culture. In this regard, an anthropological investigation is the condition to a comprehensive appreciation of multiculturalism, and a contribution to the broadening of the contemporary legal discourse about cultural defence.

I should note, however, that this article deals mostly with the traditional structure of criminal law. It acknowledges the debate but will not delve into whether the courts are the appropriate arena for discussing the acceptance of cultural practices and the importance of considering alternative forms of justice.

1. THE MULTICULTURAL RIDDLE

Multiculturalism is often accused of promoting localism and divisiveness. However, much that is accounted for under multiculturalism, or rather blamed on it, including deviations such as an excessive relativism, are derived from misguided and reified notions of ethnic and religious identities, as well as from a Romantic view of the idea of nation.

Gerd Baumann (1999) speaks of a 'multicultural riddle': a paradox that can be solved by a recasting of its terms. He points out that only by rethinking the relations between and among nationality, religion and ethnicity is it possible to devise a viable multicultural philosophy.

The riddle is then how to establish a state of justice and equality between and among three parties: those who believe in a unified national culture, those who trace their culture to their ethnic identity and those who view their religion as a culture (Baumann 1999: vii). Due to static views of culture as a 'thing' rather than a dialogical process of construction of meaning, ethnic, religious and national identities are misrepresented into essentialist notions, as if culture would be a giant photocopying machine that reproduced identical elements in a quasi-biological manner (Baumann 1999: 24–6).

Under the surface of this misconception of uniformity, there is an oversimplification of complex realities. Distorted ideas of nationality, ethnicity or religious identity create 'a unified ideological construct called French culture or European civilization or the Muslim way of life' (Modood 2013: 86).

As William H. McNeill (1986: 4) reminds us, 'the ideal of an ethnically unitary state was exceptional in theory and rarely approached in practice'. In this period, when the nation-state is in crisis and we talk of a post-Westphalian era, it is important to bear in mind that the ideal of ethnic uniformity was already controversial at the rise of modern European countries. Two well-known examples can provide us with a glimpse of the problem: the sharp analysis of Eugen Weber (1977), demonstrating the construction of the modern French culture ('Peasants into Frenchmen'), and the famous quote from Massimo d'Azeglio, one of the architects of the Italian Unification: 'We have made Italy. Now we must make Italians' (Hobsbawm and Ranger 2012: 267).

Indeed, the idea of ethnicity, in relation to multiculturalism, is primarily used in opposition to the idea of nationality (or nationalism). In this sense, ethnicity challenges the belief in a uniform concept of nationality, exposing the variety of ethnical origins in contemporary nation-states.

We cannot forget, however, that during the formation of the modern nation-states the notion was of a unified ethnic origin: the idea of nation as a 'superethnos', a congruence between geographical and ethnic (at least potentially) boundaries (Scherrer 2003: 9–10). The idea was that a legitimate government should rule only over citizens of the same ethnos. However, as its premise, ethnicity is itself frequently misunderstood and the appeal to a uniform shared culture is feeble, as we shall explore in the next section.

Similarly to the demands of ethnic minority groups, religious groups present demands of recognition beyond religious freedom and the toleration of classical liberalism, crossing into the debate about essentialism and defying the ideal of national uniformity.

Essentialist views of nationality, ethnicity and religious allegiances generate deterministic approaches to multiculturalism and the cultural defence. By solving the multicultural riddle, we avoid the trap of turning cultural elements into deterministic factors of human behaviour. The key to this process is to overcome a static view of cultural identity.

2. CULTURAL IDENTITY

The tendency to refer to cultural elements as determinant in human conduct and the mere belonging to a cultural group as a conclusive proof of this condition is questionable: a cultural norm or practice cannot be objectively identified and culture is not static. In fact, in view of contemporary anthropology, multiculturalism approaches that endorse reified views of culture regarding cultural defence cannot be sustained.

The idea of a personal identity forged by and dependent on the collective identity, in a process of replication, so that members of the same ethnical or religious group would all act in the same way, like clones (Baumann 1999: 137–8), represents a risk of reaching an 'ecological' (Habermas 1994: 128–30) or 'conservationist' (Raz 1995: 181) view of cultures.

Like culture, identity is not static. To use the definition of the sociologist Manuel Castells (2010: 6), identity, as it refers to social actors, is the 'process of construction of meaning on the basis of a cultural attribute, or a related set of cultural attributes, that is given priority over other sources of meaning'. It is not a mechanism that creates differences that do not exist, but a discourse that organises and gives sense to the cultural differences.

For instance, in the process of building ethnical boundaries it would not be the cultural elements that defined the ethnic group so much as the subjective notion of the group about the boundaries. Indeed, Fredrik Bark, one of the most influential contemporary anthropologists, published in 1969 an essay arguing that 'members of an ethnic group could, through contact with other groups, cease to exhibit their separate cultural traits and yet still perceive themselves as distinctive and different from their neighbours' (Poulter 1998: 6).

The fundamental advantage of this way of reasoning is to divert from the commonplace essentialist view of ethnic identities as 'genuine' or 'authentic', in contrast to other identities which are 'manufactured' or 'imposed' (Miller 1995: 135). In fact, an ethnic identity is a dialogical 'social imaginary' process, a narrative which bounds community in 'time and space, in history, memory, and territory' (Rattansi 1995: 258). Thus, ethnicity is a process, a product of a group's actions.

Culture is a continuous process of making. The essentialist approach to culture as heritage does not subsist in the light of the evidence of this processual nature of culture. If culture itself is an ongoing process, our adherence to a culture, and the extent of that adherence, presumably also changes over time, which means that cultural identity is not at all fixed. One way to refrain from the misconception of having culture as a 'thing' is to replace the term 'identity' with the notion of 'identification', so that we embrace fluidity and no longer expect any identity to be fixed and immutable (Baumann 1999: 137–8). Indeed, identity is not immutable throughout a person's lifetime; on the contrary it is in a continuous accumulative process (Maalouf 2000: 20).

On the other hand, a fluid identity or identification should not lead to scepticism toward social groups, as if they were only fiction. The key point here is that groups are 'real not as substances, but as forms of social relations' (Young 1990: 44). Social groups do not exist in isolation from individuals, neither are they a mere aggregation of indistinguishable homogeneous individuals. Social groups are the result of shared constructed cultural meanings, which partially constitute each person's identity.

The lack of a proper analysis of the role and attributes of culture underestimates both culture and cultural rights, reducing the problem to a question of mere 'cultural survival', oblivious to the positive aspects of cultural change (Cowan et al. 2001: 18).

But what constitutes culture? How exactly does culture affect human behaviour? What are the social and political processes in its regard? To what extent may law and institutional practices consider culture? Both in the liberal and in the communitarian perspectives on multiculturalism, community and culture are taken for granted, as universalised abstractions, 'empirically and logically prior to the question of rights' (Cowan et al. 2001: 17–18).

Like the continuous movement of culture, the concept itself has undergone transformations over time. However, the results of the long process of theoretical revision of the concept of culture within the field of anthropology have not yet been incorporated into other social sciences, or into law. Since the 1970s, the concept of culture has been subjected to criticism and extensively revised, though the social sciences and humanities still use notions that are no longer accepted by anthropologists (Giglioli and Ravaioli 2004).

One notion of culture that is no longer accepted in anthropology, but still permeates cultural studies, is Tylor's classical definition: 'Culture or Civilization, taken in its wide ethnographic sense, is that complex whole which includes knowledge, belief, art, morals, law, custom, and any other capabilities and habits acquired by man as member of a society' (Tylor 1973: 63).

This definition opposes culture to nature and covers all non-biological elements (Giglioli and Ravaioli 2004: 271), hence considering culture as a 'thing', not a process. Tylor's definition of culture remained the dominant one in anthropology for the first half of the twentieth century, and began to be challenged only in 1951, with Talcott Parsons' definition, which was re-elaborated and refined through the years and finally perfected by Geertz (1973). In this new depiction, the concept of culture is no longer contrasted to biology (this contrast is now taken for granted), but to social organisation (Giglioli and Ravaioli 2004: 272).

Geertz traces the rise of the concept of culture back to the overthrow of the view, dominant in the Enlightenment, of human nature as 'regularly organized, as thoroughly invariant, and as marvellously simple as Newton's universe'. This perspective considered the universal origin of desires and passions in an immutable structure, where the differences among people, regarding beliefs and values, customs and institutions, over time and places, consisted only of mere accretions, or distortions of 'what is truly human – the constant, the general, the universal – in man' (Geertz 1973: 34–5). This modern ideal of humankind engendered an idea of liberation from the burden of local attachments (Remote 2000: 143), though it took a reductionist approach towards the variability of human manifestations.

It was in this context that anthropology attempted to find a path to a more viable concept of human, one which would include culture and its variability. In fact, modern anthropology defies the Enlightened view of a universal 'Man' free of particularities, sustaining the impossibility of drawing a line between what is natural, universal and constant and what is conventional, local and variable.[1]

Having liberated the concept of humankind from the invariable perspective, the new goal became to locate it amid the diversity of customs. This has taken several directions, but they have proceeded through a 'stratigraphic' view of the relations between biological, psychological, social and cultural factors in human life: humankind was looked at as a 'composite of levels'. This was (and still is) an appealing view for academic purposes and led, at the level of concrete research and specific analysis, to a hunt for universals in culture that, despite a diversity of customs, could be found everywhere in about the same form (Geertz 1973: 37–8).

Tylor's definition is part of this context, which is ultimately a version of the Enlightenment's notion of universal conceptions of the right, real and just.[2] Against this universalistic approach, Geertz proposes a systematic relationship among diverse phenomena, replacing the 'stratigraphic' view of the relations between the

---

[1] Geertz (1973: 37 ff.) argues, however, that, away from a uniformitarian view of humanity, anthropology may turn to a cultural relativism that is as much an aberration as the banners of cultural relativism and 'cultural evolution'.

[2] In this regard, I would also like to allude to this extract: 'The major reason why anthropologists have shied away from cultural particularities when it came to a question of defining man and have taken refuge instead in bloodless universals is that, faced as they are with the enormous variation in human behavior, they are haunted by a fear of historicism, of becoming lost in a whirl of cultural relativism so convulsive as to deprive them of any fixed bearings at all' (Geertz 1973: 43–4).

various aspects of human existence with a synthetic perspective, based on two ideas. First, that culture is best seen as a set of control mechanisms – plans, recipes, rules, instructions – for governing behaviour. And second, that people are dependent on such mechanisms. For Geertz, there is no such thing as human nature independent of culture, since we are simply incomplete animals who complete ourselves through culture. The boundary between what is innately controlled and what is culturally controlled in human behaviour is therefore loosely defined (Geertz 1973: 37–43).

While the Enlightenment's image of humans divested of culture renders the differences between individuals secondary, Geertz proposes a compromise between a general theoretical understanding and a circumstantial understanding, between the definition of a person by innate capacities alone and his or her actual behaviours: 'Becoming human is becoming individual, and we become individual under the guidance of cultural patterns, historically created systems of meaning in terms of which we give form, order, point, and direction to our lives' (Geertz 1973: 52).

This processual perspective encapsulated by Geertz goes beyond the notion that culture is an external and superior entity to the person and overcomes the anachronistic idea of culture as internally coherent and homogeneously shared by the members of a community (Giglioli and Ravaioli 2004: 269).

However, this 'new' notion of culture perfected by Geertz is applied with some difficulty to social reality, which has led some anthropologists to refute the instrumentality of this concept (Giglioli and Ravaioli 2004: 269). Indeed, the complexity of the concept of culture has often resulted in controversy about the nature and relevance of culture to the contemporary world (O'Hagan 2002).

Despite the complexity that anthropology lends to the culture concept, cultural identity is currently being used in a quasi-biological manner in the discourse about ethnicity (and religion), relying upon outdated views of culture, so that a 'group of people "has" a culture in the way that animals have fur, inherited as genes are inherited, rather than as a repertoire people create or use to adapt or changing social condition' (Merry 2001: 42). This distortion is also present in the legal discourses about culture, exposing the contradictions between universal ideals and particular pretensions.

3. CULTURE AND LAW

The undeniable reality of increased cultural diversity has highlighted the presence of cultural conflicts in criminal law. Indeed, the growing cultural diversity within the borders of nation-states has heightened the interest in the debate about criminal cultural conflicts. In this process, multiculturalism has become a theoretical reference and has underscored some contradictions in criminal law.

Multiculturalism challenges the fundaments of the liberal nation-state, mainly the principles of equality and universal individualism. Since these are core values of modern criminal law, multiculturalism therefore tests the very bases of the penal system. It poses a challenge to an absolute idea of equality, compelling an account of the Aristotelian concept of equality, so that like cases are treated alike and different cases differently (Truffin and Arjona 2009: 118).

Modern criminal law has dialectical roots in the Enlightenment and Romanticism. With rationality as an aspiration, the Enlightenment brought into the penal theory the logic of universal individualism (Norrie 2001: 21), but this logic refers also to the construction of the nation-state, which has a Romantic origin. From this Enlightenment basis, 'homo juridicus' was deemed a rational, calculating man, isolated from the social and moral circumstances in which the crime occurs as well as from the local culture. However, this process often ignores how the background of the majority culture or, from a different angle, the national culture, is reflected in criminal law. The awareness of these roots is fundamental for understanding the role of culture within criminal law and to locate criminal law in a cultural perspective.

These dialectical roots represent a paradox between the claim of a law free of particularism ('culture' in the plural) and its cultural nature related to the dominant values ('culture' in the singular) (Monceri 2007: 83–4). Indeed, law has developed conceptually mainly as the antithesis of culture, in the sense of tradition, myth and customs. At the same time, modern criminal law is an achievement of the Enlightenment culture and the process of civilisation that led to nation-states (Coombe 2006: 22–3), being in this sense identified with the emerging national cultures.

This leads to the debate about the limits of legal universalism, which has gained strength with the growth of migratory movements and the demands of recognition of autochthonous peoples. Although there have been marked social (and cultural) differences since its origin, modern criminal law was established taking into account an idealised homogeneous society. This concealing of differences is exposed by the multicultural demands.[3]

However, that does not make the ideal (or myth) of universal individualism pointless and dispensable; it only means that we must be aware of its limits.[4] On the other hand, it is also true that law and legal reasoning have universalistic aspirations, but this does not imply that universalism must be ethnocentric. In a multicultural society, by means of democratic procedures, different cultures should be able to reach consensus through deliberation and agree about universal norms for the broad community.[5]

What is the role of law in this process? Could criminal law become the confluence for social cohesion in a multicultural society? The answers to these questions

---

[3] In fact, the pursuit of a homogeneous nation-state was usually accompanied by violence and oppression, including genocide (De Maglie 2010: 3).

[4] Regarding this perspective, I quote McNeill (1981): 'Our social existence depends on shared values, symbols and meanings, proclaimed and acted upon, at least sometimes, by hundreds, thousands, and millions of persons'.

[5] In this sense, the processual universalism sustained by Seyla Benhabib, cited by Mohr (2005: 90–1).

lie in the opposition between the claims of universal rights and the multiculturalist recognition of particularities, which could be balanced only through deliberative procedures that account for cultural difference.

Multiculturalism 'pushes thinking on criminal justice issues towards political theory, because it makes it much more important than before to theorize about the premises of the authority of law' (Nuotio 2014: 67). This political perception of the debate reminds us that the issues raised by the cultural defence approach are part of a larger debate concerning multiculturalism (Coleman 1996: 1094). In fact, it would be meaningless to view the cultural defence isolated from the contemporary multicultural political context.

4. THE POLITICAL SPHERE

An effective multicultural policy has to go beyond an idealised view of cultural heritage towards a demythologising view. Culture is not always pretty: it involves 'the good and the bad, the attractive and the unattractive, reasons for pride and reasons for shame' (Bissoondath 1994: 87). We cannot pick only the aspects that we appreciate.

Furthermore, an effective multicultural theory should care about values. The right to recognition cannot represent a blank cheque to all ways of life and practices (Bauman 2001: 80). Indeed, the challenge underlying multiculturalism is to understand how cultural diversity may contribute to a 'better, richer, pluralistic society' (Lernestedt 2014: 45). In this perspective of values, criminal law represents an 'important and distinct dimension to the general multicultural debate' (Lernestedt 2014: 45), because of its role as mediator of different ways of life.

The accentuation of ethnic and religious identities in mere opposition to nationhood results in a dangerous space for divisiveness (Bissoondath 1994: 186), tending to diminish the role and autonomy of the individuals, placing them in stereotypical confines (Bissoondath 1994: 212). The positive self-fulfilment role of culture is turned into an object for display, devaluating the inherent value of culture itself (Bissoondath 1994: 88), in a static view of human personality.

In this framework, citizenship could be a secure place for the meeting of cultural diversity, an instrument to engage minorities in a dialogical process, a 'reasonable basis of social unity' (Rawls 2005: XXXVI). Indeed, the ascription of rights is the mechanism of social cohesion through which differences can be respected.

In other words, this is a perspective of a reshaping of the public sphere, so that social meanings, including citizenship, could be reconstructed through a more comprehensive and democratic public representation, aiming to circumvent the tendential advantage of dominant groups. We must overcome an enclosed idea of citizenship that excludes all others. It is a question of political justice (Walzer 2000: 60).

At the same time, we have to bypass the idealised views of nation, because, in the end, nationalism is also a form of moral particularism (Young 2000: 251). The challenge is to reach cohesion beyond cultural diversity. In this sense, from the awareness of the procedural nature of nationality follows that the unity of the *demos* 'ought to be understood not as if it were a harmonious given, but rather as a process of self-constitution through more or less conscious struggles of inclusion and exclusion' (Benhabib 2005: 675).

Multiculturalism, if the procedural nature of nationality and ethnicity is adequately understood, could then be, contrary to expectations, a mechanism of unification rather than division (Caniglia 2003: 48), effacing the idea of a hostility of multiculturalism towards the nation-state.

In fact, citizenship is the only possible point of cohesion in a multicultural society.[6] Neither nationalism nor patriotism will bind together the different groups in a multicultural society. The only way to reach this in a pluralistic society is through a constant negotiation to accommodate naturally different interests, and the overcoming of a monistic view of citizenship (Modood 2013: 116–17).

Moreover, the idea of citizenship accommodating cultural diversity is a way to preserve the values represented by the formal and material expansion of citizenship rights since the seventeenth century. This, however, is viable only through a reframing of the idea of universality, as will be discussed below.

5. THE UNIVERSALITY OF HUMANITY

In the confrontation between the idea of nationhood and other collective allegiances, seeking a pluralistic concept of citizenship is the way to circumvent divisiveness. Accommodating differences requires a departure from the humanistic notion of universal citizenship. Universality does not have a metaphysical nature. It is a material goal reachable through procedural commitments. In this regard, Zygmunt Bauman claims:

> Universality of citizenship is the preliminary condition of all meaningful 'politics of recognition'. And, let me add, universality of humanity is the horizon by which all politics of recognition, to be meaningful, needs to orient itself. Universality of humanity does not stand in opposition to the pluralism of the forms of human life; but the test of truly universal humanity is its ability to accommodate pluralism and make pluralism serve the cause of humanity – to enable and encourage 'ongoing discussion about the shared conception of the good. (Bauman 2001: 140)

---

[6] Along these lines, Modood (2013: 113): 'The ideas of equality that are implicit in the practice of citizenship can be used to highlight how certain challenges to those ideas of equality are not being met, or need to be rethought, of how the facts and mechanism of negative difference have to be more seriously explored and highlighted and overcome by allowing the flourishing of positive difference.'

We need, then, to inquire about the concept of universality emulated in our legal system. The discourse of human rights can be used as paradigm for this purpose. Indeed, due to their roots in European liberalism, human rights face criticisms of eurocentrism and unfeasibility of their universalistic pretension, sharing, in this sense, a connection with the demands of multiculturalism (Maffettone 2003: 201).

However, contrary to static and homogeneous views of traditional cultures, what can be observed is that minority groups undertake a process of cultural appropriation of human rights. Although produced in the 'central' West, human rights are now being 'appropriated around the globe by other peoples and transformed in various ways in different locations' (Merry 2001: 47).

In fact, despite their opposing origins, universalism and relativism are not irreconcilable with regard to human rights. Borrowing Dembour's perspective, we can say that they work in a pendulum motion, so that we can locate human rights in an unstable in-between position (Dembour 2001: 56).

The challenge is to overcome the presumptuous approach of the 'righteousness' of human rights, which excludes the experience of the other. This does not represent the rejection of a universalistic aspiration or the embrace of a cultural relativism, but recognises that a broader view of human rights should include the perspective of minorities (Dembour 2001: 58).

Dembour, recalling Peter Fitzpatrick, remarks that the universal can never be established by itself, but is always accessed by the specific, in the sense that it represents a particular historical experience. The Universal Declaration of Human Rights, for example, although representing a pretension of universality, was in fact 'drafted by people who looked at the world from a particular window' (Dembour 2001: 75).

The common project of building democratic constitutional states, in a multicultural context, can and should be seen not as an enterprise of people sharing an ethnic and cultural common identity, but rather an agreement among diverse and conflicting groups, in a way that the civic coexistence is guaranteed by law. In other words, this project is not the mere reproduction of the majoritarian will, but an attempt to reach harmony among citizens, regardless of their identities (Ferrajoli 2007: 50–1).

With this perspective of citizenship as a meeting point of differences, Luigi Ferrajoli affirms that fundamental rights are compatible with cultural diversity, arguing that most of the criticisms against multiculturalism are based on a misinterpretation of the concept of universalism. For Ferrajoli, axiological or sociological definitions, which identify the concept, respectively, with moral or ideological theories, are not adequate. Indeed, in neither of these two perspectives can fundamental rights be understood as universal. Instead, the logical meaning of universalism is that of a universal ascription of rights. That is, fundamental rights are universally and equally bestowed to citizens (Ferrajoli 2007: 57–8). In fact, its premise is the equivalence between equality and the universalism of fundamental rights, so that they are ascribed *iura omnium* by abstract and general norms (Ferrajoli 2007: 104).

This view of the universalism of fundamental rights is not only compatible with the respect of differences demanded by multiculturalism, but it is also their main guarantee. Ferrajoli points out two reasons for this. First, the universal ascription of fundamental rights is a guarantee against the majority and against anybody – including, in this class of rights, the protection of cultural manifestations. In fact, the category of fundamental rights includes the rights of freedom, being the freedom of conscience, the first fundamental liberty and the fundamental right *par excellence* concerning the protection of personal and cultural identity, alongside the freedom of thought and expression, religious freedom and other fundamental rights that are also tools for the protection of diversity (Ferrajoli 2007: 58–9).

The second reason for considering fundamental rights instrumental to the protection of difference in multicultural contexts is the fact that these rights substitute the 'law of the jungle' with a law that protects the weakest, including his or her cultural manifestations and identities (Ferrajoli 2007: 59–60).

However, Ferrajoli's main point, regarding the compatibility of fundamental rights and multiculturalism, is the distinction he makes between the universal legal form and its original philosophical basis. He argues that, despite the concept of universalism being the product of a specific political and moral experience, it is not necessary to agree with its theoretical sources in order to recognise the intrinsic value of the universal ascription of fundamental rights (Ferrajoli 2007: 60–1). Indeed, the notion of universal ascription of fundamental rights should be recognised as an independent value *per se*. In Barry's (2002: 286) words: 'It does not have to be valid unconditionally to be valid universally.'

6. CONCLUSION

Multiculturalism poses the question of how cultural aspects affect the delivery of criminal justice services. There is a certain tension between a widespread perception that defendants want the courts to excuse their behaviour based upon their culture, and the perspective that only with a proper understanding of the offenders' culture and its impact on their behaviour can the courts accomplish their role. This conflicts appear in different guises, often with multiculturalism accused of promoting localism and divisiveness.

On the other hand, essentialist views of culture and the so-called cultural relativism can lead to a 'boutique multiculturalism' (Fish 1997: 8), which picks and chooses only the easy parts of the discourse, ignoring the negative side of cultures and practices that do not contribute to a better pluralistic society. This concern is, and must be, central to the debate on criminal law and culture. Otherwise, we may similarly risk instilling a kind of 'boutique cultural defence' (Lernestedt 2014: 45), one which selects only a 'favoured "snapshot" version' of the culture in question (Jeremy Waldron cited by Scotti (2014: 462)).

Multiculturalism is frequently criticised for being an essentialist philosophy. However, it actually challenges the essentialist ideas of solid and monolithic national identities, highlighting the variance and discrepancies under the surface of a national unified identity. A viable multicultural philosophy needs to go beyond reified views of nation, ethnicity and religious identity, the three pillars of multiculturalism. In order to overcome such reified notions that undervalue cultural diversity, we have to understand how cultural identity bears on these three poles.

In fact, the unveiling of a reified notion of ethnic and religious identities, as well as of a Romantic view of the idea of nation, discloses the fragility of claims of cultural recognition based on deterministic ideas of culture, as if all members of a cultural group would be clones of the same matrix. In this vein, multiculturalism points towards an amplification of the idea of culture. Only a processual or dialogical view of culture has a place in contemporary anthropology.

From a political point of view, a possible response to the challenges related to the rising cultural diversity in contemporary societies lies in the enlargement of the concept of citizenship, so that cultural differences may take shelter under a common civic sphere. In this perspective, citizenship could democratically embody a wider cultural reference (Nuotio 2014: 86). By the same token, the duty to respect the law would rest on the civic role of the member of a political community, not in his or her cultural allegiances (Nuotio 2014: 76).

Regarding criminal law, we may not have as optimistic an approach as Bernardi's (2006: 128), who sees criminal law as the ultimate locus in which to settle multicultural conflicts and make social harmony possible. We could, however, still agree with him in regard to the need for a greater openness to the Other in criminal law theory. This approach inevitably requires a better understanding of culture.

Moreover, we must acknowledge modern criminal law as a political construct, in opposition to notions of a natural law and universal morality. Indeed, the legitimacy of criminal justice needs to be built on political bases. However, the political dimension of criminal law and the function of universal ascription of rights are usually undervalued in some approaches to cultural defence.

We cannot forget how important it is that criminal law may provide equal guarantees to all citizens, regardless of status, focused on acts rather than on subjects, in contrast to a view of the law as moralising, applicable only to certain categories of people. The fact that an action can be traced back to the defendant's cultural allegiances does not mean that his or her conduct can be justified, especially when the recognition of cultural evidences challenges the fundamental rights of others.

Modern criminal law is the result of a process of building up legal values: a civilisational achievement. In fact, we are not merely conditioned by laws from the 'outside'. Rather, we are part of the creation of social meanings, and legal meanings become part of the image of ourselves, in a way that 'our own purposes and understandings can no longer be extricated from those meanings' (Sarat and Kearns 2006: 7–8).

Indeed, it is possible for a national community, even as it recognises the liberty of the individual to maintain his or her allegiances to minority groups and to carry out traditions and cultural practices, to maintain, in a multicultural context, the perspective of outer limits, that is, of minimum standards to be followed by every citizen regardless of his or her allegiances. Ultimately, this means that the very notion of universalism needs to be reframed.

However, in imperfect or dysfunctional political and criminal systems, where we have an excess of criminalisation beyond the minimum standards of behaviour that should be the aim of criminal law, the conflict between cultural rights pretensions and criminal law provisions emerges in the practice of criminal law justice, so that this kind of conflict can be accommodated only in the particular – or, in other words, case by case. Kimmo Nuotio (2014: 84) makes an interesting observation about the tendency to deal in this manner with cultural diversity at the judicial level: 'We would not be willing to compromise the whole system by making cultural exceptions to the rules, but in individual instances this may be acceptable.'

Legal meanings are produced performatively, so that the law already has in its genesis the flexibility to respond to cultural changes (Rosen 2006: 92–3). In fact, law is itself an element of culture, even though this feature does not commonly appear as a solution to the issues related to culture in criminal law, but instead as obstacles to a law open to cultural diversity.

To harmonise universal ideals and particular cultural aspects on each case, it is indispensable to bring to the foreground the relation between culture and law, in order to avoid the double trap of cultural relativism and void universalism. The legal discourse is located in this unstable in-between position, and the knowledge of anthropology and political theory are two equally indispensable tools to navigate it.

Bibliography

Barry, B. M. (2002), *Culture & Equality: An Egalitarian Critique of Multiculturalism*, Cambridge, MA: Harvard University Press.
Bauman, Z. (2001), *Community: Seeking Safety in an Insecure World*, Cambridge: Polity.
Baumann, G. (1999), *The Multicultural Riddle*, New York: Routledge.
Benhabib, S. (2005), 'Borders, Boundaries, and Citizenship', 38(4) *PS: Political Science & Politics*, 673–7.
Bernardi, A. (2006), *Modelli Penali e Società Multiculturale*, Torino: Giappichelli.
Bissoondath, N. (1994), *Selling Illusions: The Cult of Multiculturalism in Canada*, Toronto: Penguin Books.
Caniglia, E. (2003), 'Il multiculturalismo come forma sociale del postmoderno', in R. Boudon, E. Caniglia and A. Spreafico (eds), *Multiculturalismo o comunitarismo?*, Roma: Luiss University Press, 23–48.

Castells, M. (2010), *The Power of Identity: The Information Age - Economy, Society, and Culture (Information Age Series, vol. 2)*, 2nd rev. edn, Chichester: Wiley-Blackwell.
Coleman, D. L. (1996), 'Individualizing justice through multiculturalism', 96 *Columbia Law Review*, 1093–157.
Coombe, R. J. (2006), 'Contingent Articulations: A Critical Cultural Studies of Law', in A. Sarat and T. Kearns (eds), *Law in the Domains of Culture*, Ann Arbor, MI: University of Michigan Press, 21–64.
Cowan, J. K., M.-B. Dembour and R. A. Wilson (2001), 'Introduction', in J. K. Cowan, M.-B. Dembour and R. A. Wilson (eds), *Culture and Rights: Anthropological Perspectives*, Cambridge: Cambridge University Press.
De Maglie, C. (2010), *I reati culturalmente motivati, Ideologia e modelli penali*, Pisa: ETS.
Dembour, M.-B. (2001), 'Following the Movement of a Pendulum: Between Universalism and Relativism', in J. K. Cowan, M.-B. Dembour and R. A. Wilson (eds), *Culture and Rights: Anthropological Perspectives*, Cambridge: Cambridge University Press, 56–79.
Ferrajoli, L. (2007), *Principia Iuris. Teoria del diritto e della democrazia*, Roma: Laterza.
Fish, S. (1997), 'Boutique Multiculturalism, or Why Liberals Are Incapable of Thinking about Hate Speech', 23(2) *Critical Inquiry*, 378–95.
Geertz, C. (1973), *The Interpretation of Cultures*, New York: Basic Books.
Giglioli, P. P. and P. Ravaioli (2004), 'Bisogna davvero dimenticare il concetto di cultura? Replica ai colleghi antropologi', XLV(2) *Rassegna Italiana di Sociologia*, 267–98.
Habermas, J. (1994), 'Struggles for Recognition in the Democratic Constitutional State', in A. Gutmann (ed.), *Multiculturalism: Examining the Politics of Recognition*, Princeton, NJ: Princeton University Press, 107–48.
Hobsbawm, E. J. and T. O. Ranger (2012) [1983], *The Invention of Tradition*, Cambridge: Cambridge University Press.
Lernestedt, C. (2014), 'Criminal Law and "Culture"', in W. Kymlicka, C. Lernestedt and M. Matraver (eds), *Criminal Law and Cultural Diversity*, Oxford: Oxford University Press, 15–46.
Maalouf, A. (2000), *On Identity*, London: The Harvill Press.
Maffettone, S. (2003), 'Liberalismo, multiculturalismo e diritti umani', in R. Boudon, E. Caniglia and A. Spreafico, *Multiculturalismo o comunitarismo?* Roma: Luiss University Press, 201–22.
McNeill, W. H. (1981), 'Make Mine Myth', *New York Times*, 28 December 1981 <www.nytimes.com/1981/12/28/opinion/make-mine-myth.html?mcubz=1> accessed 9 September 2019.
McNeill, W. H. (1986), *Polyethnicity and National Unity in World History*, Toronto: University of Toronto Press.
Merry, S. E. (2001), 'Changing Rights, Changing Culture', in J. K. Cowan, M.-B. Dembour and R. A. Wilson (eds), *Culture and Rights: Anthropological Perspectives*, Cambridge: Cambridge University Press, 31–55.

Miller, D. (1995), *On Nationality*, Oxford: Clarendon Press.
Modood, T. (2013), *Multiculturalism*, 2nd edn, Cambridge: Polity.
Mohr, R. (2005), 'Some Conditions for Culturally Diverse Deliberation', 20(1) *Canadian Journal of Law and Society*, 87–102.
Monceri, F. (2007), 'Multiculturalismo: Disincanto o Disorientamento del Diritto?', in G. De Francesco, C. Piemontese and E. Venafro (eds), *Religione e religioni: prospettive di tutela, tutela della libertà*, Torino: Giappichelli.
Norrie, A. (2001), *Crime, Reason and History: A Critical Introduction to Criminal Law*, London: Butterworths.
Nuotio, K. (2014), 'Between Denial and Recognition: Criminal Law and Cultural Diversity', in W. Kymlicka, C. Lernestedt and M. Matraver (eds), *Criminal Law and Cultural Diversity*, Oxford: Oxford University Press, 67–88.
O'Hagan, J. (2002), 'Conflict, Convergence, or Coexistence? The Relevance of Culture', in R. Falk, L. Edwin and J. Walker (eds), *Reframing the International: Law, Culture, Politics*, New York: Routledge, 187–217.
Poulter, S. (1998), *Ethnicity, Law and Human Rights: The English Experience*, Oxford: Oxford University Press.
Rattansi, A. (1995), 'Just Framing: Ethnicities and Racism in a "Postmodern" Framework', in L. Nicholson and S. Seidman (eds), *Social Postmodernism: Beyond Identity Politics*, Cambridge: Cambridge University Press, 250–86.
Rawls, J. (2005) [1993], *Political Liberalism*, New York: Columbia University Press.
Raz, J. (1995), 'Multiculturalism: A Liberal Perspective', in J. Raz, *Ethics in the Public Domain*, Oxford: Clarion Press.
Remote, F. (2000), *Prima lezione di antropologia*, Roma-Bari: Laterza.
Rosen, L. (2006), *Law as Culture: An Invitation*, Princeton, NJ and Oxford: Princeton University Press.
Sarat, A. and T. R. Kearns (2006), 'The Cultural Lives of Law', in A. Sarat and T. R. Kearns (eds), *Law in the Domains of Culture*, Ann Arbor, MI: University of Michigan Press, 1–20.
Scherrer, C. P. (2003), *Ethnicity, Nationalism and Violence: Conflict Management, Human Rights, and Multilateral Regimes*, Aldershot: Ashgate.
Scotti, G. (2014), 'A Constituição de 1988 como marco na luta por reconhecimento dos direitos fundamentais dos povos indígenas e quilombolas no Brasil – a natureza aberta dos direitos no estado democrático de Direito', in C. Clève and A. Freire (eds), *Direitos Fundamentais e Jurisdição Constitucional*, São Paulo: Editora Revista dos Tribunais, 457–76.
Truffin, B. and C. Arjona (2009), 'The Cultural Defense in Spain', in M. Foblets and A. Renteln (eds), *Multicultural Jurisprudence: Comparative Perspectives on the Cultural Defense*, Oxford and Portland, OR: Hart Publishing, 85–120.
Tylor, E. B. (1973) [1871], 'Primitive Culture', in P. Bohannan, *High Points in Anthropology*, New York: A. A. Knopf.
Walzer, M. (2000), *Spheres of Justice: A Defense of Pluralism and Equality*, New York: Basic Books.

Weber, E. (1977), *Peasants into Frenchmen: the Modernization of Rural France – 1870–1914*, London: Chatto & Windus.
Young, I. M. (1990), *Justice and Politics of Difference*, Princeton, NJ: Princeton University Press.
Young, I. M. (2000), *Inclusion and Democracy*, Oxford: Oxford University Press.

Chapter 5

Cognitive Populism: A Semiotic Reading of the Dialectics Type/Token

Massimo Leone

Omnia mala exempla ex rebus bonis orta sunt.
Sallust, *Catilinaria*, 51.27

1. INTRODUCTION: STAGING SCRIPTS

In Quentin Dupieux's 2018 movie *Au Poste !* (English title: *Keep an Eye Out*), Louis Fugain, the protagonist, calls the police after finding a corpse in a pool of blood in front of his apartment building one night. Police detective Buron then inflicts on him an ordeal in the form of an overnight interrogation, asking him increasingly surreal questions. The film narrates the confrontation by continuously breaking the common rules of cinematic logic. In the filmic visualisation of Fugain's answers to Buron, the suspect comes across some of the characters that he has met at the police station, a feature that contradicts the chronology of narration; at one stage, the former can even clearly visualise the story that the latter is telling him. He can also sometimes be seen by the detective when it is his turn, Fugain's, to narrate. Eventually, when the interrogation seems to have reached a dead end, the police station suddenly turns into a theatre stage, and Buron and the other police officers reveal themselves to be in fact actors and actresses, applauded by the audience at the end of their enacting the interrogation. Fugain is, therefore, relieved but, after having dinner with the whole theatre troupe in a local brasserie, he finds out to his despair that he is going to be arrested again so as to be forced to participate in the same staged interrogation the following day. His legal ordeal, turned into a theatrical show, might never come to a definitive end.

The movie explores a short-circuit between reality and representation: on the one hand, Buron seems to suspect Fugain for real, with real consequences; for instance, the suspect loses his freedom to leave and go home. On the other hand, Fugain is actually turned into the involuntary protagonist of a play whose destiny is to be put on stage over and over again, representing an interrogation that will never cease either with his condemnation or with his acquittal. The continuous interferences between the interrogation and the visualisation of the stories shared through it prepare the revelation of this overlapping between the two dimensions of reality and representation.

This confusion lends itself to two readings: in the first, *Au Poste !* reads like a reflection on the complex semiotics of visual and, in particular, filmic storytelling: at least from Roland Barthes' (1968) theorisation of the reality effect, it is well known that, when a *mise en abyme* or 'story within a story' is represented, the fact itself that a narrative is contained within another analogous narrative attributes to the latter an aura of reality (Ankersmit 1989). This is even more striking in visual embedding: in a movie, for instance, whenever a character tells a story and this story is visualised by the movie, this bestows on the main filmic narrative a greater connotation of realism (Fischer and Nänny 2001). *Au Poste !*, like other non-conventional or post-modern narratives before it, plays with the formal conventions of this rhetoric, disenchanting it: contrary to what is expected, characters in the embedded visual narration meet with those in the embedding one, interacting with them. In this way, the separation between the two dimensions that the formal structure of the *mise en abyme* usually guarantees, playing a central role in its rhetoric of realism, is disrupted, with the opposite result of creating an 'unreality effect', affecting both the containing visual narrative and the contained one. In *Au Poste !* one starts disbelieving the reality of the interrogation, but this sceptical attitude soon invests the movie in its entirety, with the consequence that it ends up looking like a surreal apologue (Orban 1990).

This apologue, however, does not bear only on the artificiality of narrative conventions but also, more generally and ambitiously, on the conventionality of the specific institutional practices that the film represents. Most of the movie consists in the surreal scene of an interrogation presented as the discursive genre characteristically meant to find evidence as regards the facts involved in a trial. *Au Poste !* seems to suggest that such a genre, and more generally the discursive template of the trial, which crucially comprises interrogation, entails a certain degree of rituality, marred by the implacable stupidity of bureaucracy and the inextricable paradoxes of theatricality (Chaemsaithong 2019). These two aspects, a disenchanting perspective on the rhetoric of realism and an equally disillusioning perspective on the rhetoric of trial, are however intertwined: if the interrogation, and the trial to which it leads, is an ancient and complex rhetorical machine to construct an aura of realism around the description of facts and events, then deconstructing the classic filmic representation of it also inevitably casts a shadow of doubt on the juridical institution of the trial itself (Kavanagh 1972).

2. THE ULTIMATE NATURE OF SCRIPTS

To this regard, the reflection of the philosophy of law intersects the one offered, in various ways, by structural linguistics and semiotics. In most modern attempts at dispassionately grasping the main mechanisms of meaning, both in verbal and non-verbal language, consideration of the dialectics between token and type has been pivotal (Wetzel 2006). In language, meaning is indeed hard to explain without accounting for the capacity, entailed by the human faculty of language itself, of activating the switch between the general representation of a meaningful pattern and its actual, particular occurrence (Bromberger 1992). Such ability is necessary at all levels of the structural functioning of the sign: it is essential in the recognition of the phonic or graphic expression of meaning in verbal language (Bromberger and Halle 1986), beyond the discrepancies of singular utterances, as well as in any form of conceptualisation (Zemach 1992). Human beings are able to perceive singularities in both expression and content but the form itself of culture encourages them to disregard idiosyncrasies and to concentrate, instead, on the relation between the utterance and the general type to which it can be ascribed (Wolterstorff 1970).

Such dialectics between perception of singularities and conceptualisation of generalities has been studied and denominated in various disciplines with diverse terminologies, 'token and type' being, perhaps, its most diffused version in structural perspectives. In any case, in the dimension of narration, this dialectics is crucially linked with an issue of scripts (Mandler 1984; Mattozzi 1987). Such issue is key in the legal discourse of interrogation and trial also (Heffer 2005). In the first, events are usually recounted according to a script, which is moulded by the powerful but invisible rhetoric of common sense. It would be naive, nevertheless, to believe that these narrative scripts hamper the otherwise unhindered expression of the singularity of the real, for the real itself is, to a significant extent, predetermined by scripts.

It is exactly by subverting these scripts (those of legal narration but also, more deeply, those of the emergence itself of facts) that surreal movies like *Au Poste !* produce an effect of ironic estrangement. This subversion, however, is doomed to be surreal for reality itself is actually controlled by quite rigid scripts. Events do not usually happen in surprising ways, and it is only for artistic purposes that their being nothing but tokens of pre-existent types is represented through a playful consideration for alternatives. From the strictly structural point of view, a token is different from a type, for the former contains material but also semantic traits that do not belong to the latter, that are not crucial to evoke it, but that nevertheless are not pertinent either to evoke an alternative type (Wetzel 1993). Tokens, therefore, contain semantic residues that, strictly speaking, are not relevant as regards the social construction of meaning. The impertinence of the arts, then, precisely consists in magnifying those aspects of a token that are not pertinent, in order to convert them to alternative tokens of non-existing types (Wolterstorff 1975).

Here the non-existence of types that ironic stories represent must necessarily give rise not to the idea of an alternative reality but to that of a surreal dimension, which can receive and maintain a status only in the very special discourse of the arts. The scripts that somehow govern the production of facts and meanings are indeed socially constructed through long-period interactions that absolutely escape individual agencies. It is evident that a human being cannot speak a singular language (Wittgenstein's idiolect), but this evidence must also be connected with another piece of evidence which is more difficult to accept: reality itself does not produce significant exceptions. Accidents in the regular coming about of tokens are not a real disruption of the cultural machine producing meaning in a human community because the production itself of accidents is somehow stereotypical (Leone 2018).

That is, ultimately, what most moral and legal discourse does: on the one hand, it ratifies the regularity of certain behaviours (like not terminating the life of other human beings, for instance), whereas, on the other hand, it typifies the exceptions to these regularities (there are many different ways of murdering someone but they all inevitably converge toward recurring types). Whenever, on the contrary, residual tokens of this typology are themselves attributed the status of types, the result is absurd. Given that this dialectics excludes the significance of impertinent exceptions at both the level of representation and that of reality itself, then the very dialectics between types and tokens is, in fact, a rhetorical field, in whose perimeter the discourse of exemplification characteristically unfolds (Peirce CP 4.423; 8.334; Greenlee 1973).

3. SCRIPTING RHETORICS

What happens, indeed, when the locutions 'for instance' or 'for example' are uttered? The surreal effect of the abovementioned movie stems exactly from the production of impertinent tokens that do not properly exemplify a type. Watchers of a crime movie expect that it will present them not with the type of the murder but with a specific token of it, which both refers to it, and is, therefore, recognisable as its token, without for that reason entirely overlapping with it. The degree of experimentation can go from one extreme to the other along a spectrum. At the one end, a commercial movie can fill the filmic representation of a police interrogation with all the elements that are contained in its cultural and cinematic type (or script). The result of this exhaustiveness is usually both reassuring and kitsch (Putz 1994): the scene will be universally recognisable as one representing a police interrogation, yet it will be its exhaustiveness itself to irradiate a feeling of inauthenticity (Umbach and Humphrey 2018). Similarly, love affairs never manifest themselves with all the traits of a love affair, for something is always missing. Movies that, on the contrary, represent this completeness might be sentimentally reassuring but are ultimately unbelievable. At the other end of the spectrum, however, representations that eliminate some central aspects of a type for the sake of originality end up being surreal and absurd, to the extent that the cultural script they refer to is not recognised if not through the filter of irony.

In between the preposterous adhesion to a type and the equally farfetched divergence from its semantic kernel, one finds good exemplification and efficacious examples. A good example contains enough elements of a cultural type so as to be recognised as its instance, yet it does not contain so many of these elements as to give rise to an effect of inauthenticity. Indeed, the rhetorical power of examples precisely resides in the fact that they allow discourse to gain specificity, and to even allude to the utopia of singularity, but without loosening the relation with generality and, as a consequence, with the domain of intelligibility, which rotates around conceptualisation, typologies and universals.

4. SCRIPT IDEOLOGIES

In an effort of meta- and self-reflection, what would be a good example of the theory abstractedly exposed thus far? And, symmetrically, what would be a 'bad' example of it? Answering this question in a straightforward manner would itself be ingenuous, for it would neglect a fact that the history of legal discourse and, more generally, the history of exemplification betrays: those discursive constructions that would have been considered as good examples in past centuries appear totally unconvincing nowadays. Reading the classics of early modern Christian moral theology, for instance, one is struck by the abundance of examples taken from ancient, often non-Christian, history (Van Den Akker 2018). The moral imperative of justice, for example, was often evoked with reference to the historical and mythical 'Judgment of Cambyses'. Coeval readers of these works of early-modern moral theology would read the narratives of these ancient and mythical examples and receive them as actual specifications of an abstract principle. That, however, cannot be the case in the present time, in which the aura of singularity and concreteness of ancient Greek and Roman historical episodes is inexorably lost, not to speak of the persuasive power of mythology (Carr 2018).

A currently effective example must still strike a good balance between the necessity of being recognised as the token of a conceptual type and the equally important need to be appreciated as more specific than the type itself; yet the measure and style of this rhetoric of specificity varies, and not only because of the change in the cultural references through which examples might be created (the decline of mythology, the emergence of popular culture), but also because the necessity itself of examples is subject to cultural and historical variation. Present-day continental philosophy, for instance, has a tolerance for abstraction without examples that is certainly greater than that of contemporary US philosophy, where the sentence 'could you give me an example?' as regards, for instance, the theorisation of the narrative patterns of meaning, is very likely to be prompted in response to an abstract academic presentation.

Thus, to complete the exercise of meta- and self-reflection initiated above, to a French semiotician an article like the present one would sound just as acceptable, although it would not contain any concrete examples; to such a reader, the abundance of exemplification would actually give rise to a kitsch effect analogous to that of exceedingly romantic Hollywood movies; to a US philosopher, however, this article would probably sound irritating at some stage, for it would fail the reader's implicit request to pass from the level of type and abstract theorisation to that of its tokens and exemplification, which almost inevitably must take the rhetorical form of a story.

That is why the movie *Au Poste !* reads so continentally irreverent: it mocks the practice of legal storytelling by representing a scene that contains all the elements of its type, albeit subverted through the magnification of impertinent token residues. Shouldn't the police detective, at a certain point in the interrogation, start smoking a cigarette and even tempt or seduce the suspect with the prospect of smoking a cigarette too? Well, that does happen in *Au Poste !*, but there the smoke begins to come out from a hole in the policeman's stomach, which is physiologically absurd but turns into a psychoanalytical detail meant to evoke the possibility of a nightmare and, simultaneously, the porous nature of reality itself.

5. THE POPULIST SCRIPT IN EDUCATION

Propensity to the rhetoric of exemplification depends both on a specific philosophical attitude and on the cultural epoch in which it manifests itself. Exemplification, especially in the form of storytelling, has acquired an abnormal relevance in many present-day discursive domains. This is evident, for instance, in the academic arena. Examples are requested more and more not only in relation to disciplines that traditionally seek to capture the facets of social reality for practical purposes, such as law or economics, but also to traditionally highly abstract disciplines such as theoretical philosophy or general semiotics.

Nevertheless, the rhetorical force of examples and their capacity to bestow a reality effect on the concepts that they exemplify, is sometimes paradoxical. In teaching semiotics to undergraduates, for example, conveying the main tenets of Louis T. Hjelmslev's glossematics is often quite strenuous, precisely because glossematics itself was conceived as an extreme attempt at developing a formalised understanding of language. Hjelmslev's writings certainly provide examples, but their rhetorical relevance is lesser than, for instance, that of examples in Umberto Eco's general semiotics and even lesser than in Roland Barthes' works of semiotic divulgation. Explaining Hjelmslev through examples indeed somehow contradicts the Danish linguist's project itself, which precisely consisted in the aim of grasping the generalities of language without significantly referring to its singularities. For the sake of clarity, however, examples must be provided to undergraduate students as regards this topic; Hjelmslev's characteristic dialectic of form, matter and substance as strata of the planes of both expression and content, for instance, can be exemplified through the simple image of a child that takes amorphous sand from a seashore and, with the help of some concave plastic forms, turns it into the substance, or formed matter, of castles or starfish. Interestingly, however, what most students tend to remember during the examination is not the type exemplified by the token, but the token itself; not the abstract functioning of the dialectics of matter, form and substance in language, but the story of the child playing with sand.

In many other domains of academic communication, the necessity of conveying a highly abstract and theoretical discourse through examples also leads to a paradoxical replacement of types and tokens. The replacement is paradoxical: on the one hand, Saussure's famous example of the train is essential to somewhat concretely render the abstract idea of structure; on the other, identifying this example with the very concept that it exemplifies means betraying the initial purpose itself of abstract conceptualisation. In reality, it is the abstract concept of structure that is created in order to explain how the gestalt of a train works, yet, the gestalt of a train ends up being essential for explaining how a structure functions.

6. THE CONTAGION OF COGNITIVE POPULISM

The increasing allure of examples, to the point that they end up replacing the types that, as tokens, they should help to exemplify, cannot be simply explained with reference to a supposed decrease of cognitive abilities. If examples, and especially narrative examples, are in fashion, this must be accounted for in relation to broader cultural trends. One of them could be evoked with the label of 'cognitive populism'. Undergraduate students are not the only ones to believe that, so to speak, 'theory does not speak to them'; to have the impression that theory, which was elaborated precisely to encompass the generalities of a certain domain of human experience, is unable to do justice to what actually happens to them; to what they see and hear and experience around them; to the singularity of their perception of the domain that theory seeks to abstractly capture.

In other contexts too, examples are rhetorically considered not only as subservient to abstraction but as actually independent from it, as if theory could be replaced by an unarranged collection of examples; as if the idea itself of the type could be supplanted by an empirical and inductive gathering of tokens (that is, the teaching style of many self-defined 'practical' courses that promise not to teach any theory but, more effectively, a series of case-studies, which are another rhetorical version of example).

Populist medicine

In an apparently unrelated domain but one that is actually connected with education, that of medical diagnostics, the need for a more and more personal understanding of the patient is felt, to the point that an academic discourse on the necessity of a 'narrative medicine' has been developed (Charon 2017). In some of its extreme forms, the narrative approach to diagnosis encourages doctors not to consider the illnesses of their patients as tokens of pathological types but as types in themselves, irreducible to any generality. On the one hand, such an approach voices a legitimate desire for the repersonalisation of the relation between doctor and patient, especially as regards the storytelling and the hermeneutics of suffering; on the other hand, however, it is underpinned by the same 'cognitive populism' that underlies the urgent demand for exemplification in the academic discourse: medicine is not able to grasp the singularities of patients; doctors only know about the frustrating commonalities of suffering but are unable to capture and even less to treat the individuality of pain. In its most subversive form, cognitive populism applied to medical discourse gives rise to pernicious forms of self-diagnosis and self-medication: only the patient, with the help of the internet, can find an appropriate answer to his or her pain, for all doctors do about it is humiliatingly consider it as the occurrence of a type, if not as the instance of a statistic.

Populist law

The domain of law is not immune from the effects of general disintermediation on the emergence of cognitive populism and its new rhetoric of exemplification, a rhetoric in which, paradoxically, examples actually become pseudo-singularities whose relation to an overarching type is irremediably lost. As 'theories do not prepare for real life' in universities, and as 'doctors do not understand patients' in hospitals, so 'judges do not consider individual cases' in trials. The law seems not to be able to fully grasp the particularities of people's situations, whose singularity is emphasised not simply as an exception, or evoked as a partial token of a more general type, or narrated as an example, but as a dimension of life that the discourse of law, with its institutions, is no longer able to account for.

Populist politics

Needless to say, the logic of exemplification is perverted in the political discourse too (Müller and Precht 2019), where the token-type dialectics that is inherent, for instance, to the political and economic typology of classes, yields to a political rhetoric in which individuals are not members of a class but centres of a political singularity that old ideologies are not able to do justice to. In this, as in the previous domains, the demise of the classical understanding of exemplification gives rise to a stylistic frenzy, in keeping with which, in fashion as in education, in medicine as in law, in politics as in tourism, what matters is the continuous reaffirmation of the force of singularity over generalisation.

7. THE SUBVERSION OF SCRIPTS

Multiple reasons subsist for this thirst for minute exemplification in all domains, for this rejection of the dialectics type-token, for a multiplication of personal stories and case-studies. In order to formulate some hypotheses about them, it should be underlined that, in these trends, what preoccupies is not the renewed and emphasised attention for singularities; on the contrary, what is worrying is the decline of any effort to consider this attention as instrumental to a better articulation of theory; examples are not sought in order to enrich and nuance theory, but to replace it. Technically, this happens because, in the abovementioned dialectics, an example must introduce, within the discourse of theory, a fragment in which a lesser level of abstraction coexists with a greater degree of detail and concreteness; examples do serve to let people 'see better' what theory is about; they should also serve, however, as points of departure for an inductive-deductive movement in which the example not only visualises but also somewhat challenges the exemplified theory. If the example is treated as a token, and not simply as a type, then it should be read not as a mere story illustrating what the concept is about, but also as the story that the concept, in its abstraction, could not possibly capture. That, however, is meant to promote not the elimination of the type but its re-articulation for the sake of a more efficacious categorisation of 'the real'.

The real, however, is exactly part of the problem here. The idea that there might be such a thing as an existential, social, economic, political and legal 'reality' whose richness and unpredictability is impossible to capture through any type is evidently a romantic one. Semiotics and other intrinsically 'cynical' disciplines have embraced as their mission precisely the task of deromanticising this idea of reality, for instance through showing that there is a pattern, and therefore a language, in most apparently individual social activities, including those that are represented and marketed as the epitome of exclusivity (such as having a romantic relationship, for instance).

8. THE INFRASTRUCTURE OF COGNITIVE POPULISM

Social life is not only evidently patterned by these invisible lines of common sense but also increasingly formatted through logics of large-scale industrial production of profits. That is manifest in the first domain analysed by the present chapter, that of education: present-day undergraduates have less freedom in shaping their own *cursus studiorum* than a student of twenty years ago, for most public universities today can survive only through cutting the costs entailed by the customisation of learning; the same goes for patients in public hospitals and citizens on trial: a increasingly smaller number of people can now afford singularity.

On the one hand, the standardisation of social patterns for the sake of economic profit (but also as a consequence of the increased demographic density in fewer and fewer areas of the planet, and mainly in cities) is bringing about a typological frustration. In the crucible of big numbers, individuals feel less and less represented in their supposed particularities. This is giving rise to the violent rejection of types in every field, including that of the discursive formation of the public opinion. Reading the content of social networks today exposes one to the desperate spectacle produced by an unceasing as well as inane effort of differentiation.

On the other hand, various forms of cognitive populism hijack and market this thirst for singularity. Mass fashion paradoxically promises to everyone the achievement of an individual style through the personal recombination of a range of items that must be necessarily kept within a limited range for the needs of industrial production. The idea of achieving singularity in furnishing a house with IKEA items is simply a mirage. Similarly, students are attracted by storytelling, patients by the allure of auto-therapy, and voters by the idea of a grassroots politics that is necessarily illusory because it is based on the idea that there might be a social reality somehow more real than the representations of it that circulate in the social sphere.

The dialectics of type and token is rejected in favour of a rhetoric of pseudo-exemplification: the global sociocultural system needs the production and diffusion of standardising patterns on the one hand, whereas on the other hand it sells populist antidotes to this same standardisation. People who painstakingly and often ridiculously strive to fashion their own educational, medical and political style do so through platforms that invisibly force them to uniformity.

9. THE MASOCHIST SCRIPT OF IRONY

One of the surprising and sometimes pernicious consequences of this paradox is the hyper-proliferation of the ironic discourse, embraced by many, especially by the younger generations, as the only possible escape from the patterns of social life. One, two, three, multiple levels of irony coat any individual position in the semiosphere, and especially in its digital communication, for it is only through this childish game of superposing negations, and negotiations of negotiations, that one can gain a certain idea of singularity, of being out of the multitude, of being a type of its own kind. This ironic escape from the standardisation of life and its representation in global and mass culture is illusory also because irony itself becomes a standard and actually the most trivial of the tokens. A machine with little effort can now produce jokes that circulate on the internet, such is their lack of originality.

10. THE MASOCHIST HERO

In no domain is this absurd effort of demonstrating one's special singularity more evident than in that of the discursive construction of heroes. Exemplification does not concern only discourse but also people; to express this idea more in line with the perspective of semiotics, one should rather say that people too sometimes turn into discursive elements in a rhetoric of exemplification. That is evident in the case of religions, for instance: throughout the history of the Church, saints have also been canonised as examples of virtue, ideal role-models following whom the faithful could shape their conducts of life in keeping with the moral Catholic orthodoxy at a certain stage of its historical development. Saints, however, were not simply ideal types but also tokens of a range of values that the Church would consider as central in its general project of the moral structuring of society. The functioning of secular heroes, including those of the various sports, is not completely different; in this case, too, champions should not only 'fence for themselves' but exemplify an array of attitudes deemed as the most appropriate in their relations with other sportspeople, with their audience and with themselves.

This 'DIY' logic, however, characterises more and more this dimension of exemplification. Self-aggrandising narratives proliferate on the web, so that each person becomes his or her own hero, a role model that is carefully crafted and presented to others, except that the others too have the same virus, and as a consequence the social networks pullulate not only with examples without types, but also with examples without followers. As in many other contexts of digital life, a lot of emphasis is put on giving and a decreasing importance on receiving: people write more than they read, give opinions to others more than they listen to others' opinions, and seek to set an example more than they follow one. In this multitude of solipsistic little heroes, not only does nobody follow anybody else's example, but any attempt to extol the virtues of an overarching hero is frustrated by a pitiless game of belittling anything that could jeopardise the desire for micro-singularities. A particularly kitsch form of this heroic micro-representation of the self is that of the new martyr: everyone, from the PhD student to the train commuter, feels obliged to present their life as special, not so much for its successes as for its singular pain, for the unease that stems from an individual life and must, therefore, attract the attention of an audience.

11. THE QUEST FOR A NEW SCRIPT

Feeling special and presenting oneself as such is one of the most intense activities of today's society, a preoccupation that is at odds with any dialectics of token and type and with any truthful logic of exemplification, but one that is fuelled, on the contrary, by cognitive populism in all its forms. One is therefore left with the following question: if the pseudo-singularisation sold by populist marketing offers no authentic escape from the standardisation of meaning, and if ironic subcultures do nothing but reinvigorate the same frustration that they pretend to dispel, is there really no alternative to the two extremes of either completely yielding to an idea of multitudinous regime of meaning and to that of cultivating solipsistic utopias? Can the thirst for singularity lead to something different than the violent disintermediation of populism?

So as to recapitulate the conceptual path followed thus far: structural conditions like the increase in the world population, demographic hyperdensity in a few, essentially urban, areas of the world, the consequent necessity to efficiently organise the infrastructure of vast human multitudes, the creation of super-communities in the digital world and, above all, the logics of large-scale industrial production introduce the logistic need for growing standardisation in the patterns of meaning that regulate social and cultural life. On the one hand, the semiosphere consubstantially is a patterned structure in which it is de facto impossible to semiotically exist without yielding to the codification of a common sense; this regards not only cultural productions but also behaviours that seem to belong to the 'natural' and personal dimension, such as the various ways of satisfying primary physiological needs, for instance; on the other hand, when the structural conditions mentioned above manifest themselves, patterns become more numerous, more rigid and concerning a greater amount of production.

Many individuals do not react to the mass production of meaning: they just accept it, and live with and through it. Many other individuals, however, depending on a complex matrix of socio-economic determinations, feel the frustration of not being able to express an individual life. They feel singular inside, but they live generally outside. They somehow consider themselves as superior to, or simply different from, the patterns of meaning that prevail in the community, but do not find a way of getting rid of them. This frustration is, as suggested earlier, largely induced: if on the one hand the market injects standards and uniformity in the semiosphere so as to suit its logistic needs, on the other hand it sells pseudo-antidotes against such standardisation of meaning in the paradoxical market of subversion and subculture. The market sells us Zara clothes with the right hand, and vintage clothes in the shop next to Zara with the left hand. It would be naive to believe that either of these options is better than the other, for they are mutually dependent.

The frustration and, at the same time, the utopia of singularity generated by the global logistics of the new digital world bring about intolerance for everything that seems to sacrifice the particularities for the sake of abstracting commonality therefrom. The effects of this intolerance have been enumerated and analysed with reference to various domains, in which disintermediation ultimately stems from the urge not to submit the illusion of singularity to the global machinery of meaning. The dialectics between type and token, which is the essential epistemological fulcrum of mediation, is, therefore, rejected; what is cultivated, instead, is the utopia that tokens might turn into independent types, in a semiosphere essentially composed of unique social monads. To a certain extent, the global marketing of styles seeks to suit this illusion and produces gigantic profits. This 'market of styles', nevertheless, must be conceived as much wider than the one existing in the mere domain of fashion. This is a revealing area of human life, in which styles are indeed bought and sold as a pseudo-antidote to the frustration of singularity, yet this global market of styles is more all-encompassing, since it ultimately stems from general cognitive populism, which is the real answer to the frustration of singularity.

Examples and exemplification, as underlined earlier, are the primary victims of this cognitive style. That does not mean that they are eliminated, for, on the contrary, exemplification becomes increasingly central in many discursive domains; what happens is that exemplification is denaturalised into a cognitive travesty of it. Examples are no longer tokens to help the reference to a type, but rather tokens that seem to rebel against any idea of type, surreal stories that inductively accumulate without leading to any abstraction, exactly like the interrogation in *Au Poste !*

12. EXAMPLES AS NARRATIVE GRADIENTS

As explained earlier, what is requested from an example is that it introduces a gradient in the cognitive line of a discourse, a gradient thanks to which whoever receives an example is rhetorically induced to believe that the abstract argument or value is more perceptible. The post-Greimassian theory of the actant observer is suitable to technically explain the nature, cause and effects of this gradient: all of a sudden, at the appearance of the usual locutions 'for example' or 'for instance', or through other similar meta-signs, the receivers of a discourse are invited to follow an actant observer that promises them to let them wear a different pair of lenses, lenses thank to which they, the receivers, will actually see what the argument or value is about not only in greater detail but also in the narrative form of a story. That is why, if examples are always micro-narrations, their insertion is actually a *mise en abyme* that retroacts on the more abstract discursive line which they are part of. When I say 'for instance', I take the interlocutor to another level of cognitive perception, yet this leap is not isolated and independent from but functional to the subjacent discursive line. The example must cast an aura of authenticity on the abstract argument, which in turn must validate the epistemology of the example.

This circularity between type and token is broken as a result of the diffusion of cognitive populism. First of all, people cease to see themselves as living examples. Existential roles are increasingly rejected; a logic of *bricolage* and stylisation is embraced instead. Today, few would aspire to become 'ideal fathers' or 'role-model mothers'; what is much more intriguing, and is bought and sold as such with its plethora of gadgets, is, conversely, the idea of being a 'one of a kind' father or mother, someone who receives tradition and its patterning roles but customises them for the sake of an increasingly pressing aesthetics of self-aggrandising and singularity. The result is often kitsch; nothing, indeed, is more pathetic than sophisticate stereotypes stemming from the strenuous effort not to yield to stereotypes; it is exactly what happens to the hiker who climbs an impervious mountain only to realise that what he or she has reached is not a solitary and unspoiled paradise but a base camp littered by a myriad of previous attempts at singularity. Although it is a scientific fact that our faces are a visual gestalt resulting from a combination of a few basic facial ingredients, nobody ever takes into account that his or her face might be not a uniquely singular interface for interacting with the world but a biological pattern itself, on which culture leaves traces that are even more standardised than those of nature (Leone 2017).

13. KITSCH DANDIES AND KITSCH JIHADIS

The spasmodic quest for singularity, the political market of cognitive populism and the accrued speed of digital global communication transform along these lines all the domains of meaning production, in which the inevitable cognitive hierarchies of mediation are also rejected with regard to the subservience of examples and tokens to arguments and types. It is, therefore, relevant to wonder whether there might be any alternative to the vicious circle of singularity frustration and cognitive populism, and if such an alternative might also entail a different consideration of the dialectics between type and token, example and argument. For instance, an alternative might consist in embracing a sort of ontological quietism, accepting that singularity is actually an illusion and that strong patterns structure both the natural and the social life of individuals. Such would be the stance of a sort of neo-pre-modernism, in which traditions are held as unshakeable and roles as unmovable, and discourse would return to resort to old-fashioned examples and heroes, characterised by a strong emphasis on hierarchy and mediation. This return to the innocence of pre-modernity and its conception of singularity, however, is not only impossible, given the cultural memory of modernity, but also somehow dangerous; indeed, it is in the alluring fundamentalisms of all kinds, and in particular in the religious and political ones, that such a utopia of strong mediation is concretised. Even if one suspended the judgment on the ethical consequences of such re-adoption of pre-modern ethics – especially in terms of the often violent subjection of all minorities that it entails – it would remain the case that fundamentalism is a form of rebellion that does not escape the market of subversion. After all, young jihadists too are sold a pseudo-antidote to the frustration of their singularity, although this antidote does not consist in the bricolage of an illusorily personal style but in the adoption of an ideology in the name of which all styles are violently abolished for the sake of extolling and defending a unique way of life, that fundamentalist patterning of the existence in which singularity is not regained individually but within a community battling against the surrounding chaos. Fundamentalism, however, also from the aesthetic point of view, is no less pathetic and kitsch than dandyism.

14. CONCLUSION: LOVING EXAMPLES

Exemplification consists in grafting, within a text, a parenthetic textual fragment adhering to a different genre and style. The latter usually features both a lower level of abstraction and a higher degree of narrativity than the former. In other words, most exemplifications propose that the receiver proceeds from a textual dimension essentially based on generalisation to one tending to singularity. Such singularity, however, can never result in idiosyncrasy, for that would lead to the production of a *hapax legomenon*, as the Greeks would designate a word that occurs only once in a context, that is, to an example that exemplifies nothing but itself. A good example, on the contrary, contains both figurative details and a narrative structure whose level of concreteness nevertheless maintains an effective proportionality with the exemplified abstraction. The example figuratively and narratively embodies the abstraction, but it is not so detailed and specific that other examples could not do the same (although within a hierarchy of efficacy), or that the same example could not exemplify a different abstraction. The relation between principle and example must be one of significant proportionality, not one of bijection.

In an effort to define some of the structural dynamics that establish such 'significant proportionality' of the example in the legal discourse as well as in the other patterning structures of the semiosphere, it is relevant to refer to the rhetorical, linguistic and semiotic literature on the figure of hypotiposis, the rhetorical figure of 'vivid depiction'. Many of the defining elements of exemplification (but not all of them) can indeed be detected in this rhetorical figure, which analogously consists in grafting a more detailed figurative textual fragment onto less detailed figurative textual content. Through a hypotiposis, a token is proposed in such a way as to be detached from the type that culturally subsumes it and so as to highlight the singularities of the token itself. This operation, however, is sterile if it does not lead to a better functioning of the same dialectics between type and token. A good example is neither one that exclusively visualises a type nor one that limits itself to express a token, but one that encourages a better re-articulation of the relation type-token itself. In political terms, for instance, the crisis of intermediation and representation cannot be solved by the production and marketing of pseudo-idiosyncratic styles, but in the production of a new common sense in which singularities can nevertheless emerge and, above all, be compared. That is the main point that the global noise of the digital quest for singularity is neglecting: the quest for singularity is not a disease in itself but becomes such when it turns subservient to the goals of global cognitive populism, which is nothing but a new form of *divide et impera*. On the contrary, singularities should continue to be in dialogue, and examples and tokens compared systematically with each other, precisely in order to achieve a reformulation of the overarching type so that it might encompass more of the subjacent singularities without frustrating them. Without this ability and inclination for the systematic comparison and contrast of tokens and examples, pseudo-constructions of singularity just result in the – often violent – disintegration of the inevitable abstractions that enable the constitution of a framework of common sense. Indeed, it is the community itself that requires a curtailing of singularity for the sake of coexistence; if this curtailing is too violent, and especially if it is uneven, it generates frustration; but if this frustration is hijacked by cognitive populism, and gives rise to countless micro-utopias of singularity, then what is achieved is not a better form of life, more friendly to the legitimate desire for increased identity, but a situation of potentially violent conflict, which is violent because it does not recognise a fundamental law of singularity, one that cognitive populism perniciously hides: in order to feel singular and unique, what we ultimately need is love, meaning that we need that another singularity somehow recognises ours through the same existential gesture that institutes a commonality.

Bibliography

Ankersmit, F. R. (1989), 'The Reality Effect in the Writing of History: The Dynamics of Historiographical Topology', *Mededelingen van de Afdeling Letterkunde; nieuwe reeks, d. 52, no. 1*, Amsterdam: Koninklijke Nederlandse Akademie van Wetenschappen / Amsterdam and New York: Noord-Hollandsche.

Barthes, R. (1968), 'L'Effet de réel', 11 *Communications*, 84–9; English trans. by Richard Howard in R. Barthes (1986), *The Rustle of Language*, Oxford: Blackwell.

Bromberger, S. (1992), 'Types and Tokens in Linguistics', in S. Bromberger, *On What We Know We Don't Know*, Chicago: University of Chicago Press, 170–208.
Bromberger, S. and M. Halle (1986), 'On the Relationship of Phonology and Phonetics', in J. S. Perkell and D. H. Klatt (eds), *Invariance and Variability in Speech Processes*, Hillsdale, NJ: Lawrence Erlbaum Associates, 493–519.
Carr, D. (2018), 'Moral Exemplification in Narrative Literature and Art', 48(3) *Journal of Moral Education*, 358–68.
Chaemsaithong, K. (2019), 'Deconstructing Competing Courtroom Narratives: Representation of Social Actors', 29(2) *Social Semiotics*, 240–60.
Charon, R. (2017), *The Principles and Practice of Narrative Medicine*, New York: Oxford University Press.
Fischer, O. and M. Nänny (eds) (2001), *The Motivated Sign (Iconicity in Language and Literature, vol. 2)*, Amsterdam and Philadelphia, PA: John Benjamins Pub. Co.
Greenlee, D. (1973), *Peirce's Concept of Sign*, The Hague: Mouton.
Heffer, C. (2005), *The Language of Jury Trial: A Corpus-Aided Analysis of Legal-Lay Discourse*, Basingstoke and New York: Palgrave Macmillan.
Kavanagh, T. M. (1972), 'Kafka's "The Trial": The Semiotics of the Absurd', 5(3) *NOVEL: A Forum on Fiction*, 242–53.
Leone, M. (2017), 'Socio-sémiotique des "livres à visages"', in E. Landowski (ed.), *Sémiotique et engagement*, special issue of *Nouveaux Actes Sémiotiques*, <http://epublications.unilim.fr/revues/as/5816> accessed 10 September 2019.
Leone, M. (2018), 'Designing Imperfection: The Semiotics of the Pixel', in M. Frangopoulos and E. Zantides (eds), *Design as Semiosis*, special issue, 4(1) *Punctum: International Journal of Semiotics*, 105–36.
Mandler, J. M. (1984), *Stories, Scripts, and Scenes: Aspects of Schema Theory*, Hillsdale, NJ: Lawrence Erlbaum Associates.
Mattozzi, A. (1987), 'Rewriting the Script: A Methodological Dialogue about the Concept of "Script" and how to Account for the Mediating Role of Objects', paper presented at the Dept. of Philosophy–STePS Joint Colloquium, University of Twente, September 1987.
Müller, M. and J. Precht (eds) (2019), *Narrative des Populismus: Erzählmuster und -strukturen populistischer Politik*, Wiesbaden: Springer VS.
Orban, C. (1990), 'Words and Images: The Semiotics of Futurism and Surrealism', PhD dissertation, University of Chicago, Department of Romance Languages and Literatures.
Putz, C. (1994), *Kitsch: Phänomenologie eines dynamischen Kulturprinzips*, Bochum: Brockmeyer.
Umbach, M. and M. Humphrey (eds) (2018), *Authenticity: The Cultural History of a Political Concept*, Cham: Palgrave Macmillan.
Van Den Akker, C. (2018), *The Exemplifying Past: A Philosophy of History*, Amsterdam: Amsterdam University Press.

Wetzel, L. (1993), 'What Are Occurrences of Expressions?', 22 *Journal of Philosophical Logic*, 215–20.
Wetzel, L. (2006), 'Types and Tokens', in *Stanford Encyclopedia of Philosophy* <https://plato.stanford.edu/entries/types-tokens> accessed 22 January 2019.
Wolterstorff, N. (1970), *On Universals: An Essay in Ontology*, Chicago: University of Chicago Press.
Wolterstorff, N. (1975), 'Toward An Ontology of Art Works', 9 *Noûs*, 115–42.
Zemach, E. (1992), *Types: Essays in Metaphysics* (*Philosophy of History and Culture*, vol. 9), Leiden: Brill.

Chapter 6

Exemplarity as Concreteness, or the Challenge of Institutionalising a Productive Circle between Past and Present, Old and New

José Manuel Aroso Linhares

In a limit-situation such as our own, involving the paradoxical challenges of homogenising globalisation and self-celebrating plurality (if not incommensurability), the reinvention of juridically specific exemplarity – or the possibility of giving this exemplarity an unmistakable place in legal adjudication – confronts legal discourse(s) with decisive borderline issues. On the one hand, an autonomous reinvention of exemplarity seems incompatible with a representation of the problem-controversy which, invoking the constraint of 'formal justice', imposes the methodological priority of universal rulings (MacCormick) on jurisdiction as reasoning and, with this, a normativistic (purely deontological) modus for conceiving of (juridically plausible) arguments of universality or universalisability. On the other hand, an autonomous reinvention of exemplarity seems irreconcilable with an experience of the problem-controversy which – interpreting the claim to comparability (and the intelligibility of a tertium comparationis) as an inescapable exercise in constative synchronising violence (Douzinas) – admits recreating the case-event as a manifestation of pure, unconditional singularity, thus allowing an ethical-aesthetic narrative reading.

This chapter aims to reconstitute these contrary challenges whilst explicitly considering a certain law, significantly inscribed in the possibilities of the Western Text (and as such presented as a cultural artefact, if not as an institutionalised way of life). The chosen path involves three indispensable steps: (1) to consider the incompatibility between an autonomous treatment of exemplarity and the assimilation of the legacy of formalism (even when this assimilation is significantly moderate); (2) to clarify the impossibility of reconciling exemplarity and singularity, considered from the perspective of a deconstructive narrative reading; and (3) to introduce the connection between exemplarity and concreteness and to discuss this connection whilst focusing on the institutionalisation of a reciprocally constitutive intertwinement between dogmatic stabilising and problem-solving practices.

1. THE FORMALIST-NORMATIVIST PATH AS AN ELOQUENT RENOUNCEMENT OF EXEMPLARITY

It is probably unnecessary to insist on the disintegration of the problem-controversy (or its methodological priority) – as a rejection of an autonomously rational experience of praxis and phronesis – imposed by the modern shift to normativism (from the early seventeenth century onwards). However, a few words seem relevant, if only to recall the dynamic peak of this disintegration – the nineteenth-century prescriptive construction of Legal Method – whilst significantly considering how this deliberate constructive (and more or less consciously assumed) project inspired two paradigmatic parallel answers – one established by Langdell's alleged formalism and the other due to Conceptual Jurisprudence's *naturhistorische Methode* – and these as parallel responses to unmistakably different institutional environments.

Concerning the issue of exemplarity, the relevance of invoking a certain American 'mechanical jurisprudence' has evidently to do with the way this approach assimilates judge-made law's propositions, whilst consecrating a methodical domestication of precedent, if not of the rational possibilities of distinguishing – converting the given *ratio decidendi* elements into components of an implicit abstract and generic statement of law. Notwithstanding the doubts which justifiably arise with respect to the possibility of fully identifying Langdell with this 'mechanical jurisprudence' (Tamanaha 2010: 27 ff., 49–56), the said conversion of *ratio decidendi* paves the way for reconciling analogical and deductive reasoning, or more correctly, for sacrificing the first (only apparently preserved) to the demands of the second.

The relevance of considering *naturhistorische Methode* has, in turn, to do with the concept of juridically relevant reality, whose components are invariably treated as contingently material discrete empirical facts. Beyond presupposing these facts as states of affairs in the external world objectively accessible to perceptual and representational-correspondential experiences, this concept demands an exercise in abstraction, depriving the presupposed states of affairs of their intrinsic coherence or dynamics, as well as reducing them to crude, independent, unorganised materials (Neves 2008: 178–9). This (explicit or implicit) exercise corresponds to the thesis that only the self-sufficient perspective (and the methodological priority) of universally rational propositions – which are certainly *Rechtssätze* or 'generic statements of law', but also, whenever the issue concerns the *quaestio facti*, *Erfahrungssätze* or 'generic statements of fact' – provides these materials with the extrinsic plausible coherence which they need (Linhares 2012a: 68–71). As there is only a relevant leading question – determining whether the connections selectively assumed in the presupposed generic statements (seriously taken as re-ordering patterns) are recognisable in the empirical materials or data (so that this data can be subsumed in those statements, thus generating the corresponding conclusions) – we may indeed acknowledge that the exemplarity which plays an effective role in this process is, in fact, only a pseudo one.[1]

---

[1] Concerning *quaestio juris*, the judgment of exemplarity which is allowed is evidently (and exclusively) the one which, within the process of obtaining the minor premise of syllogism, corresponds to the subsumption *qua tale* or to the affirmative answer which constructs it, whilst corroborating that the proven facts, insofar as they reproduce the characteristics or qualities predicted in the norm's hypothesis, are to be treated as exemplars-specimens of the presupposed type.

In order to experience the tensions between the legacy (or legacies) of formalism or normativism and the possibility of an authentic judgment of exemplarity, it is however more interesting to leave these strong totalising approaches (which purely and simply sacrifice the conditions allowing this judgment) and turn instead to contemporary methodical representations of legal adjudication which, whilst preserving unmistakable signs or traces (if not scars) of those legacies, contemplate alternative paths. We could invoke here Hart's treatment of discretion, reconciling an effectively non-formalistic experience of the open texture of rules (and even a consideration of analogical reasoning) with a concept of jurisdictional rules which, identifying them with a 'minimal use' of 'general classifying words', pays tribute to the Enlightenment heritage and its experience of universability (Hart 1994: 124–5). It is, however, preferable to go beyond and further (in order to get as close as possible to the borders and their alternative idioms!), by alluding to MacCormick's proposal. What makes this proposal (and with it, a certain standard theory of argumentation) such a precious field for experimentation? It is undoubtedly the way it endeavours to reconcile the challenge of genuinely practical argumentative thinking with the unequivocal acknowledgment that deductivism constitutes the core claim of law and legal adjudication.

Following MacCormick's formulations, this means on the one hand acknowledging that there is an evident tension (if not antithesis) between the 'arguable character' of 'legal discourse' and law's authoritarian framework (implicit in the rule of law), that is, between the demands of a 'concrete justification' which is unavoidably a 'locus of argumentation' and a 'nursery of rhetoric' – certainly pursued under a 'pretention to correctness' but, as such, facing several types of 'uncertainties' and 'problematic' cases (MacCormick 2005: 13, 48 ff., 277) – and the 'political ideal of legal certainty' – an 'ideal' which, beyond the constitutive reference to the 'values' of 'certainty and security', includes the so-called validity thesis and 'the constraint of formal justice' (MacCormick 1994: 53–62; 2007: 39–60). On the other hand it means defending that this tension is in fact a 'resoluble' or apparent one, precisely because the political-constitutional framework limiting *jurisdictio* as *potestas* imposes on jurisdiction as reasoning and judgment a certain concept of the legal norm (as a universal ruling and as a rational major premise) and, with this, an unquestionable (and unsurpassable) experience of juridical relevance (MacCormick 2005: 79–100). The implications of this presupposition, combining two indispensable binomials (universal/particular, general/specific) – the first one in the sense proposed by Hare – are in fact quite obvious: a concept of law (and legal system) entirely and implacably identified with universals; a distribution of those universals in different degrees of generality or specificity (ranging from statements of principle and general standards to statutory rules and judicial *rationes decidendi*); an explicit weak demarcation thesis between norms-principles and norms-rules; a methodologically paradigmatic treatment of precedents as universal rulings; and, last but not least, a rational representation of these universals as premises, giving the legitimising force of syllogism (if not directly the 'formula "R + F = C", or "Rule plus facts yields conclusion"') the sense of an 'essential truth' (MacCormick 1994: X).

It is as if, concerning law's practical discourse, the formula of subsumption and its integrating rationalising (justificatory) possibilities appears as a decisive condition of autonomy, that is, as the 'framework in which the other arguments make sense as legal arguments' (MacCormick 2005: 42). Whilst revealing a constitutive and necessary dimension of the concept of law, this structure (and its experience of universalisability) ensures in fact the compossibility (in judicial decisions) of deductive and non-deductive argumentation – a compossibility which MacCormick explores assimilating (and transforming . . . vertically!) Wrobléwski's foundational distinction between internal and external justification (giving the latter the identity of a second-order justification) – whilst simultaneously framing (and distributing), as well as rationalising, the possibilities of non-deductive argumentation. This means in fact tracing a sequence of integrated steps, which (from the global perspective of universability) explore in succession the systemic reasons for formal consistence and coherence – the latter as a diachronic-correspondential narrative coherence concerning 'facts' or as a synchronic normative one concerning 'norms' – and, if 'the case still stands open', the consequentialist reasons – that is, arguments about making sense in the world which, under the normativistic discipline, are confined to the possibilities of an 'ideal' version of rule-utilitarianism (MacCormick 1994: 104 ff.; 2005: 101 ff., 121–42, 233–6). Is this decoupage sufficiently successful to ensure a plausible conjugation of elements of deductive and non-deductive reasoning? We may agree that it is. Yet, notwithstanding the apparent preservation and even the strengthening or reinforcement of a certain methodological unity or congruence, the price to be paid is undoubtedly the rejection of exemplarity, that is, an explicit renouncement of authentic (autonomously relevant) judgments of exemplarity.

2. THE DECONSTRUCTIVE NARRATIVE READING OR THE IMPOSSIBILITY OF RECONCILING EXEMPLARITY AND SINGULARITY

What about the second step and the reflexive pole which this provides? The knotty problem is now singularity (or the phronesis/singularity connection) considered as a possibility for reconstructing an alternative type of rationality. In contrast with the previous one, does this approach (notwithstanding the different paths which cross and fragment it) offer the essential conditions for rethinking a specific (juridically relevant) judgment of exemplarity? As I have already indicated, I do not think it does . . . and it is time to show why.

Clarifying that this is unavoidably an exercise in simplification – concerning the possibility of a common ground and thus disregarding many relevant differences – I will begin by emphasising that this heterodox return to phronesis (notwithstanding the internal plurality of its paths) corresponds to, or finds its crucial horizon in, a very specific critical-philosophical approach, the construction of which, whilst resisting the metanarratives of totality opened up by Hegelian and Marxist discourses, if not directly the possibilities of dialectic-materialist critical theories, reconciles with a *sui generis* return to Aristotle two major, surprisingly diverse legacies (more or less selectively overlapping!) attributable to Kant and Nietzsche respectively. It is as if this new critical attitude or the practical philosophy, if not anti-philosophy, it engenders – *un questionnement sur les fondements [qui] n'est ni fondationaliste ni anti-fondationaliste* (Derrida 1994: 22) – on the one hand reinvents a contemporary genealogy of the practical worlds and their continuum, whilst on the other hand inscribes (integrates) an autonomous (quasi-transcendental) reconstitution of conditions of possibility/impossibility within this genealogy. The first dimension responds to Nietzsche's heritage whilst assuming a narrative reconstruction of cultural practices irradiating from their *pudenda origo* (concentrating on problems of provenience-*Herkunft* and emergence-*Entstehung*), as well as imposing a specific rethinking of perspectivism, concerned with the immanent experimentation of *Wille zur Macht* (and the circularity between genealogical reconstruction and reconstructed practices), but equally with the unconditional celebration of the 'young virtue' of *Redlichkeit* and its return to the *Text als Text*, freed from predetermined interpretations (Seibert 2006: 32–43). The second dimension involves, in contrast, a selective rewriting of Kantian arguments (and his differentiation of rationality types), presenting (recovering) these arguments as an indispensable chapter in the chain of plurality thinking (Welsch 1991: 291–4), as well as the forerunners (through the aesthetics of sublime) of a rational treatment of singularity (Aguado 1994: 31–6). Whilst not forgetting certain decisive heterodox constructive mediations – which include Saussure's arbitrariness of sign thesis and Wittgenstein's interpretive pluralism, Heidegger's claim to think against Humanism and Levinas' experience of infinite responsibility (overcoming every ontic and ontological discourse), as well as Lacan's and Legendre's decentring of subjectivity and life – the full articulation of these two main legacies is, in fact, decided in the interplay of three major contributions. The first derives from Foucault's microphysics of power (Foucault 1976: 117–27) and involves his archaeological and genealogical rewriting of *L'Âge de l'homme*, if not his aesthetics of existence, while the second assimilates Lyotard's disputes between phrases and genres de discours – as well as his incommensurability theorem (Welsch 1991: 251–6) and his experience of community as a promise (Lyotard 1990: 61–84). The third assumes Derrida's programmatological interpretation (Derrida 1988: 159, n. 16) and the way in which this (as a specific 'intersection of a pragmatics and a grammatology') involves the justice/deconstruction connection, as well as a certain economy of violence (*une philosophie de la non-violence qui [choisit] la moindre violence*) (Derrida 1967: 136, n. 1). It is as if we were invoking the (reunited or separated) spells of a political 'morality' (based on the Foucauldian experience of an immanent capillary network of powers and resistances), of an aesthetics/anaesthetics of the sublime (justified through a Lyotardian reinvention of Kant's reflexive judgment) and a radically autonomous ethics of alterity (committed to the Derridean translation of Levinas' infinite responsibility).

This is certainly not the place to continue exploring how these major contributions live together and overlap (with varying weightings) as they project their critical ethos and specific categories of intelligibility in legal discourses. As the discourses which assimilate this ethos (involving significantly different trends 'within' Critical Legal Studies and Postmodern Jurisprudences) are far from reducible to a homogeneous movement – there is, in fact, a dizzying range of possibilities, each constructing a specific puzzle from the elements at stake – I will endeavour to present a drastic simplification, concentrating exclusively on singularity or the construction of singularity. This means, on the one hand, acknowledging the role which the celebration of unrepeatability and uniqueness (if not incommensurability or *différance*) plays in this construction and, on the other hand, unveiling how this celebration sustains a transparent connection with universality or universalisability – the one which, without paradox, allows us to highlight the unconditional respect for singularity as the unique legitimate expression of an universalisable claim (Derrida 1994: 44). In order to give explicit visibility to the said three major contributions (whilst not forgetting the constitutive tensions they generate), four constructive specifications (all of which connect reflexive possibilities) seem indispensable here. The first specification highlights singularity as a 'diachronic ... dispersed arrangement of unrepeatable moments' (Douzinas and Warrington 1994: 175), whilst explicitly associating it with a positive and immanent conception of power. Its challenge is thus to unveil every microscopic manifestation of practice and discourse as a multidirectional web of powers and resistances, if not already to construct hierarchy as a relational concept (Kennedy 1992: 431). The second specification has in turn to do with the reinvention which the attention to singularity – focused on the authentic 'time of the event' ('when it happens in its discontinuous, unpredictable seriality') – allows, whilst treated as a rational 'perception' of the 'ultimate and the particular' (Douzinas and Warrington 1994: 175, 180; Welsch 1991: 281). This treatment provides in fact the privileged opportunity to bring phronesis and poiesis together (through the specific mediation of aesthesis), whilst promising a productive reconciliation between normative and aesthetic arenas.[2] The third specification converts the previous diagnoses of singularity (or their overlapping) into normative (or even prescriptive) celebrations of plurality and fragmentation (Welsch 1988: 14, 20–2). This means on the one hand introducing a negative counterpoint, one that denounces the construction and performance of a rule and the dogmatic presupposition of a criterion of comparability – if not the global institutional 'condition of being ... bound by texts that one has not read' or by 'non-arriving letters' (Goodrich 1990: 149–50) – as insurmountable exercises in violence (explicitly conceived of as violence against singularity) (Douzinas and Warrington 1991: 124–9, 134–5). This however also means, on the other hand, associating the respect for singularity with the decisive intelligibility of a hyperbolic ethics of alterity (pursued in the name of a limitless justice and from the perspective of a promise of hospitality), whilst constructing

---

[2] This promise allows us in fact to incorporate this approach in a much broader humanistic trend, highlighted by the so-called 'perception' or 'sense-perception' analogy (Nussbaum 1986: 305).

(unveiling) a practical commitment to the openness and instability of every context (Derrida 1997: 37 ff.). Last but not least, the fourth specification legitimises the microscopic experience of a community to-come: on the one hand in order to associate the condition of promising (as a permanently sought and deferred possibility) with the indispensable mediation of narrative genre and its ability to testify to the practical-cultural situation of *différend* (Lyotard 1983: 218, n. 219); on the other hand, in order to presuppose an order-*ordinans* of disseminated meanings and this one as the unique opportunity to project infinite responsibility as *undecidability* (Derrida 1988: 116; 1994: 54–5).

Does this celebration of singularity allow for an authentic experience of exemplarity? And if it does, is the experience in question (whilst concentrated upon the problem-case) compatible with the preservation of an autonomous experience of law? These are the questions which I would like to consider.

The allusion to a construction of meaning which condemns singularity to the closed actuality of a phrase-event (or imprisons it within unrepeatable and irreproducible microphenomena of power and resistance) whilst simultaneously opening it up to the never-ending circulation of signifiers and signifieds – since the limit of the frame always 'entails a clause of nonclosure' (Bearn 2000: 450–1) – is certainly sufficient to answer the first question, that is, to affirm an effective incompatibility between exemplarity and the deconstructive way of thinking of contexts and its (relatively dangerous) supplements.

Even if, on this reflexive level, the plausible answers concerning a global conception of praxis are not entirely conclusive – admitting (or even demanding) the mediation of narrative genre or the exploration of reflective judgments that do not entirely reject the consideration of exempla (as plausible steps in the search for the undetermined universal) – the projection of its possibilities in legal discourses, opening up a reformulation of our second question (is this experience of exemplarity, whilst inscribed in the interstices of a dominant experience of singularity, compatible with the preservation of an autonomous experience of law?) imposes a straight, unequivocal answer which significantly neutralises the admitted openness of the first question or, at least, condemns this openness to being conceivable only beyond law or legal relevant discourses – or, more precisely, beyond the development of the deconstructive approach which is pursued in the name of law (or at least because of law's relevance). It is precisely in this context that it is important to return to the deconstructive treatment of legal principles which Douzinas and Warrington persistently assume whilst exploring the ethical-aesthetic demands of a community-promise (Douzinas and Warrington 1994: 181–2). I refer here to the deconstructive treatment which, reducing a legal system (or its methodological relevance) to the possibilities justified by rule-oriented formalistic understanding, presupposes the norms/principles continuum, whilst defending that arguments of principle (as well as the interpretative presupposition of law-worked-by-principle) aggravate drastically the violence against singularity (Douzinas and Warrington 1991: 23–4, 55–73; 1994: 199 ff.). Presenting the defence of principles as a 'last step' in the formalist 'juridification' of 'morality' (or as a 'common symptom' of the 'process of de-ethicalisation' of the law) in fact means rejecting the possibility of presenting a concept of normative legal principles which (breaking away from the norms/principles continuum) could defend a claim of consonance (of content) between principles and practices of adjudication as an indispensable component of juridical relevant exemplarity. Once the scission between the opportunities offered by legal discourses and an authentic experience of singularity is complete (confirming that law is invariably identified with a prescriptive abstract violence and the corresponding form of universalisation), the search for the community-promise, in its absolute singularity – '[so that] each judgement passed marks the community's end' (Douzinas and Warrington 1994: 182) – is not possible without stepping outside (or demanding that the 'outside penetrates and determines the inside'), that is, without going beyond law or at least renouncing law's specific 'thirdness' – *tertialité* (Levinas 1978: 239–53) and its comparison claim (a claim which would persist even when judge-made rulings are considered specific concrete criteria). For Douzinas and Warrington, this in fact means passing 'through the ethics of alterity', as well as asking the judge to impair us as an authentic spinner of alternative tales – inventing narratives which respect 'the time of saying' and the 'requests of the contingent, incarnate and concrete other' (Douzinas and Warrington 1994: 185). Whilst assuming the task of a specific justice as dike, these narratives, albeit apparently inscribed within the possibilities of the legal system (or at least authorised by the proliferation of indeterminations and blind spots), always develop against the grain of its 'interpretive moment', which means responding aesthetically and ethically to the call of singularity. This brings us to the so-called paradox of a 'momentary principle' – a 'judgment is just if it follows and creates its momentary principle' (Douzinas and Warrington 1991, 117–20, 142–7; 1994: 132–85, 211–41) – a paradox which may, in turn, be deconstructed and reconstructed, but whose elements remain thoroughly incompatible with an authentic experience of exemplarity. The lesson at stake is in fact a transparent one: 'if there are criteria of justice, they are only momentary', arising 'at the point of their application' as 'local, partial and concrete' (Douzinas and Warrington 1994: 184–5).

3. THE INVENTION OF CONCRETENESS AND ITS ARGUMENT OF CONTINUITY

Is there anything in common between the two polarised exercises which we have considered above and their treatment of exemplarity? I would say that there is: the unproblematic identification of law (and its claim to autonomy) with a formalist approach, reducing the possibilities of an internal reflexive attitude (the experience of law as an autonomous dimension of practice and an autonomous field of knowledge) to the corresponding isolation programme for an abstract self-sufficient normative cosmos. While this presupposition corresponds, following the first path (see above, section 1), to a genuine positive assimilation of the legacy of formalism and its identifying possibilities (which remain dominant, even when they are explicitly combined with alien components), it is, however, as a justifying discursive resource – as an effective element in a context of signification or performance to be deconstructed (which, as such, will be persistently unveiled in its more or less obvious conformations) – that the same presupposition intervenes in the second path. Does this difference impose any challenges when discussing the 'place' of exemplarity in juridically relevant discourses and practices? It certainly does. Defending an argument of compatibility or consonance between exemplarity and juridicalness, whilst addressing this argument versus the first path, in fact means identifying as opponent a certain concept of law (and thus considering this concept in terms of the integrity and transparence of its cultural presuppositions, its categories of intelligibility and its *modus operandi*). Conversely, defending the same argument by confronting the conclusions of the second path means identifying as opponent a reductive misinterpretation – the one which judges the claim to formal isolation (and the constative hermeneutic field that this claim presupposes) as a necessary component of legal discourses and legal adjudication. Discussing this misinterpretation means, on the one hand, acknowledging that the aporias attributed to legal adjudication only persist (conditioning our understanding of juridicalness) when the possibilities for considering legal rules are reduced to a formalistic *in abstracto* interpretation and deductive application (Linhares 2007). However, it also means, on the other hand, denouncing the deconstructive exercise, that is, concluding that whilst allowing untouchable pre-judgments (whilst immunising the corresponding statements of necessity), this exercise for once thwarts its own agenda of taking 'the limitless context into account', that is, of surprising the supplementarity or the parergonality which opens up the frame of every context (Derrida 1988: 136). Effectively, this means acknowledging the difficulty of inscribing the deconstructed practices within an authentic interplay of *différances* or dissemination, if not the paradoxical impossibility of experiencing the recontextualisation which these practices persistently and permanently constitute. It is as if this deconstructive reading, despite its intentions, runs the risk (eloquently announced by Derrida himself) of 'settling down' or 'regressing into the system' it deconstructs – 'the system that has been, or is in the process of being, deconstructed' (Derrida 1972: 11–12).

In any case, notwithstanding these differences (and how they are assimilated by the eventual critical arguments), the way out seems to be the discussion of an alternative understanding of law, not as an arbitrary choice, but as an attempt to (critically) rethink a certain law or certain practice of law – a certain response to the problem of common life – which, as a specific way of creating communitarian meanings (irreducible, as such, to other plausible constructions of praxis and practical rationality and certainly also to other forms of collective identity), is significantly inscribed in the deployment of what may be called the Western Text (Neves 2008: 9 ff., 101 ff.; Linhares 2012b: 497–501; 2016: 432–3). This full historical-cultural contextualisation of law's acquisitions, providing the opportunity to make the most dynamic of these acquisitions (considered as *artefacta*) correspond to an effective argument for continuity (if not to an effective experience of constitutive historicity, involving a permanent rewriting of memory), allows us to focus on a specific idiom, the possibilities of which (reconstituted in our present context) are significantly different from those which (either facing the formalist paradigm of application or its deconstructive reading) we have previously considered. This is the idiom which reconciles the claim to comparability (and the universalisation it involves) with an experience of concreteness and a judgment of exemplarity, whilst simultaneously acknowledging that, concerning the European legacy (and the corresponding institutional cosmos), such compossibility corresponds to a persistent distinctive feature, if not to a major sign or trace, with an explicit aspirational potential, even when it is apparently questioned or refuted (or reduced to a subordinate role).

Resisting the critical-archaeological task that this statement may inspire – a critical-archaeological approach which, involving a deliberate interpellation of our present experience, would inevitably bring us back to the republican civitas and the invention of *controversia* and *respondere* (if not *audiatur et altera pars*) that distinguishes the rise of the secular jurists, as well as to the apparent rupture (concerning the methodological priority of problem-case) imposed by modern normativism – it is, however, indispensable to stress that it is precisely as an effective consecration of a claim to comparability (inseparable from the institutionalisation of the principle of *audiatur et altera pars* and the correlative dignity of status, identifying-demarcating a community of comparable equals) that this bright initium interests us here (notwithstanding the implacably circumscribed circle, overlapping an explicit *status civitatis* and the *munus* of *paterfamilias*, that distinguishes Roman institutionalisation). Experiencing Roman isolation of law (and its legacy) by giving priority to the claim to comparability – whilst reinterpreting (in a significantly different way) Schulz's well-known diagnosis (Schulz 1936: III, 19 ff.; Linhares 2018: 248–53) – means, in fact, highlighting the acquisition of an unmistakable microscopic model of community, involving two subject-parties and an impartial third (Giuliani 1966), as well as acknowledging that the opportunity to create distinct communitarian meaning comes immediately from the conditions of possibility which, in constituting and relating the subject-parties, give them the performative identity of positions (to be occupied) or masks (to be 'buckled').

I refer, obviously, to the conditions which, by institutionalising the opportunity (if not also the legitimacy) to claim different (contrasting) understandings of the shared situation-event and the common context-order (with the corresponding warrants-*topoi*), construct-conform these differences and the issues they explore (as sources of plausible arguments) as intrinsically compatible with a (real or virtual) practical-prudential treatment or judicative assimilation. The core of the *communitas*-artefact introduced corresponds to this possibility of treatment or assimilation or, more precisely, to a certain located invention of a *tertium comparationis*, which is (or should be) institutionalised through the possibility of the participation of a third (impartial) subject. It is, in fact, as if the *face-à-face* immediately experienced in the subject's encounter should be conventionally submitted to a constitutive interruption, that is, to a thematisation of intersubjectivity which, without paradox, would be able to generate a new kind of intersubjectivity. It is this, specified as an authentic attributive bilaterality (Reale 1982: 681–94) which, whilst relativising the subjects, makes them effectively comparable, on the one hand by imposing a reciprocally constitutive connection between spheres of autonomy and responsibility (spheres which will be, in later stages, normatively and dogmatically specified as webs of rights and duties) and, on the other hand, by supporting a relevance filter which, considering the shared situation-event, renounces the possibility of treating it as such (as an arrangement of unrepeatably singular moments).

The result is a specification of phronesis which, invoking an authentic context-order – identified with *ius quod est* and its interpretative reconstruction in *iuris prudenti*'s sentences – refuses, on the one hand, the possibility of a *respondere* which may appear as a self-sufficient (*causa sui*) expression of an inspired *voluntas* (as in the case of the pontiffs' responses) and, on the other hand, frees judicial rhetoric from the holistic continuum that the Aristotelian emancipation (secularisation) of praxis-phronesis constitutively preserved, as well as from its strict reference to the past. The construction of a claim to autonomy seems, in fact, inseparable from this change of emphasis concerning the temporal dimension, not certainly because the reference to the past loses its relevance – without the reconstitution of what really happened (in the words of Jackson, 'the story *in* the trial') there would be no possible answer to the indispensable *status coniecturalis* and the interrogation '*an sit?*'! – but rather because this reference henceforth appears organically integrated (as the 'story *of* the trial') in the present of the controversy, as a necessary condition of the render-*tribuere* (*ius suum cuique tribuere*) which, as a judgment, appeases the parties' claims (Jackson 1988). However, this specification of phronesis would not be identifiable if it represented less of a specification of *humanitas*, a word invented in this context (Heidegger 1947: 19) to translate the consecration of a community of comparable equals, namely a community which the Roman Republic could only conceive of as an implacably circumscribed circle, the intentional meaning of which represents, however, a remarkable acquisition, opening up the way to a specific institutionalisation of *audiatur et altera pars* and thus to the consecration of a pragmatic of respect (considered as a source of normative claims).

Should this pragmatic of respect and its claim for equality (as a microscopic claim inseparable from the structure of controversy and from the possibility of a rational prudential comparability) be treated as a specification of human dignity? I would say it should (Linhares 2012b). With the unsuspected help of Jeremy Waldron, I would add, more precisely, that on account of the significance attributed to a microscopically experienced thirdness – granted by the adjudicator-third and the presupposition of *jus* (as a *tertium comparationis* of warrants and criteria) – this is exactly the specification of human dignity which law's cultural project invented as its own (even though in its initial consecration this meant exploring an implacably closed circle of intersubjectivity) and which has been continuously pursued and permanently reinvented (not merely expanded within its own circle!) as an indispensable identifying claim (dignity as rank and status as an 'intrinsic', non-contingent 'legal idea') (Waldron 2011: 4–5), and also as a persistent component of a specific validity order.³ The said pragmatic and the relativising mask (which this pragmatic consecrates) are, as a matter of fact, inseparable from the principle of *audiatur et altera pars* and as such represent the invention of an autonomous and responsible subject – the inter-subjectively relativised subject who, implicitly or explicitly invoking an order of warrants and criteria, addresses him- or herself simultaneously to the other party and to the impartial third, demanding a hearing, as well as expecting a rationally judicative treatment of the controversy (Linhares 2012b). Experiencing this isolation (and its legacy) by giving priority to the microscopic invention of intersubjectivity – whilst attributing the intelligibility of a contextual resource to the concentration on private secular internal normativity – is certainly indispensable to defining a clearer counterpoint between Greek and Roman understandings of law and its dimensions. The holistic view diagnosed by Schulz as a kind of natural difficulty in disentangling law from the communitarian ethos (Schulz 1936: 20–1) acquires a completely different transparent meaning when we understand that the representation of juridicalness enabled the Greek experience to remain inseparable from a philosophy of justice and the contemplation (through the intellectual virtue of *sophia*) of a cosmic being that was read (interpreted) as a presupposed, definitive, perfect order. We may, in fact, add that this juridical relevance (brilliantly opening up the path to the future *juris naturalis scientia*) corresponds to an undifferentiated normative projection of the harmony which such an order (in its essential totality) immanently claims – as if juridicalness should assume the identity of a global *nomos* incorporated (when not diluted) in the metaphysic of the *logos* (Neves 1983: 492–506). Everything changed with the rise of the Roman jurists in the second century BC, helped decisively by a certain Hellenistic fire of Prometheus that was not due to philosophical reflection but to *Hermagorei* and stasis doctrine (Giuliani 1961: 71–111): the unavailability of the order was no longer attributed to a self-sufficient (abstract) natural law but to a *cosmos* of hypostasised institutions (*un mondo a parte, il cosmo delle*

---

³ This emphasis certainly does not exclude the acknowledgement that the political-philosophical and moral idea of dignity as value, autonomously introduced in the modern cycle (the culminating canonic expression of which is certainly Kantian *Menschenwürde*) has not been assimilated into law's practical world: it has (translated into an immediate claim of equality), first of all formally, due to a decisive understanding of statute law as norm (as the Rousseaunian *loi encore à faire*, constitutively identified with an intrinsic expression of rational universality), then substantively, following a progressive (more or less contingent) conformation of the proposed legal-politic prescriptive solutions (and the corresponding justification). The normative dimension or level in which these claims to equality are incorporated (macroscopically referred to as a self-sufficient or, at least, autonomously conceived context-order, even when predominantly understood as a system of individual rights) is, however, significantly different from the normative dimension or level (intrinsically related to the problem-case) in which the said microscopic pragmatic and its experience of dignity (albeit in some historical cycles significantly hidden or apparently reduced to a subordinate place) grows or has been growing since Roman *civitas*'s stage.

istituzione ipostatizzate, dei rapport 'calculabili'), a cosmos which one may recognise (with the mediation of a substantialised typology involving *sapientia* and *prudentia*) when assuming a kind of metaphysic of being addressed to the concrete just – in the certainty that this experience of juridicalness adds the decisive experience of an autonomisation of *jurisprudentia* as praxis to the philosophical dimension (Lombardi 1967: 31).

The specification of phronesis which this invention introduces – as a response to the challenge of ensuring that the new and the particular (corresponding to the problematic nucleus) may, in circular fashion (and inextricably), become the general and the old (Bubner 1990: 64) – has its knotty point precisely in the autonomous consideration of concreteness, that is, in the possibility of defending (most of the time, however, only implicitly) a constitutive counterpoint between analogically comparable concreteness and absolute incomparable singularity, which means giving the first a very specific normative intelligibility.

How should the relevance of this acquisition be considered today? Is it possible, in our present circumstances, to preserve a legal discourse which assumes the artefact concreteness (in its constitutive relation with exemplarity and analogical rationality) as a decisive claim (or aspiration)? I would that say it is. The defence of this possibility can certainly count on a very persuasive return of phronesis – significantly different from the one considered above, which invoked deconstruction as philosophy. I refer, evidently, to the one which we may acknowledge by considering a certain non-analytical 'rehabilitation of practical philosophy' (Gadamer, Viehweg, Riedel, Bubner) (Riedel 1972–4) and this one as a discourse of constitutive immanence, developing an internal perspective on praxis (and its foundational, regulative and constitutive moments). This is, in fact, a discourse whose conditions only became possible in the second half of the twentieth century, whilst combining (overlapping) the modern acquisition of intentional-cultural subjectivity with a practical-existential experience of historicity (as a radical constitutive historicity) – the former making us responsible for the authorship-*inventio* of our practical worlds (their goals and values), the latter submitting this invention to indispensable self-reflexive differentiations concerning the factors and conditions, but also the different dynamics and varying degrees of vulnerability to contingence (with the possibility of introducing a constitutive dialectic equilibrium between *societas* and *communitas*). In parallel with the deconstructive re-writing of phronesis (even though with different outcomes), this rehabilitation reinvents the equilibrium of Aristotelian intellectual virtues as a major experience of plurality (a paradigmatic consecration of plural rational types), whilst simultaneously exploring the autonomous possibilities of phronesis, for once freed from the prevalence or predominance (or even from the methodic priority) of theoretical claims: freed from the theoretical-speculative claims due to the pre-modern integrative horizon of *sophia* (and its institutionalisation of the connection *telos/ethos*) or from the theoretical-philosophical domestication ('consummation') of dialectics due to Hegel's legacy (forcing dialectics to forget its provenience-*Herkunft* and to breach its constitutive bond with topics) (Bubner 1990: 9, 79 ff., 88–96), but also freed from the theoretical-scientific colonisation corresponding to the hypertrophy of *episteme* and its irreversible appropriation of *technê* (*Sachkundheit*) – a hypertrophy and an appropriation which modernity consummated as (or converted into) metaphysics (Heidegger 1985: 76). This capacity to pursue the interrupted emancipation of *praxis-prattein* is indeed indispensable to confirming the dialectic structure and the dialogical-conversational intention of practical reasoning – in their constitutive relation with the existential dispositions affirmed in the subject/subject experience of *Lebenswelt* (involving a productive circle of finitude and trans-finitude, *auctoritas* and reason, tradition and rational discursivity) – if not directly to warranting the dialectic between general and particular, past and present, 'old' (presupposed) and 'new'.

This indiscriminate consideration of practical thinking is certainly a necessary reflexive horizon as we consider the argument of continuity concerning concreteness. It is not, however, a sufficient condition for developing a persuasive defence of this argument (and even less for confirming its mettle to survive in our present circumstances). Why? Quite simply because the resources-artefacts assumed in law's practical world are not determinable as pure unilateral projections of this global horizon. The impossibility of admitting an experience of this specific practical world which could be fully determined through a passive reception or assimilation of the possibilities globally inscribed in (or permitted by) this horizon (more or less explicitly treated as alternatives to be chosen) imposes in fact another step, considering (as if bottom-up) how the practices and discourses at stake institutionalise the irreducible intertwinement between old and new (the key to understanding concreteness and exemplarity). In other words, the reconstitution and defence of a plausible internal normative perspective is not easily satisfied with the mere rethinking of a subject/subject practical rationality, instead claiming an autonomously institutionalised (specifically juridical) expression of this rationality – an expression which, using a very specific idiom (due to Castanheira Neves' jurisprudentialism), I will identify as a system/problem dialectics (Neves 1995: 78–81, 152–7, 188–96, 278–83; Linhares 2016: 432 ff.).

This means considering a complex intertwinement between dogmatic stabilising and problem-solving practices – the first objectifying validity as normativity in an open, multi-dimensional or multi-layered binding legal system, the second answering the novelty of concrete controversy with an adjudicative prudential mediation or assimilation. This also means exploring how the diverse strata of this system, mobilised from the perspective of the concrete problem, participate in a kind of permanent constitutive circle which, as an authentic experience of constitutive historicity, interchanges and overlaps the tasks-roles of guiding and guide-following, specifying and transforming, fixing and developing. Whilst objectifying validity in a multi-layered system with several different (not methodologically equivalent) strata – normative principles (considered as *jus* and foundational warrants), statutes, precedents-*exempla*, doctrinal criteria (and standards) and legal reality (the latter as a constitutive experience of law in action) – and whilst assuming an incessant dynamic (open to regressive re-composition, if not a permanent beginning, determined precisely by the methodological priority of the concrete problem), the praxis of stabilisation in question and the normativity it generates are not only incompatible with a normativistic modus for conceiving of universality or universability but also irreducible to a systemic reconstruction centring on the social rule category (treating the rule or its 'uses' of 'general classifying words' as the only pattern of comparability permitted by law). On the contrary, these practices claim a reflexive (methodological) experience capable of distinguishing between, on the one hand, foundational warrants and criteria[4] – which means disrupting the traditional continuum between principles and norms! – and, on the other hand, different kinds of criteria (statutory, dogmatic, jurisdictional) – which means treating judicial rulings as full concrete adjudicative decisions, inseparable from the case and from a specific context of realisation (and also from an explicit analogical rationality) (Linhares and Gaudêncio 2015: 185 ff.). It is as if the perspective of concreteness on the one hand restored interpretation to its fully normative (not hermeneutical) 'integral sense' of 'the realisation of law' (an 'integral sense' which is incompatible with any methodologically plausible splits between interpretation and application, interpretation and filling of gaps), whilst on the other hand enabling us to move beyond a purely topical assimilation of legal materials, not only distinguishing the systemic layers that should be assumed and treated as warrants and criteria, but also attributing different presumptions of bindingness or normative force to these layers, all treated as (explicit or implicit) rebuttable presumptions (whose refutation determines a particular burden of contra-argumentation)[5]. When we explore this unique way of experiencing and assimilating the particular and new, we may indeed understand that the participation in the general and the old which this institutionalised way claims (that is, the permanent presupposition-reinvention of an autonomous system involving, as strata, diversely binding warrants and criteria) gives legal adjudication the rational identity it needs, precisely the one which allows us to treat it not only as a decision

---

[4] A foundational warrant (*fundamento*) is a rationale which gives specific intelligibility or an autonomous sense to a certain field or domain of practice (mainly identifying the commitments that constitute this field): the rationale justifies a plausible conclusion, even though it does not propose a solution or a type of solution (i.e. it does not free us from the discursive effort, which is indispensable to reaching the solution). The rule or criterion is an available ('technical') device or apparatus, which can be immediately mobilised ('convened') to resolve a given problem and/or provides a plausible scheme for finding the corresponding solution (albeit requiring a discursive effort in concretisation or realisation). The normative principles (extended by some doctrinal models that constitutively specify and reinvent those principles) should be methodologically treated as foundational warrants or rationales. Statutes, judge-made law and all the other dogmatic models are (or should be assumed as) criteria.

[5] With principles (as warrants) benefiting from a presumption of communitarian validity, statutes (as criteria) from a presumption of political-constitutional pedigree or authority-*potestas*, legal dogmatic models (as warrants or criteria) benefiting from a presumption of rationality or rational conclusiveness and, last but not least, precedents-*exempla* (as criteria) benefiting from a singularly contextualised presumption of correctness (*justeza*).

but also as a judgment, if not already as a judicative decision (Neves 1995: 30–4) – that is, an adequate treatment-assimilation of a concrete controversy which is also and inseparably a unique realisation of systemic intentions and claims.

However, is this step sufficient in order to corroborate the argument of continuity concerning concreteness (as the possibility of autonomising a specific juridical context of realisation)? Is the desired point of equilibrium (or reversibility) between problem and system an attainable one when the contexts of meaning and the contexts of realisation which frame the practices of adjudication (whilst simultaneously interfering with the practices of systemic stabilisation which they presuppose) appear increasingly wounded by plurality and fragmentation? Do these signs of disintegration not favour, on one hand, the closeness and the dogmatic violence of principles and criteria, whilst on the other hand condemning any claim of concreteness to uncommunicable singularity? I think this step is sufficient and that all these risks (eloquently denounced by the deconstructive idiom) can be significantly attenuated under the (absolutely necessary) condition that the legal system itself, through the mediation of one of its strata (legal doctrine) directly assumes the thematisation of pluralism and fragmentation. This means, in fact, defending that legal dogmatics should develop itself effectively beyond its natural practices, explicitly considering adjudication's *modus operandi* through the plural spectrum which only a genuine methodological meta-dogmatic research, in its internal specific way, provides. In fact, this intensified attention to performance and its heterogeneous possibilities, converting disparately esoteric approaches into an integrated exoteric testimony of plurality (eventually with the resource to piecemeal narrative), today seems indispensable, not only as doctrine constructs its own *novum* (anticipating criteria) but also as it reconstitutes the dynamics of the legal system in general and the contents of normative principles in particular. It is indeed as if we could distinguish a very specific reflexive burden as a contextual condition essential to giving presumption of rationality (and *auctoritas*) the sense and the success it needs in a limit-situation such as our own: a reflexive burden which does not, in itself, overcome the violent effects of dogmatic isolation and problematic fragmentation, but has the advantage of submitting (treating) the corresponding threats and the intrinsically juridical search for plausible modes of equilibrium as an authentic thematic core (whose reflexive outcomes may be normatively incorporated). This is, however, another story, to be told in another place and time.

Bibliography

Aguado, M. I. Peña (1994), *Ästhetik des Erhabenen. Burke, Kant, Adorno, Lyotard*, Wien: Passagen Verlag.

Bearn, G. (2000), 'Differentiating Derrida and Deleuze', 33 *Continental Philosophy Review*, 441–65.

Bubner, R. (1990). *Dialektik als Topik. Bausteine zu einer lebensweltlichen Theorie der Rationalität*. Frankfurt am Main: Suhrkamp Verlag.

Derrida, J. (1967), *L'écriture et la différence*, Paris: Éditions du Seuil.
Derrida, J. (1972), *Marges de la philosophie*, Paris: Éditions Minuit.
Derrida, J. (1988), *Limited Inc*, Evanston, IL: Northwestern University Press.
Derrida, J. (1994), *Force de loi. Le 'fondement mystique de l´autorité'*, Paris: Galilée.
Derrida, J. (1997), *Adieu à Emmanuel Levinas*, Paris: Galilée.
Douzinas, C. and R. Warrington (1991), *Postmodern Jurisprudence: the Law of Text in the Texts of Law*, London: Routledge.
Douzinas, C. and R. Warrington (1994), *Justice Miscarried. Ethics, Aesthetics and the Law*, New York and London: Harvester Wheatsheaf.
Foucault, M. (1976), *L'Histoire de la sexualité, I, La volonté de savoir*, Paris: Gallimard.
Giuliani, A. (1961), *Il concetto di prova. Contributo alla logica giuridica*, Milano: A. Giuffre.
Giuliani, A. (1966), *La controversia. Studi nelle scienze giuridiche e sociali della facoltà di giurisprudenza dell' Università di Pavia*, vol. XXXIX, 81–216.
Goodrich, P. (1990), *Languages of Law, From Logics of Memory to Nomadic Masks*, London: Weidenfeld and Nicolson.
Hart, H. L. A. (1994), *The Concept of Law*, 2nd edn with postscript, Oxford: Clarendon Press.
Heidegger, M. (1947), *Über den Humanismus*, Frankfurt: Vittorio Klostermann.
Heidegger, M. (1985), *Vorträge und Aufsätze*, 5th edn, Pfullingen: Neske.
Jackson, B. (1988), *Law, Fact and Narrative Coherence*, Liverpool: Deborah Charles Publications.
Kennedy, D. (1992), 'The Politics of Hierarchy', in J. Boyle (ed.), *Critical Legal Studies*, New York: New York University Press, 427–46 (first published in 1983 as 'Legal Education and the Reproduction of Hierarchy', 32(4) *Journal of Legal Education*, 591–615).
Levinas, E. (2004) [1978], *Autrement que l'être ou au-delà de l'essence*, Paris: Le Livre de Poche.
Linhares, J. M. A. (2007), 'Dekonstruktion als philosophische (gegenphilosophische) Reflexion über das Recht. Betrachtungen zu Derrida', 93(1) *Archiv für Rechts- und Sozialphilosophie (ARSP)*, 39–66.
Linhares, J. M. A. (2012a), 'Evidence (or Proof?) as Law's Gaping Wound: a Persistent False Aporia?', 88(1) *Boletim da Faculdade de Direito*, 65–89.
Linhares, J. M. A. (2012b), 'Law's Cultural Project and the Claim to Universality or the Equivocalities of a Familiar Debate', 25 *International Journal for the Semiotics of Law*, 489–503.
Linhares, J. M. A. (2016), 'In Defense of a Non-Positivist Separation Thesis Between Law and Morality', 4 *Rechtsphilosophie. Zeitschrift für Grundlagen des Rechts*, 425–43.
Linhares, J. M. A. (2018), 'Law and Opera as Practical-cultural Artefacts, or the Productivity and Limits of a Plausible Counterpoint', in M. Manzin, F. Puppo and S. Tomasi (eds), *Multimodal Argumentation, Pluralism and Images of Law (Studies on Argumentation and Legal Philosophy)*, Trento: Università degli Studi di Trento, 241–66.

Linhares, J. M. A. and A. Gaudêncio (2015), 'The Portuguese Experience of Judge-Made Law and the Possibility of Prospective Intentions and Effects', in E. Steiner (ed.), *Comparing the Prospective Effect of Judicial Rulings Across Jurisdictions*, Cham: Springer, 185–202.

Lombardi, L. (1967), *Saggio sul diritto giurisprudenziale*. Milano: Giuffrè.

Lyotard, J. F. (1983), *Le différend*, Paris: Éditions de Minuit.

Lyotard, J. F. (1990), *Pérégrinations. Loi, forme, évènement*, Paris: Galilée.

MacCormick, N. (1994) [1978], *Legal Reasoning and Legal Theory*, 2nd edn, Oxford: Clarendon Press.

MacCormick, N. (2005), *Rhetoric and the Rule of Law*, Oxford: Oxford University Press.

MacCormick, N. (2007), *Institutions of Law. An Essay in Legal Theory*, Oxford: Oxford University Press.

Neves, A. Castanheira (1983), *O instituto dos 'Assentos' e a função jurídica dos Supremos Tribunais*, Coimbra: Coimbra Editora.

Neves, A. Castanheira (1995), *Metodologia jurídica. Problemas fundamentais*, Coimbra: Coimbra Editora.

Neves, A. Castanheira (2008), *Digesta – escritos acerca do direito, do pensamento jurídico, da sua metodologia e outros*, vol. 3, Coimbra: Coimbra Editora.

Nussbaum, M. (1986), *The Fragility of Goodness. Luck and Ethics in Greek Tragedy and Philosophy*, Cambridge: Cambridge University Press.

Reale, M. (1982), *Filosofia do Direito*, 9th rev. edn, São Paulo: Saraiva.

Riedel, M. (1972–4), *Rehabilitierung der praktischen Philosophie*, 2 vols, Freiburg: Rombach Verlag.

Schulz, F. (1936), *The Principles of Roman Law* (rev. and enlarged trans. from *Prinzipien der römischen Rechts*, 1934), Oxford: Clarendon Press.

Seibert, Th.-M. (2006), 'Dekonstruktion der Gerechtigkeit?', in S. Buckel, R. Christensen and A. Fischer-Lescano (eds), *Neue Theorien des Rechts*, Stuttgart: Suhrkamp, 29–55.

Tamanaha, B. Z. (2010), *Beyond the Formalist-Realist Divide. The Role of Politics in Judging*, Princeton, NJ and Oxford: Princeton University Press.

Waldron, J. (2011), 'How Law Protects Dignity', the 2011 David Williams Lecture at the University of Cambridge, *New York University School Of Law, Public Law Research Paper no. 11-83* <http://papers.ssrn.com/sol3/papers.cfm?abstract_id=1973341##> accessed 1 February 2013.

Welsch, W. (1988), 'Einleitung', in W. Welsch (ed.), *Wege aus der Moderne. Schlüsseltexte der Postmoderne-Diskussion*, Weinheim: Acta Humaniora,

Welsch, W. (1991), *Unsere postmoderne Moderne*, Weinheim: Acta Humaniora.

Chapter 7

What is Happening to the Norm? Gender as Paradigm of a Deformalised Neo-legal Positivism

Silvia Niccolai

1. LEGAL REALISM IN THE AGE OF PHILOSOPHICAL DECONSTRUCTIVISM

Philosophical and political deconstructivism is largely inspirational for today's critical legal theories, which are showing a renewed vigour in Italy. Here, a new wave of legal realists affirms that opposing 'practices of oppression' means imagining strategies that focus not on the individual, seen as separated from the social structure, but on a collective 'we', constituted by a complex mixture of various types of norms: legal, political, social. In this postmodern frame, new critical legal theories reformulate the most classical realistic commitment against legal positivism and formalism.[1]

It is undeniable that, when transposed on the juridical level, philosophical deconstructivism brings along anti-formalist implications. Nevertheless, does it also imply substantive changes at the level of the idea of 'norm' and of 'law' that is used, compared to those ideas used in a traditional, legal-positivist context?

Not much: this is the position which I will advocate in this chapter. Exploring the concept of norm that philosophical deconstructivism adopts could lead one to discover that this latter presupposes an idea of norm not that far from that which is centred on the heteronomy of command, and which used to be typical of legal positivism. This latter, in the European continental experience of the twentieth century at least, owes a great deal of its long-lasting success to having been able to combine the heteronomy of the command with the democratic and constitutional foundation of the juridical order: in this frame, the legal norm has been regarded as the product of progressive political addresses, and the tool of their affirmation.

This may explain why, in today's anti-formalistic views – interested in the reform of society – the norm remains what it has always been in modern times: a useful (and somewhat authoritarian) tool for the promotion of progress.

In this chapter, I will compare some aspects of Judith Butler's thought, prominent in contemporary philosophical deconstructivism, with certain aspects of a contrasting view, the Italian feminist thought of sexual difference. It is precisely in the dominant paradigm of Butler's thought, the gender norm, that I believe we

---

[1] See the collected essays in Bernardini and Giolo (2017).

can find the signs of a resurgence of imperativistic conceptions of law, diluted in some sort of deconstructed pan-normativism which in the whole recalls the features of legal positivism much more than one would expect.

It goes without saying that in this short chapter I will not be able to give a complete exposition of Butler's thought, nor of that of the feminism of difference. Neither will I be able to do justice to the complexity and ramifications of either of them; the same goes for the conceptions of law, or the philosophical ideas, which I will call into question.

My hope is that by piecing together some portions of considerably broader paths of thought, history and practice, suggestions can arise that will be useful for perceiving something of what is happening today to a cardinal idea in legal imaginary, practice and discourse: the idea of norm.

2. NORMS, LAWS, RULES: A SHORT ITINERARY WITHIN THE PAN-NORMATIVE UNIVERSE OF JUDITH BUTLER

If deconstructive thought has on the legal level anti-formalist consequences, this is due to its tendency to consider the legal norm and the social norm as substantially indistinct. Deconstructivism assumes that legal regulations always imply a certain social idea of normality, of value, of good, of useful or just. Thanks to their cogent and prescriptive character, legal norms impose and preserve a given, socially accepted, idea of normality; when the coincidence between social normality and the normality prescribed by the juridical norm gets lost, the juridical norm tends to lose its effectiveness; but the circularity between the social norm and the juridical norm implies that what emerges on the social level is destined to become normative also on the juridical level. This idea recurs in Judith Butler's thought.[2] According to her, although equivalent 'neither to rule nor to law', the norm 'is, in the context of social practices, standard of normalization' and 'often presents itself in the guise of the law' but, on the other hand, 'the norm only persists as a norm to the extent that it is acted out in social practice'.

> A regulation is that which *makes regular*, but it is also, following Foucault, a mode of *discipline and surveillance* within late modern forms of power; it does not merely constrict and negate and it is, therefore, not merely a juridical form of power . . . As an operation of power, regulation can take a legal form, but its legal dimension does not exhaust the sphere of its efficaciousness . . . regulation is thus bound up with the process of *normalization*. (Butler 2004: 55)

> A norm is not the same as a rule, and it is not the same as a law. A norm operates within social practices as the implicit standard of normalization. (Butler 2004: 41)

---

[2] In and of itself, this idea corresponds to the assumption that law is never neutral with respect to the socially dominant forces, and certainly has Marxian or even Hegelian roots (if we accept the materialistic reading of Hegel's thought famously offered by, among others, Herbert Marcuse).

'Normativity' has a dual character: on the one hand 'it refers to the aims and aspirations that guide us, the precepts by which we are compelled to act or speak to one another, the commonly held presuppositions by which we are oriented and which give direction to our actions'; on the other hand it 'refers to the process of normalization, the way that certain norms, ideas and ideals hold sway over embodied life, provide coercitive criteria for normal "men" and "women"' (Butler 2004: 206).

The norm is thus both 'that which binds' and 'that which excludes' (Butler 2014: 301).[3] Between these two poles swing the dynamics of recognition: 'on the one hand the norms seem to indicate the regulatory or normalizing function of power, but from another perspective, norms are precisely what binds individuals, forming the basis of their ethical and political claims' (Butler 2004: 219).

Two aspects stand out: on the one hand, criticism of the norm coexists with a declared 'desire for norms'; on the other hand, the deconstruction of existing norms is performed by subjects that are always collective. A 'desire for norms that might let one live' is what, for Butler, determines the critical relationship with the rules of recognition given, and this critical relationship, in turn, depends on 'a capacity, *invariably collective*, to articulate an alternative, minority version of sustaining norms and ideals that enable me to act' (Butler 2004: 3). This idea has been repeatedly affirmed by Butler for the rights of homosexual or transgender people and for women, the 'viability' of whose life 'depends upon an exercise of bodily autonomy and on social conditions that enable that autonomy'; self-determination in relation to one's body is made effective 'by forms of autonomy that require social (and legal) support and protection' (Butler 2004: 12).[4]

Gender is a norm, Butler maintains, and the gendered subject is the product of a particular form of subduing; what is wrong with gender is not its being a rule, which, as such, constitutes, dominates, produces the subject. What is wrong with gender is its being understood as (and thereby its functioning as) that particular rule that subdues in the sense of sexual binarism, thus impoverishing the semantic field of gender. The criticism and deconstruction of this rule makes room for other regulations, deconstructed and denaturalised, and therefore more welcoming.[5]

These are the issues that outline 'an agenda[6] for the future' (Butler 2004: 14) with which scholars and activists can tackle the urgent questions of a 'social transformation' that even passes, by necessity, through the struggle for law. Since what is real is determined by power (Butler 2004: 215), the latter, the power, is at the centre of contention: those who are excluded from the 'real' because of the rules that determine it today cannot become real unless they, in turn, have access to the normative. Although the space of law and that of the normative do not

---

[3] The original wording is as follows: 'we see the "norm" as that which binds us, but we also see that the "norm" creates unity only through a strategy of exclusion'.
[4] The Italian translation here adds: 'and that must be guaranteed by welfare' (Butler 2014: 46).
[5] 'Gender has a way of moving beyond that naturalized binary' (Butler 2004: 42–3).
[6] 'A political agenda' in the Italian translation (Butler 2014: 48).

coincide, the state of the first is symptom and primary condition of the operation of the latter.

These positions lead to aporias, which became unavoidable around the theme of same-sex marriage, in which Butler famously warned the LGTBI movement against the risk of 'institutionalisation'. In turn, these aporias are avoidable in only one way: by keeping the critical register always open, that is to say, provoking continuous revisions and shifts within the normative structures that are progressively determined in the unstable relationship between social reality and regulations (Mastromartino 2017: 241).

It is apparent here that the deconstructive conceptions that emphasise the link between social and juridical norms render good service to law, understood as the machinery that dispenses statutes, rules and regulations. The continuous adaptation to the emerging social change represents, for the law, an opportunity to renew its binding link with reality, to maintain its grip on it and to demonstrate that it is an irreplaceable instrument to affirm the real and recognised character of experiences, subjectivities, values.[7]

The normative and the symbolic

According to Butler, 'the shared presuppositions that guide and govern our actions' are part of the normative. The normative, then, with its indistinction between the juridical and the social, takes the place of the 'symbolic'. 'Symbolic' is a highly elaborate concept in Lacanian psychoanalysis, which we can define as what institutes 'the order of the intelligible and the thinkable' (Ferrando 2017: 220). It is in the light of the symbolic, 'the background of the possibilities represented', that we interpret both 'what happens to us and our desire' (Fanciullacci 2017: 85).

Butler's distancing from the concept of symbolic is explicit, and has very pragmatic motivations: 'The changes in the symbolic take a long, long time. I wonder how long I will have to wait?' (Butler 2004: 212).

Here, Butler is interrogating the feminist thought that has conceived sexual difference as belonging to the symbolic order. According to Butler, if the sexual difference is assumed to be symbolic, the failure of feminism is decided, which for her is a 'social transformation' movement. 'What happens to the task of feminist theory to think social transformation, if we accept that sexual difference is

---

[7] One way to reinforce the link between life and law is through judicial action: the trial can offer a valid scene where it can be shown that some norms provoke exclusion, discrimination or disadvantage at the cost of ways of living or of being which are outside the idea of social normality accepted by the law. This can provoke a revision of existing norms. The analysis that Condello (2018) develops around the dynamics of the 'extraordinary case' that realigns the correspondence between norm and reality is easily explained from this point of view. It goes without saying that the motive according to which law is always behind the times and real life and therefore must continuously be changed in order to adapt to them is an intimately realistic assumption , and originates from a criticism against 'statualism', 'normativism' and 'formalism' which is far from new.

orchestrated and constrained at the symbolic level? If it is symbolic, is it changeable?' (Butler 2004: 212, italics mine).

These positions, which, perhaps intentionally, limit the indeterminate expression 'feminism' to a monodimensional meaning,[8] are based on two assumptions. The first relates to the fact that, in Butler's view, to pronounce the idea of sexual difference is very close to affirming compulsory heterosexuality; thereby, to say that the sexual difference refers to the symbolic involves the risk of placing heteronormativity beyond 'social contestation', beyond the reach of social and political protest, in the sphere of what is necessary and unchangeable. This is enough to make inadvisable the placing of the sexual difference within the symbolic. The second position, which I want to emphasise here, is that whatever meaning is assigned to the idea of 'symbolic', this latter certainly refers to something that cannot be attacked or changed by the means of institutional, normative or social reforms. In essence, the preference towards thinking that 'man' and 'woman' are sociological concepts (Butler 2004: 212) is due to the fact that, when placed in the social, those concepts appear governable and reformable with social measures (for example a protest which results in a new legislation or provision, a bill, a judicial strategy for 'civil rights'), something which is impossible to think and affirm with regard to what is placed in the symbolic. The concept of symbolic that Butler adopts is, in turn, a manifestation of the 'normative'; it is in a normative (performative) way that the symbolic manifests itself, provoking certain ways of being more than others (Zamboni 2017b: 9). Butler affirms, however, 'that the distinction between symbolic and social law cannot finally hold' given that 'the symbolic itself is the sedimentation of social practices' (Butler 2004: 44). This allows her to affirm that the symbolic is subject to a 'critical practice'; in this way, Butler achieves exactly the conclusion that (in her view) the understanding of the symbolic as 'final authority' precludes. The symbolic therefore is not 'law', Butler maintains, but 'variable' laws: 'to contest symbolic authority' means to affirm that the norm, 'in its necessary temporality, is opened to a displacement and subversion from within' (Butler 2004: 47).

It may be said that for Butler the symbolic is a complex of prescriptions that in the reality of things are social but are ideologically assigned to the sphere of the symbolic. The claim to the symbolical tends to make some prescriptions immutable. The denial of the symbolical thus has the meaning of bringing the symbolical down in the sphere of the normative, which is to say in the realm of those prescriptive but changeable ('variable') regulations that constitute the 'human'. This implies that the symbolical, like the normative, is something that changes thanks to power, is the object of acts of disposition (and will). This also implies that different conceptions – challenging the dominant symbolical/normative order – can be affirmed, in the name of their intrinsic justice, by the force of other norms.

---

[8] Feminist thinkers that consider the sexual difference as belonging to the symbolic describe feminism as a political and symbolic movement, not a social one (Zamboni 2017a).

Therefore, the contestation of the existence of the symbolical goes together with the idea that everything that constitutes the human is modifiable by human intention, will and action, and that this constitutive and modifying action is expressed through power. It has actually been observed that in Butler's conceptions 'the term "power" [functions as] the all-encompassing interpretant of reality' (Zamboni 2018: 9).

Symbolical: a tool by which humans are constructed or the means by which humans can make present their reality to each other?

It is common knowledge that a line of fracture runs between the thought of Judith Butler and that of European feminism, and in particular Italian feminism which is known as the 'thought of sexual difference'. There is less awareness of the fact that this fracture runs exactly along one line: the location of sexual difference in the symbolical or in the social, and, ultimately, in the idea of 'symbolical' that is adopted.

Unlike Butler, Italian feminism does not see in the symbolical the instrument (or an aspect) of the power that constitutes and conforms the subjectivities, but the principal tool of mediation that singular human beings use to signify themselves and their experiences, their feelings, judgments and opinions. Unexpected and unrecognised ways of being, even if originating from an individual experience, can change mentality and behaviour at a general level, because, affirming themselves at the level of the symbolical, they become commonplace. In other words, Butler sees the symbolical as a rather objective force which organises itself notwithstanding and against the singularity, and in order to constitute it, whereas Italian feminism views the symbolical from the perspective of the subjective experience; this latter is considered to be what constitutes the symbolic. The symbolical level is thereby universal because it is filled by the subjective experience in its continuous 'becoming' made of discourse and experiences that, through the medium of language, people exchange with each other.[9] The analogy with a 'genuine' idea of market is explicit: 'The so-called free market could be only a huge copy of the unceasing exchange that passes through bodies and words, by which we get generated and re-generated, together with the entire world' (Muraro 2009: 8).

The lack of attention to the fact that it is precisely on the issue of the symbolic that 'gender' and 'sexual difference' theories split, is mainly due to a terminological question. What we know as 'thought of sexual difference' would have been better called 'politics of the symbolic', according to one of the greatest thinkers of this movement (Muraro 2006), but since the term 'symbolical' seemed at risk

---

[9] However, Italian feminism's idea of the symbolic distances itself on several points from the traditional Lacanian assumptions and from their North American reception (the one that Butler keeps in mind). Among these are the idea that 'we can create symbolic by introducing unforeseen in the order symbolic' (Muraro 1991: 126) and the idea that it is part of the symbolic 'the contingency of the real; the awareness that things happen and that anything can happen' (Muraro 2006: 151).

of sounding obscure and purely intellectual for most people, another entered into use in its place, which has had certain costs.

In particular, the fact that the feminism of the symbolic is known as 'feminism of sexual difference' has drawn on these conceptions charges of essentialism and heteronormativity, which do not affect their substance at all, since if this feminism has spoken of sexual difference it has done so in order to introduce the idea of 'a free sense of difference outside of sexual roles' (Cigarini 1995: 35) and with the aim of recognising and nominating such a 'free sense' when and where it makes itself visible. In fact, the thought of sexual difference is not a social theory that suggests action and reform programmes (and in this sense a political agenda), but a thought that has devoted itself to putting into words 'something that had already been there, in the political practice of women' (Muraro 2006: 159), a political practice started by saying 'I am a woman'. This foundational feminist statement ('I am a woman') is a symbolic gesture: by pronouncing it (in words and facts), each woman chooses positively to be such, she assumes and interprets subjectively the 'objective' role in which she, being born as woman, has 'found' herself to be. Thus, by uniting her body to her words, a woman can make of an imposed and endured condition, that of being woman, one chosen and loved instead. With this, the existing symbolic established order, which does not contemplate the woman as a subject that speaks as such (as a subject of the enunciation: Fanciullacci 2017), is already disrupted and reopened with respect to the synthesis it had previously achieved:

> I think that freedom consists concretely in being able to make of a human condition imposed, like that of women, the occasion for a greater existence . . . Until now women have thought that being born women was an obstacle, a negative value. When the value of difference has been affirmed, obviously this condition has become an element of enrichment, of modification of what exists. (Cigarini 1995: 121–2)

Saying 'I am a woman' is therefore a symbolic gesture that introduces a 'transgressive cut in the common sense and produces critical sense' (Cigarini 1995: 241); 'the accepted fact becomes the ordering principle of experience and saves the thought. Reality itself frees itself from the grip between blind repetition of self and becomes something other than itself' (Muraro 1991: 75).[10]

By saying 'I am a woman', each woman rediscovers her singularity as inserted into a female genealogy. The latter, as we are going to see, refers to the mother-daughter relationship, the relation on the denial of which the patriarchal symbolic order is constructed and preserved.

What is distinctive about the thought of sexual difference is affirming that every single person can feel real, can tell his or her truth, and therefore operate in a transformative sense, even on the public level, outside the mechanisms of power

---

[10] Muraro's seminal book, *L'ordine simbolico della madre* has now been translated into English; see Muraro 2017; on her thought see, recently, Cesarino (2018).

and without resorting to it, simply breaking the foundational interdict of patriarchal thought, the denial of the link between body and speech.

Even the thought of sexual difference, like Butler's, starts from the subjective experience of a woman who, seeing her own reality denied, begins to doubt that it is real – with all the unhappiness that derives from this – because outside of herself her reality is not recognised: no one more than a woman in a patriarchal history experiences the denial of herself, of her value and meaning. In order to resolve this painful condition, the thought of sexual difference points to the idea that singularity is real, that each human being makes true experience of her (or his) reality, can express it in language and can make it visible in the relationships that she (or he) directly undertakes with others. An individual woman, an individual human being can do this, and for one precise reason: because coming into the world language was transmitted to her, and language is the first symbolic resource. Before learning from social constructs that, in order to talk and think, in order to exist socially, a woman must renounce her sexed body and make herself a neutral subject,[11] every woman (and indeed every person) has experienced a moment in which body and word come together. This moment occurs in the mother-child relationship, the original couple in which everyone learns to speak and acquires confidence in the correspondence between words and things, a correspondence demonstrated and guaranteed by the other party in the relationship, who understands, replies, interacts, responds.

The maternal relationship is the image of an 'authority that is not power', whose function is to give assurance to the possibility of each person to vary and diverge, to be other, and to be recognised for what she is and feels, because it has given credibility and consistency to our words and our existence.

> The opposition between what is innate in us and what is acquired, between the biological and the cultural, the natural and the historical have a limited validity. They are not worth from the point of view of the coming of life to the world: from this point of view everything is inborn and everything is acquired. Similarly, we can say for the opposition between the logical and the factual: in the creative relationship of the world, when the world is born together with us and our learning to speak, the sense is coincident with being true. Here we find the point of view in which the logical and factual necessity ceases to oppose each other and are one and the same necessity. (Muraro 1991: 75)

The symbolic is then the language, and the maternal relationship represents (or makes present) the creative character of the language, composed of interaction between the speaker and the rules of language. For this reason, the symbolic, as the language, is living; the source of its changes is the subjective experience, that is to say the individuality which, from the beginning of life, has a relation with

---

[11] Or before learning, being born man, the expectations of an imposed masculinity; or before learning, all of us, the expectations of an imposed sexual orientation.

the other. In fact, according to the thinkers of sexual difference, the work of the symbolic (as well as the work of language) has one distinctive characteristic: no one can play it alone; it is a relational game.

> The ability to speak is given to us only through bargaining with the mother and it is the fruit of it. Knowing how to speak means knowing how to put the world into the world and this we can do in relation to the mother[12], not apart from her. (Muraro 1991: 49)

The primary experience of learning to speak, which each of us has lived, if recovered, if made to resurface, restores confidence in language, gives us confidence in our ability to put in words what, in our lived experience, we have discovered to be true; confidence, also, in the fact that what we are and what we say will be heard and understood by others. This will happen, if one keeps in mind the need to go through 'what others have in mind' (Muraro 1991: 67).

Another idea of 'norm'

The reflection on language as a field in which the symbolic is formed and transformed allows one of the greatest thinkers of the thought of sexual difference to grasp a dimension of the 'normative' that in the idea of the 'binding' and/or 'excluding' norm adopted by Butler disappears: the rule as to what makes a game, the game of language, possible, and therefore serves the subject to voice herself:

> Natural or maternal languages (the true languages) differ from the artificial ones because they are in a living relationship with reality, they are never indifferent to it. They change with the changing reality and they participate to the change freely, or, better, in the same way as the human beings involved do, actively and passively. I speak of mutation, which is the aspect of the life of language that makes that more evident to us. In all its aspects, including grammatical and syntactic, the language responds finely and constantly to the requirements of signification, so that nothing of the experience is excluded, if possible, from the possibility of expressing itself. (Muraro 1991: 83)

Therefore, 'the meaning and the real world are in relation to each other, they are in a circle, and this forms the true world' and 'the world in which the new can emerge, develop and make sense, is *a circle of body and words*' (Muraro 1991: 80, italics mine).

---

[12] Or 'with whom for her' (Muraro 1991): the mother is symbolically the 'figure of the exchange', of the symbolic exchange that continuously occurs between speakers in the language. 'In order to signify herself as a woman, every woman needs that sexual difference is significant for herself; and so that sexual difference be significant in itself, the mother figure must be made significant as a figure of origin' (Libreria delle donne di Milano 1997: 138): this is the reason why the thought of sexual difference has developed the conception of the 'symbolic maternal order'. It is an order that puts at the centre not the mother, but the mother/child relation as a civilised/civilising form of generatingthe human.

By seeing that the symbolic is made by language, on the one hand, and by restoring the adherence between body and words, on the other hand, the thinkers of sexual difference have saved, from an all-encompassing notion of law and norm – a deterministic, heteronomous and entirely prescriptive notion that leaves only the alternative between subduing or transgressing – a different dimension. This dimension safeguards the possibility and the necessity that between the subjective experience and the 'norm' there is a connection, free and open in its outcomes.

> The normativity of language translates the authority of the mother [as one can see from] how it is exercised: *not as a law but as an order* and as a living order because it is instituted. In fact, the linguistic order is maintained not through the strict observance of its rules but through its incessant transformation that allows it to reform itself despite and even thanks to the innumerable irregularities of our speech. (Muraro 1991: 69, italics mine)

The word 'rule' (*regola* in Italian) has often been used in order to express the idea of a norm that makes something possible for the subject. Luisa Muraro states:

> For my way of thinking, which is always also a feeling because of my attachment to the matrix of life, the *rules* are not separable from their reason or from the *substance of life that is regulated*, so that respecting them always has the characteristics of a loving act, whatever they are, including the rules of grammar. The *law*, on the other hand, does not express anything other than the impersonal necessity that there is a law, while *in its contents it is always empty and revisable*. (Muraro 1991: 82, italics mine).

In another important step, Muraro formulates the basic principle of the symbolic maternal order, the principle of 'always considering what is in the mind of others':

> The exchange between speakers can be regarded as an exit from the perfect identity of oneself with oneself (the identity of the stone), to start existing in the commonplace. A commonplace that is formed and reformed in the availability of everyone to represent things according to the other, of what is present also to the other. (Muraro 1991: 66)

'According to the principle of "passing through what is present also to others", there are no limits to what can be said but only rules, or rather a single rule, immanent to the same speakability: recognizing the need for mediation', so that 'the speakability of what is present to me will grow *with the respect for the rule*' (Muraro 1991: 68, italics mine).

Does freedom need norms?

In her refutation of the symbolic, Butler states two points: all norms are given to human beings from something external to their lived experience and all norms can be changed thanks to collective actions inspired by will or intention. In its affirmation of the symbolic, the feminism of sexual difference affirms instead that there are norms that arise from human action and experience, and can be changed by it, but not as an effect of planned acts of will or intention, just as they were not born through willpower. As I have anticipated, when developing this idea, Italian feminist thinkers often resort to the word 'rule' as opposed to 'norm'. This has implications that stand out in the Italian language. The authoritative *Treccani Italian Dictionary* tells us that:

> *Norma* (norm) is a rule of conduct, established by an authority . . . which has *the purpose of guiding the behaviour of individuals or of the community* . . .
> *Regola* (rule) is the orderly and constant way of taking place that is found in almost all of the facts, in the field of nature or of human action; *the enunciation of this mode*, which may or must be taken as a norm in similar cases.[13]

On the one hand, in Butler's world, we have the norm as the 'cause' of a behaviour, individual or collective, as it determines it (the norm as guidance); on the other hand, in the feminism of the symbolic's world, we have the rule as a 'means', to be used to obtain a result that is of subjective interest (the rule of language used by the speaker as a medium to show others what she is and thinks, according to her point of view): 'There are no absolute norms but only rules more or less *suitable for obtaining a result*' (Muraro 1991: 65, italics mine).

Accepting or not accepting the symbolic means thinking very different things that have to do with the normative, the norms and the rules. As a consequence, in the different conceptions that animate Butler's thought, on the one hand, and the thought of the symbolic, on the other, the jurist recognises the different views of law at work.

The Italian philosopher of Law Alessandro Giuliani has explored the difference between two conceptions of the norm, sometimes using the words 'norm' and 'rule' to name them. In one conception, the idea of norm is based on the relationship of cause and effect (the norm is what is established in view of the achievement of certain goals: it guides behaviour); in the other conception, the norm is based on the relationship between means and end (the norm is then the rule usable by each person to achieve their ends in the juridical field: a means to a subjective end).

Giuliani's vigorous research aims at saving the juridical experience from being reduced to a technique of social engineering that, devoted to prescribing to humans what they must be, want and do, has its source outside of itself, in political power, for example, and certainly not in the subjective experience. When law is reduced to social engineering the subjective experience is what must be shaped (or constructed) by the norm in view of the purposes of general interest.[14]

According to Giuliani, the heteronomous and causalistic conception of the norm is at the root of every authoritarian conception of law, 'authoritarian' being the views that conceive law as a tool to impose on women's and men's values and ends. The identification of the norm with the act that comes from a (political

---

[13] Translated by the author.
[14] See particularly Giuliani (1954) and (1957).

or social) power leads fatally to such a result. This notion of norm, hypostatised in contemporary conceptions, hides the possibility (historical, not merely theoretical) of recognising that, instead, 'the concept of norm is connected to that of human action and every action implies a choice' (Giuliani 1954: 169).

Giuliani's critique is addressed primarily to Kelsensian normativism, but it does not apply only to normativism or legal positivism; instead, it is also explicitly oriented towards the sociology-based, anti-formalistic trends of legal realism. The latter, which conceive law in instrumental terms, as a technique of social engineering, criticise of course the formal notion of juridical norm, on which positivism and normativism are built. Nonetheless, they hold and reinforce the idea, which is pivotal in all forms of legal positivism and normativism, that law on the one hand is driven by factors external to the sphere of individual human action, such as cultural or economic superstructures, and, on the other hand, serves to determine, guide and direct that action.

Giuliani returns the juridical to the sphere of individual human action, emphasising that the norm 'is something that, in a given community, is considered immanent to activities that are repeated and that are in a certain sense predictable, as certain activities are felt as a means suitable to achieve certain results: *these are the juridical forms*' (Giuliani 1954: 177, italics mine). Norms instead become mere form, mere abstraction, as they lose contact with individual human action and its subjective motives.

Bearing in mind the connection between the notion of norm and that of activity and of human conduct, according to Giuliani, an investigation of norms different from the traditional one becomes possible, an investigation interested not in studying and defining how to give norms to individuals, but in studying how juridical norms are formed in human conduct. Keenly interested in a 'non-preceptive normative science',[15] Giuliani, in his studies, refers back to the *regulae iuris* of the V *Book of Digest*.

A human idea of the rule

How did rules that say that there is no obligation to do impossible things (*impossibilium nulla obligatio est*) or that the other party has to be listened to (*audiatur et altera pars*) originate? Such rules are certainly prescriptions, but they also have a descriptive element: at their basis lies a sympathetic observation (that is, the observation made by a human of the same nature as those observed) of some constants of human experience, of characteristics common to all, which are common not for ontological or metaphysical reasons, but because they are observable as such (Giuliani 1954: 112–13). If it is prescribed that we cannot deduce the impossible in a contract, it is because we have observed and we know that no human being can perform the impossible. These principles are thus 'maxims

---

[15] The 'normative' is for Giuliani the science of the human conduct (Giuliani 1954: 171–2).

of experience' drawn from the observation of human nature, 'interpretations of behaviours': the *regulae* highlight dimensions of the concept of norm that have been forgotten due to the concentration on the norm's sole prescriptive component. The understanding of norm as prescription, external to human action, is also due to the modern propensity to separate the 'ought to be' (considered in its turn the essence of the normative moment) from the 'being', which is to say, from the plane, always changing, but also rich in recurrences, of the reality of the experience that individuals make by observing themselves and their peers. Likewise, the principle *audiatur et altera pars* proceeds from the limit of human intelligence in the knowledge of the truth, having observed it, knowing that conclusions based on one's point of view are easily erroneous and therefore harmful; the *regula* appeals to the intersubjectivity of evaluation as guarantee against arbitrariness, another possible – because it is visible – manifestation of the human.

In the *regulae iuris* Giuliani sees the manifestations or the product of the autonomy of the legal experience from the will and power of an external authority – political, social or scientific. Guided by a subjective and intuitive method, the classical Roman jurists

> saw the law not as a complex of norms or imperatives, but as an interpretation of the juridical aspects of human conduct and action: if we open the Title of the Digest *Regulae iuris* we do not find many definitions or conceptual arrangements indeed, but rather interpretations of behaviour: *Eius est nolle qui potest velle. Non vult heres esse qui ad alium transferre voluit hereditatem.*

Therefore

> as for the eighteenth-century economists, the phenomenon of exchange was not something imposed, that it should take place according to norms, but something human that could be understood because it was the natural result of the cooperation and efforts of many men, likewise, in the Roman jurists' view, the law was not the product of a legislator, nor even of a constituent assembly, but a natural reality produced by the human actions that could be observed and understood. (Giuliani 1957: 139)

The *regulae* are 'interpretations of behaviour'; this idea recalls that the norm is not only the object of interpretation, but it is in itself interpretation, interpretation of behaviour, of human facts appreciated in their individual meaning, in accordance with the idea, expressed by the word *ius*, that the law derives from the needs of individuals to satisfy individual ends.

The *regulae* are the result of the individual capacity of choice (which Giuliani calls 'conscience') and of the ability of (wo)men to interact with other (wo)men in the world, of their sociability (which is for Giuliani the equivalent of 'moral'). They testify that the law is a human fact, that is, that it refers to the individual, animated by the ability to act, to want, to perceive values. Law is thereby constantly changing but around some constants; as such, it is not the result of a planning activity, but of an enormous number of individual actions, born of the reality of inter-individual needs and exchanges interpreted in the light of a 'reason' capable of 'sympathy'. Thus, the foundations of a truly universal law are discovered, universal because it is common to all humans: 'Roman Law ignored the notion of norm, because it departed from an atomistic and individualistic conception of society' that is, a conception in which society is not something that overlaps the individuals or encompasses them: in the Romans' view, the society 'remained a society of equals . . . The term "*ius*" as used by the Roman jurists of the classical age shows us that the law stemmed from the needs of individuals to satisfy individual ends' (Giuliani 1957: 139). This perspective, Giuliani emphasises, according to which the formal act is the action that conforms to a norm, not the action conformed by a norm, reminds us that law does not exist only as the imposition of some people on others; rather, it stems from a subjective experience – that of those who make use of it in view of their subjective ends.

The norm intended as a prescription, based on a causalistic mechanism, which can also be conditional or 'nudging' (legal norms are established in order for certain results to be achieved on a social level), is displaced entirely on the plane of the 'ought to be', and this emancipates the norm from the necessary relationship (which can also be understood in terms of measure or limit) with the human and subjective foundation of legal experience. The heteronomy of norm expresses the becoming of the law 'something external to human activity' (Giuliani 1954: 169), whose contents and scope can expand indefinitely: having assumed a completely heteronomous conception of law has stamped within the law the mark of excessive 'insistence on what changes' (Giuliani 1957: 50), which expresses the concern to make the law more and more efficient with respect to the purposes of governance of society. In these views the study of law is resolved in that of social control and social technique: it only deepens the idea of law as a means of achieving the goals of society, not of individuals. This idea, according to Giuliani, will be brought to completion by the anti-formalist movements and is also reflected in an activist conception of legal science.

Gender: the anti-caste device of a new legal Romanticism

I will leave the reader to recognise the connections, which seem to me rather noticeable, between Giuliani's *regulae* and the Italian feminists' 'rules'. For my part, I will signal, albeit quickly and without pretension of completeness, the connections between Butler's philosophical activism, committed to suggesting a social theory suitable to support a political reforming action,[16] and the idea of law as instrument of social engineering.

To start with, I have to restate that 'the creation of symbolic is a political work that does not allow itself to be thought within that paradigm for which the subject (eventually the collective one, for example an assembly) *has mastery over the*

---

[16] See on this Marcuse (1966: 376 ff.).

possible effects of his volitions' (Fanciullacci 2017: 59, italics mine). If this is true, Butler's distrust in the symbolic is the expression of a voluntarist attitude, the first traces of which have historically undeniably arisen with the revolutionary ambition of reforming society through the law; an aptitude which can be incorporated both into positivistic views of law and into anti-formalist views. However, Butler's opposition to the symbolic recalls indeed a romantic and sentimental, intuitive yearning for justice, which is by definition in conflict with exegetical formalism. But from a historical point of view, the first reaction to formalism in Europe can be traced back to the 'legal romanticism' that contested the formalist curving of the German Historical School in the name of the desire to 'create the norm' (Giuliani 1954: 22) and is at the origin of the first anti-formalistic wave, the *Interessenjurisprudenz*. However, the aversion for formalism that is proper to every realist trend does not contradict the fundamental assumption of legal positivism, which is to conceive of the law as an instrument, a mere technique, destined to be filled with contents from the outside, because it has broken all connections with the concrete, singular experience. This is why legal realist trends have very often resulted in an updating of legal positivism.[17]

We can therefore say, first and foremost, that Butler sides among those who conceive of law as modernity has conceived of it, which is to say as a tool for social engineering, an idea that can have both formalist and anti-formalist types. One should never forget that positivism, after all, was a form of juridical realism.

Further, there is in Butler's thought a certain degree of imperativism. The Butlerian idea of normative is focused on the prescriptive, binding and conventional character of the norm. The norm is what determines an 'ought to be', and a norm is effective to the extent that it manages to guide and constrain people's behaviour (which is to say, that it has a grip on society). The norm is conventional because what it prescribes is by definition changeable, having been established, every time, on the basis of what is useful, right or good, concepts which, in turn, are provisional and unstable. All of this brings us back towards a fully legal positive environment, since the distinctive element of legal positivism can be seen in the idea of norm that this latter has generally stated, the norm as a given, which imposes itself on human activities, but does not originate from them.

The fluid and fragmented conception of the subject that characterises Butler's thought matches with

> the ideal of a society that determines autonomously (and collectively) the norms according to which to conduct and organize the moments that constitute its life. It is the idea according to which the most radical autonomy is participation in the collective exercise of autonomy. (Fanciullacci 2017: 76)

Thus, at the bottom of Butler's deconstructive thought we find the topic of a democratism centred on the nexus between autonomy and the democratic ideal. This is

---

[17] Giuliani (1958, 1979).

combined with the remarkable presence, in her thinking, of the ideal of progress, with its dose of ethics, signalled by the recurrence of the 'endless movement of a liberation never objectively possessed but always pursued, in a sort of asymptotic "aiming to the Best" [that is] genuinely Hegelian' (Guaraldo 2014: 18).

All this ends up in the ideal of equality as an anti-caste principle. The opposition to the placing of sexual difference in the symbolic, the opposition to the adoption of the symbolic perspective in political analysis and philosophical thought has a precise consequence. It makes unthinkable (or unacceptable) differences that do not originate in the choice of the person, in an individual preference. Instead, when placed in the symbolic, sexual difference is a difference that is not adopted in the name of choice, but is a difference in which a person finds him- or herself to be. This is, of course, very challenging towards the modern pluralist liberal-based views, where society is

> represented as a plurality of individuals, each of which has its own preferences and can orient herself on values that deserve equal respect to that reserved for the values on which others are oriented . . . Given this assumption, how can sexual difference be a difference that makes a difference in terms of ideas and values? How can it be that what is considered first and foremost an individual, is associated with certain values and certain norms on the basis of the fact that he or her is characterized *by a difference that is not herself to have placed?* (Fanciullacci 2017: 27, italics mine)

In the framework of liberal pluralism, in which the differences admitted are only those that result from individual choice and preference, sexual difference, when seen as a condition to which the individual gives sense, but which does not depend on him or her, tends to be perceived as the equivalent of a status, thereby an enemy of equality.

In this sense, Butler's idea of gender norm can be seen as an aspect of equality as anti-caste principle[18] coherent with and functional to the concept of pluralism proper to liberal individualism.

All this can well explain the reasons for the success of Butler's thought among contemporary progressive scholars, who recognise in it the same ideals of liberal pluralist democracy that were once conveyed into positivistic conceptions of law and that these latter no longer support today, having lost their substantive premise, which was trust in a functioning and responsive political arena. But it reduces the innovative and transgressive character of this thought with respect of the classical assumptions of a juridical modernity based on the idea that the conditions of freedom of human beings depend only on 'provisionally benevolent' institutions (Rudan 2018). After all, since the age of French social thought, philosophical criticism, which makes societal disorder and injustice recognisable, has gone together with the idea of a governing authority able to contrast, with its rules, that disorder and injustice.[19]

---

[18] As interpreted by Sunstein (2009).
[19] See on this Marcuse (1960: 376 ff.).

Bibliography

Bernardini, M. G. and O. Giolo (eds) (2017), *Teorie critiche del diritto*, Pisa: Pacini Giuridica.
Butler, J. (2004), *Undoing Gender*, London: Routlege.
Butler, J. (2014), *Fare e disfare il genere*, ed. F. Zappino, Milano: Mimesis.
Cesarino, C. (2018), 'Mother Degree Zero?', in C. Cesarini and A. Righi (eds), *Another Mother*, Minneapolis, MN: University of Minnesota Press, 303–20.
Cigarini, L. (1995), *La politica del desiderio*, Parma: Pratiche.
Condello, A. (2018), *Between Ordinary and Extraordinary. The Normativity of the Singular Case in Art and Law*, Leiden: Brill.
Fanciullacci, R. (2017), *La generazione della libertà femminile e la tessitura dell'universale*, in C. Vigna (ed.), *Differenza di genere e differenza sessuale*, Napoli-Salerno: Orthotes Editrice, 47–101.
Ferrando, S. (2017), *Oltre i paradossi della differenza: la pratica politica del simbolico. Per una discussione di Joan Scott*, in C. Vigna (ed.), *Differenza di genere e differenza sessuale*, Napoli-Salerno: Orthotes Editrice, 205–23.
Giuliani, A. (1954), *Contributi a una nuova teoria pura del diritto*, Milano: Giuffré.
Giuliani, A. (1957), *Ricerche in tema di esperienza giuridica*, Milano: Giuffré.
Giuliani, A. (1958), 'Dal positivismo "benthamiano" al realismo giuridico', in A. Giuliani, *Il pensiero americano contemporaneo*, Milano: Edizioni di Comunità, 117–63.
Giuliani, A. (1979), *Introduzione*, in C. Perelman, *Logica giuridica e nuova retorica*, Milano: Giuffré, V–XXX.
Guaraldo, O. (2004), *Prefazione* to J. Butler, *Fare e disfare il genere*, ed. F. Zappino, Milano: Mimesis, 9–27.
Libreria delle donne di Milano (1997), *Non credere di avere dei diritti*, Torino: Rosenberg & Sellier: (published in English as *Sexual Difference: A Theory of Social-Symbolic Practice*, ed. The Milan Women's Bookstore Collective, trans. P. Cicogna and T. De Lauretis, Bloomington, IN: Indiana University Press, 1990).
Marcuse, H. (1966), *Ragione e Rivoluzione*, Bologna: Il Mulino (first published as *Reason and Revolution, Hegel and the Rise of Social Theory*, New York: Oxford University Press, 1954).
Mastromartino, F. (2017), *Contro l'eteronormatività, La soggettività* queer *davanti al dilemma del riconoscimento giuridico*, in M. G. Bernardini and O. Giolo (eds), *Teorie critiche del diritto*, Pisa: Pacini Giuridica, 231–47.
Muraro, L. (1991), *L'ordine simbolico della madre*, Roma: Editori Riuniti.
Muraro, L. (2006), *L'ordine simbolico della madre*, 2nd edn, Roma: Editori Riuniti.
Muraro, L. (2009), *Al mercato della felicità. La forza irriducibile del desiderio*, Milano: Mondadori.
Muraro, L. (2017), *The Symbolical Order of the Mother*, ed. T. Murphy, transl. F. Novello, New York: State of New York University Press.
Rudan, P. (2018), 'Il corpo vivente nelle relazioni per J. Butler', *Il Manifesto*, 16 June 2018, 11.

Sunstein, C. R. (2009), *A cosa servono le Costituzioni*, Bologna: Il Mulino (first published as *Designing Democracy*, New York: Oxford University Press, 2001).
Zamboni, C. (2017a), 'Un movimento che si scrive passo passo', in Diotima (ed.), *Femminismo fuori sesto. Un movimento che non può fermarsi*, Liguori: Napoli, 5–22.
Zamboni, C. (2017b), *La pratica dell'inconscio. Un ponte tra 'Psychanalyse et Politique' Antoinette Fouque e il pensiero femminista italiano*, Milano: Libreria delle donne.

Chapter 8

Hypothetically Speaking: How to Argue about Meaning

Karen Petroski

Hypothetical examples are a pervasive feature of legal discourse in the United States, my home jurisdiction. Law professors base class discussion on questions about hypothetical scenarios. Examinations, in law school and for licensing purposes, ask test-takers to read descriptions of imagined occurrences and analyse the legal implications of the events described. Advocates and judges use hypothetical examples to explain and justify rules and describe the limits of their application. But unlike some related legal discourse practices, such as the case method and analogical reasoning, the legal use of hypothetical examples has not been systematically studied.[1]

This chapter examines the use of one type of hypothetical example by justices of the US Supreme Court in three recent terms. The chapter focuses on the justices' use of hypothetical utterances – invented 'samples' of language use – in the service of arguments about the ordinary meaning or original understanding of statutory or constitutional language. Ordinary-meaning analysis has received significant recent scholarly attention (e.g., Slocum 2015), and some of the rhetorical techniques associated with such arguments, especially judges' reliance on dictionary definitions, have also been discussed and criticised at length. This chapter shows that judges making ordinary-meaning arguments seem to support them with language-use hypotheticals just about as often as with dictionaries. If judges' use of dictionaries deserves attention, then so might their use of language-use hypotheticals.

When judges and justices support their arguments using hypothetical scenarios or examples, including language-use examples, they are not just offering premises for the conclusions reached in particular cases, but also providing their readers with examples of acceptable argument forms. Judicial opinions function as records of decision and as how-to guides for lawyers and judges. Because of the outsize influence of the US Supreme Court on US legal education and practice, Supreme Court justices' explanatory practices are especially likely to serve as models in this way. The focus on Supreme Court opinions in this chapter is, then, not motivated solely by those opinions' status as legal authority, but just as much by the opinions' institutionalisation as discourse models in the US legal sphere.

---

[1] For limited exceptions, see Gewirtz (1982); Mitchell (2004); Petroski (2018: 121–50); Strassfeld (1992).

The pages that follow briefly review some recent work on the rise of ordinary-meaning analysis and the use of dictionaries to support such arguments. The chapter explains what is special about language-use hypotheticals and how they differ from related (and equally often used) kinds of hypotheticals. It documents the pervasive use of this kind of reasoning in the Court's recent output and considers how language-use hypotheticals might affect their readers through some examples from recent terms. The chapter is an initial contribution to – and, hopefully, a partial justification for – a more robust scholarly discussion of the role of hypothetical discourse and examples in legal activity.

1. THE RISE OF ORDINARY MEANING ARGUMENTS

Justice Antonin Scalia joined the US Supreme Court in September 1986 and remained an Associate Justice until his unexpected death in February 2016. Many observers seem to believe the Court's approaches to constitutional and statutory interpretation shifted markedly over the forty years of Justice Scalia's tenure. In particular, by the time of his death, in statutory cases almost all of the justices had come to emphasise textual analysis focused on the 'ordinary meaning' of particular words and phrases, and in constitutional cases all had come to accept the importance of the 'original understanding' of the words used in the Constitution. Justice Scalia was a champion of these positions (see, e.g., Scalia 1997; Scalia and Garner 2012), but his textual focus is now shared by justices across the ideological spectrum (see Petroski 2018: 165–71).

The two approaches (ordinary meaning and original understanding) differ in some ways, but judges committed to the primacy of one are often also committed to the other, and the approaches share an emphasis on detailed analysis of the linguistic meaning of legal prescriptions. The discussion below focuses mainly on 'ordinary-meaning' arguments, but the survey discussed in the next section included constitutional cases, and there is little difference between the two approaches for the purposes of this discussion. Judges use similar justificatory techniques for conclusions about meaning in statutory and constitutional cases, as later sections of this chapter explain in more detail.

Legal academics have commented at length on the increased judicial focus on text and language. Scholars have documented the prevalence of text-focused approaches among judges (e.g., Cross 2009; Gluck 2010); they have considered the ideological implications of a focus on text rather than statutory purpose or legislative objectives (e.g., Benesh and Czarnecki 2009; Cross 2012); and they have debated the merits of specific techniques for analysis of ordinary meaning and original understanding, including canons of interpretation and, more recently, dictionary definitions of words appearing in statutory and constitutional provisions.

In 2013, James Brudney and Lawrence Baum published a comprehensive review of the use of dictionaries in statutory analysis in Supreme Court opinions. Brudney and Baum surveyed Supreme Court opinions issued between 1986 and 2011 and found 'a major increase in usage' of dictionaries over that period (2013: 488). Analysing the functions played by dictionary citations in the opinions, Brudney and Baum concluded that the justices often use dictionaries in a 'casual' and 'opportunistic' way (2013: 490). Brudney and Baum did not find that this use was particularly ideologically driven; it wasn't the case, for example, that conservative justices cited dictionaries more often than liberal judges. Brudney and Baum concluded that justices' increased use of dictionaries might 'stem from the Justices' conception . . . that dictionaries . . . can be promoted to audiences as objective and neutral proxies for ordinary meaning' (2013: 490).[2]

Much recent commentary on this phenomenon has pointed out how this conception of the authority of dictionary definitions rests on apparent misunderstandings of how dictionaries are compiled (e.g., Brudney and Baum 2013: 502–15). Judges do seem to select dictionaries and definitions that support their conclusions, and it is common for judges to rebuke their colleagues for cherry-picking dictionaries and definitions to support conclusions reached on other grounds. But the justices' reliance on dictionaries has not abated.[3]

Criticism of reliance on dictionaries has, however, apparently spurred interest in alternative methods of justifying ordinary-meaning and original-understanding arguments. One alternative receiving recent high-profile support is the use of corpus linguistics. Linguistic corpora are searchable databases of actual examples of language use (in, for instance, newspapers from a particular language region).[4] In a recent article, Utah Supreme Court Justice Thomas Lee and Stephen Mouritsen argued for the use of corpus linguistics, noting that '[w]hen we speak of *ordinary* meaning, we are asking an empirical question – about the sense of a word or phrase that is most likely implicated in a given linguistic context'. Linguists, the authors explain, have developed 'computer-aided means of answering such questions', namely, searches in appropriate corpora (Lee and Mouritsen 2018: 795). Some of the justices on the US Supreme Court seem inclined to take such an approach. In one dissenting opinion from the Court's 2014 term, for example, Justice Samuel Alito reproduced the fourteen sentences including the phrase 'because of' that appeared in the *Washington Post* on the day the case was argued before the justices.[5] He did this in support of his argument about the ordinary meaning of that phrase in the statute at issue (for a brief discussion, see Petroski 2018: 68).

---

[2] Other significant discussions of judges' use of dictionaries are Aprill (1998); Calhoun (2014); Harvard Law Review (1994); Thumma and Kirchmeier (1999); and Weinstein (2005).

[3] In just the final month's worth of opinions from the Supreme Court term preceding the preparation of this chapter (June 2018), for example, the justices cited dictionaries in nine cases: *Florida v. Georgia*, 585 U.S. ___ (2018) (Thomas, J., dissenting); *Trump v. Hawaii*, 585 U.S. ___ (2018); *Carpenter v. United States*, 585 U.S. ___ (2018) (Thomas, J., dissenting, and Gorsuch, J., dissenting); *Wisconsin Central Ltd. v. United States*, 585 U.S. ___ (2018) (majority opinion and opinion of Breyer, J., dissenting); *Pereira v. Sessions*, 585 U.S. ___ (2018) (majority opinion and opinion of Alito, J., dissenting); *Minnesota Voters Alliance v. Mansky*, 585 U.S. ___ (2018); *Husted v. A. Philip Randolph Institute*, 585 U.S. ___ (2018) (majority opinion and opinion of Breyer, J., dissenting); *Lamar, Archer & Coffrin, LLP v. Appling*, 584 U.S. ___ (2018); *Hughes v. United States*, 584 U.S. ___ (2018).

[4] In addition to Lee and Mouritsen (2018), see, e.g., Gries and Slocum (2017); Mouritsen (2010).

[5] *Texas Dep't of Housing & Community Affairs v. Inclusive Housing Project, Inc.*, 576 U.S. ___ (2015) (Alito, J., dissenting) (slip op. 4 n.2).

As the next section explains, the justices have also used another 'casual' and 'opportunistic' method of supporting their conclusions about the meaning of legal provisions: samples of language use not pre-existing the justices' opinions, but rather created for the argument at hand. This technique might be motivated by concerns similar to those voiced by advocates of corpus linguistics. But it poses problems of its own.

2. A SURVEY OF LANGUAGE-USE HYPOTHETICALS IN JUDICIAL OPINIONS

The justices who use language-use hypotheticals in cases turning on the interpretation of legal texts – all of the current and recent members of the US Supreme Court – seem to regard hypothetical examples of language use as an effective way to make points about language meaning.

A typical example appears in *Reynolds* v. *United States*, decided on 23 January 2012. *Reynolds* concerned a provision of the federal Sex Offender Registration and Notification Act (SORNA), a statute the Supreme Court has recently addressed repeatedly. The provision in question says, 'the [US] Attorney General shall have the authority to specify applicability of the requirements' of SORNA to sex offenders convicted before SORNA's effective date in mid-2006. The Court accepted the case because courts of appeals had reached different conclusions about the meaning of this provision; six had held that in the absence of a 'specification' by the Attorney General, SORNA did not apply to people convicted of sex offences before mid-2006, while five had held that if those people had previously registered under similar state laws, SORNA might apply to them.

The justices analysed this case as turning largely on the meaning of the language quoted above, especially the phrase 'authority to specify the applicability'. Justice Breyer, writing for seven justices, opted for the first of the two interpretations, noting at the start of his analysis,

> the [provision] says that the Attorney General has authority to specify the Act's 'applicability,' not its 'nonapplicability.' And it consequently is more naturally read as conferring the authority to apply the Act, not the authority to make exceptions. That is how we normally understand a term such as 'authority to specify' in the context of applying new rules to persons already governed by pre-existing rules. If, for example, the Major League Baseball Players Association and the team owners agreed that the Commissioner of Baseball 'shall have the authority to specify the applicability' to the major leagues of the more stringent minor league drug testing policy, we should think that the minor league policy would not apply unless and until the commissioner so specified. (440)

Justice Scalia dissented. In an opinion joined by Justice Ginsburg, he noted,

> I do not share the Court's belief that to 'specify the applicability' more naturally means, in the present context, to 'make applicable' rather than to 'make inapplicable.' . . . The example the Court gives, the Commissioner of Baseball's 'authority to specify the applicability' of more stringent minor-league drug testing policies to the major leagues . . . is entirely inapt, because it deals with a policy that on its face is otherwise not applicable.

Since the major leagues are not covered by the policies, the Commissioner's 'authority to specify [their] applicability' can mean nothing else but the authority to render them applicable. What we have here, however, is a statute that states in unqualified terms that '[a] sex offender shall register' . . . and that the Court rightly believes was meant to cover pre-Act offenders. (448–9)

This exchange contains several notable features present in many opinions containing language-use hypotheticals. First, as Justice Scalia observes, Justice Breyer presents his hypothetical authorisation language as being used within a context in some ways similar to the case at hand and in some ways different, enabling Justice Scalia to rebut the point by drawing on familiar techniques for countering arguments by analogy. The hypothetical context is also an everyday, accessible context, not a technical one. Justice Breyer's example is not, however, just analogous to the issue in *Reynolds*; his example is useful, if it is, because of readers' more or less automatic, intuitive assessment of the hypothetical utterance he presents. Justice Breyer does not explain how that understanding might come to be; he seems to assume that it will crystallise out of the example as a reader works through the opinion. At the same time, his example also implicitly prescribes a particular understanding of the hypothetical utterance as appropriate (a prescription accepted by Justice Scalia). These features – the selection of an everyday setting, the absence of any expressed link between hypothetical utterance and its 'natural' meaning, the blurring of persuasion and prescription – are not unique to this set of opinions, but rather recur in case after case.

The justices use techniques like this to support conclusions about statutory or constitutional meaning roughly as often as they use dictionaries. Table 8.1 tallies use of the two kinds of support in opinions issued during three recent terms.

Table 8.1 Support for arguments about ordinary meaning in US Supreme Court opinions, 2011–14

	2011 term (2011–12)	2012 term (2012–13)	2013 term (2013–14)
Contemporary dictionaries	5	3	2
Historically specific dictionaries	8	7	9
Law dictionaries	4	3	3
Total opinions citing dictionaries	**11 (14%)**	**12 (15%)**	**10 (14%)**
Examples of appropriate usage	8	5	12
Examples of misuse	4	5	10
Total opinions relying on usage examples	**10 (13%)**	**9 (11%)**	**16 (22%)**
Discussions of reader response	5	5	14
Absurd analogies	3	5	6
Usage back-and-forth	4	5	6
Total cases yielding merits opinions	**77**	**79**	**74**

The appendix to this chapter provides some more detail about the bases for these tallies. The tallies derived from my review of all of the opinions in the cases decided on the merits in the three terms in question. The counts are of cases yielding merits opinions that incorporated these tactics, not of opinions; the counts would be higher if they included separate opinions.

The counts are also of a very specific kind of hypothetical: samples (or 'mentions') of language use apparently generated for the case at hand (or, less often, quoted from an earlier opinion in which the samples played a similar role). This kind of hypothetical is distinct from three kinds of closely related hypotheticals, two of them also recorded above.

Examples of application

The most common kind of hypothetical used in statutory and constitutional cases does not present a hypothetical utterance, but describes a hypothetical scenario to which the legal language at issue would clearly either apply or not apply. In the 2011-term case *Judulang v. Holder*, for example, Justice Kagan clarified the application of several terms in the immigration statute at issue by presenting a simplified hypothetical scenario: 'Consider, for example, an alien who entered the country in 1984 and committed voluntary manslaughter in 1988. That person could be charged (as Judulang was) with an "aggravated felony" involving a "crime of violence".'[6] Such hypotheticals are like language-use hypotheticals in that they are usually generated for the case at hand, draw on accessible, everyday scenarios and depend on readers' intuitions (specifically, their intuitions about the circumstances under which use of a particular term would be appropriate). They are unlike the language-use hypotheticals examined here in that, as noted, they do not present a hypothetical sample of language.

Discussions of reader response

The next most common related kind of hypothetical, one not always clearly distinguishable from language-use hypotheticals, mentions a hypothetical sample of language in the service of an argument about the effects of the language in question rather than its meaning. In the 2012-term case *Salinas v. Texas*, for example, Justice Breyer dissented from the majority's conclusion that a person in police custody who stays silent when informed of his or her right to an attorney has implicitly waived that right. Justice Breyer observed, 'Suppose the individual says [when questioned by police], "Let's discuss something else" or "I'm not sure I want to answer that"; or suppose he just gets up and leaves the room.' Then, after citing cases holding that such responses would not imply waiver, Justice Breyer asked, 'How is simple silence in the present context any different?'[7] The

---

[6] *Judulang v. Holder*, 565 U.S. 42, 57–8 (2011).
[7] *Salinas v. Texas*, 570 U.S. ___ (2013) (Breyer, J., dissenting) (slip op. 11).

point made by hypotheticals of this sort concerns pragmatics rather than semantics; the occasional fuzziness of the distinction between semantics and pragmatics is the reason these hypotheticals are not always clearly distinguishable from language-use hypotheticals. These kinds of hypotheticals are tallied in Table 8.1 as 'Discussions of reader response'.

Absurd analogies

A more clearly distinguishable but fascinating kind of hypothetical involves a justice's generation of an obviously absurd utterance – often presented *as* an utterance – to highlight the logical flaws in a party's or judge's argument. An example appears in Justice Alito's 2012 opinion in *Rehberg* v. *Paulk*:

> Petitioner says there is no reason to distinguish between a person who goes to the police to swear out a criminal complaint and a person who testifies to facts before a grand jury for the same purpose . . . But this is like saying that a bicycle and an F-16 are the same thing. Even if the functions are similar as a general matter, the entities are quite different.[8]

In another opinion from the 2013 term, *Riley* v. *California*, Chief Justice Roberts criticises the logic of the government's argument as 'like saying a ride on horseback is materially indistinguishable from a flight to the moon'.[9]

These kinds of hypotheticals often involve criticism of an analogy drawn by another party or judge, but sometimes highlight other logical missteps; they are tallied in the table above as 'Absurd analogies'. These hypotheticals differ from language-use hypotheticals in that the justices use this technique not to make a point about word meaning, but to criticise the logic of another's argument. But because many of these hypotheticals mention hypothetical statements, one could consider these to be hypothetical examples of language misuse.

These four types of hypothetical example are, of course, just a subset of those the justices use in their opinions. The frequency of use of these devices contrasts strikingly with the paucity of critical analysis addressing them, especially given the amount of commentary addressing techniques that often accompany use of such hypothetical examples, such as dictionary definitions. For further discussion of the wider variety of hypotheticals appearing in the Court's contemporary output, see Petroski 2018: 121–50.

3. THE FUNCTIONS AND EFFECTS OF JUDGES' SPEAKING HYPOTHETICALLY

The judicial use of hypothetical examples of any kind depends on certain linguistic signals and cognitive capacities in readers, some of them acquired in law school, others more broadly shared by the literate members of a culture. When a

---

[8] *Rehberg v. Paulk*, 566 U.S. 356, 372 n.3 (2012) (Alito, J.).
[9] *Riley v. California*, 573 U.S. ___ (2014) (slip op. at 16–17) (Roberts, C. J.).

competent reader encounters one of these signals, that reader knows to consider the material that follows under a different aspect.[10] The signals include commands like 'Consider'; parenthetical markers like 'for example'; modal auxiliaries such as 'would' and 'could'; and conditional constructions, like 'as long as'. Signals like these instruct readers to suspend their commitment to at least some aspects of the material readers had been considering up to that point. These signals prompt readers to engage in something like cognitive experimentation, an activity that has much in common with some forms of play (see, e.g., Stalnaker 2014).

This feature of hypothetical discourse helps to justify its popularity as a pedagogical device, particularly in legal education. Law students' encounters with hypothetical scenarios help students understand the limits of application of legal rules but also, more basically, which aspects of their 'real-world' commitments to suspend when they apply such rules. Play is a vital developmental activity for young humans; it allows them to learn how their bodies work and what they are capable of. Play also helps children learn how to manipulate symbols and inhabit cultural roles, as in games of 'house', 'doctor' or 'war'. In play, children and adults normally know themselves not to be acting in earnest, and they can experiment with actions they might not be willing to take outside the play 'envelope' (Bogdan 2013: 36, 63, 77, 84–5). Acquiring expertise in any area, including legal reasoning and understanding legal rules, requires a similar kind of offline practice analogous to the 'quarantined' play of young animals and children (e.g., Feltovich et al. 2006).

Among the things one can learn through play are cultural 'scripts'. Psychologists and cognitive scientists use this term to describe individuals' routinised conceptualisation of typical scenarios, allowing the individuals to form expectations and predict certain behaviour. A classic illustration is the restaurant script (Schank and Abelson 1977). When you enter a restaurant and are shown to a table and given a menu, then even without speaking with anyone, you will likely understand that someone will probably return to your table and that you will then communicate about what you would like to eat, based on the contents of the menu. Scripts of this kind are the basis for what laypeople, lawyers and judges refer to as 'common sense' and 'intuition'. Such scripts allow us to explain our intuitions about what is possible and normal, both within and outside of legal culture. And we acquire these culturally based scripts by playing interactively with other people.

Some scripts are professional: they are the routines that experts learn to internalise. The hypotheticals used in legal education are both cultural and professional. In their education, lawyers-in-training learn not only rules, but also how

---

[10] In a recent book, Justice Ruth Bader Ginsburg quotes a mid-twentieth-century quip by Thomas Reed Powell: 'If you think that you can think of something inextricably attached to something else without thinking about the thing it is attached to, then you have a legal mind' (Ginsburg 2016: 298). One can read this observation as a cynical comment on lawyers' detachment from the real world and their tendency to 'go meta', but it is also possible to read the quotation as a compact insight into the peculiarities of legal cognition and its dependence on the kind of play discussed in the text.

to talk and write about them (see generally Mertz 2007). The use of hypothetical scenarios in the classroom prompts students to imagine, offline, systems of relation and response between imagined agents. To do this, learners must internalise heuristics that enable them to predict the agents' behaviour. Students learning to be lawyers internalise heuristics allowing them to predict the behaviour of other members of the guild; in the process, they also learn how to talk and write about those legal-behavioural scripts. In the US, lawyers-in-training learn which kinds of statements are acceptable in legal culture largely from Supreme Court and other appellate opinions.

It is in this sense that the justices' hypotheticals are how-to guides as well as situation-specific reasoning tools. Even hypotheticals that justices seem to offer merely for illustration may become focal points for and well known to large numbers of students, lawyers and judges. Language-use hypotheticals are just as susceptible to attaining this kind of canonical status as other kinds of hypotheticals; for example, the 'no vehicles in the park' hypothetical generated by Henry Hart (1958) has become canonical in US legal education (see Schauer 2008; Schlag 1999). But even single-use hypotheticals serve as models for readers of how to argue about the meaning of language. The next section of this chapter will consider some of the potential problems with this dynamic.

4. THE PITFALLS OF LANGUAGE-USE HYPOTHETICALS

The justices' frequent use of language-use hypotheticals encourages lawyers to use the technique themselves. It seems like a relatively easy and even fun justificatory technique. But when we look closely at the work such examples are being asked to do, they do not always hold up logically. The ease of grasping the samples of language use when reading them can mask logical jumps and missteps. In the absence of any systematic understanding of the use of hypothetical examples in justification, however, it is not possible to do more than criticise each hypothetical on its own terms. The justices often do this; Table 8.1 tallies such criticisms as instances of 'Usage back-and-forth'. But a more categorical critique is also possible.

One problematic feature common to the justices' reliance on dictionary definitions and language-use hypotheticals is their use in a kind of analysis that Victoria Nourse has recently labeled 'petty textualism' (2016: 106). While Nourse focuses on statutory interpretation, judges and lawyers use the same approach in constitutional cases that turn on 'original understanding'. Nourse describes petty textualism as 'a highly problematic *method of dissecting text*' (2016: 106) that 'proceeds as follows: the interpreter pulls one or two or five words out of a lengthy statute, holds them up as chunks of text, declares the words plain, and, as plain, ends the case' (2016: 107). Nourse points out, rightly, that this mode of analysis is problematic not only because it '[d]econtextualiz[es]' the language in question but also because it trivialises the judicial role: 'The great judges of yesteryear ... knew justice demanded more than wordplay' (2016: 107).

The justices use dictionary definitions and language-use hypotheticals, together or separately, at the second step of this kind of argument, the 'declares the words plain' step. Nourse does not discuss this step at length, although she accurately observes that judges seem to perform it 'unconsciously ... silently, without thought' (2016: 109). The opinions surveyed for this chapter contain many examples of petty textualism substantiating Nourse's criticism. In each term, several cases yielded multiple opinions using multiple dictionaries, often alongside language-use hypotheticals, as the principal support for assertions about 'plain' or ordinary meaning, or original understanding.

Sometimes the justices focus mainly on dictionaries. In the 2011 term, for example, the Court decided *Taniguchi* v. *Kan Pacific Saipan*, a case turning on a 1978 statute providing for the award of litigation costs to prevailing parties in some federal lawsuits. *Taniguchi* specifically concerned whether 'compensation to interpreters', part of the costs described in the provision as awardable to a prevailing party, 'covers the cost of translating documents' (562). To answer this question, Justice Alito, author of the majority opinion, cites definitions of 'interpreter' from six general-purpose dictionaries published in the 1970s (566–7), as well as three law dictionaries (567), before explaining at length the reasons for the Court's rejection of the petitioner's own dictionary-based argument (567–9). Justice Ginsburg's dissent directly responds to Justice Alito's dictionary citations by citing other definitions provided in the same dictionary editions he consulted (575–6); she also presents lengthier discussions of other courts' application of 'interpreter' to translators (576–9), as well as the purpose of the cost-shifting statute (579–81). *Taniguchi* perfectly illustrates the points made by critics of the judicial use of dictionaries; it also demonstrates how easily a petty-textualist approach to an interpretive issue can get sidetracked into a kind of dictionary-definition stalemate.

The opinions in *Taniguchi* contained no language-use hypotheticals, but this is more the exception than the rule. Several cases from each of the terms surveyed for this chapter generated opinions relying on both dictionary definitions and language-use hypotheticals in similar debates about plain meaning. In the 2012 term, for example, the Court decided *Kirtsaeng* v. *John Wiley & Sons*, which concerned the application of a provision of the federal Copyright Act allowing 'the owner of a particular copy or phonorecord lawfully made under this title' to resell the copy. As decided by the Court, the case turned on whether to give the statutory phrase 'lawfully made under this title' a 'geographical interpretation' or a 'non-geographical limitation' (529). The latter interpretation would allow resale of foreign-printed copies in the US without violating the Copyright Act; the former interpretation would not, because foreign-printed copies would not be 'lawfully made under this title' on a 'geographical interpretation' of the phrase. Justice Breyer cited two dictionaries to support his argument for the non-geographical interpretation, as well as to rebut an argument for the geographical interpretation. In that rebuttal, he also offered on a language-use hypothetical, noting 'the uncertainty and complexity arising out of the [respondent's] effort to read the necessary geographical limitation into the word "applicable" (or the equivalent) [which appeared in the respondent's brief as a paraphrase of the statutory phrase "under this title"]'.[11]

> Where, precisely, is the Copyright Act 'applicable'? The Act does not instantly protect an American copyright holder from unauthorised piracy taking place abroad. But that fact does not mean the Act is inapplicable to copies made abroad. As a matter of ordinary English, one can say that a statute imposing, say, a tariff upon 'any rhododendron growing in Nepal' applies to all Nepalese rhododendrons. And, similarly, one can say that the American Copyright Act is applicable to all pirated copies, including those printed overseas. (531–2)

Note how this passage drifts away from the statutory language at issue. In this discussion, Justice Breyer takes a petty-textualist approach not to the statutory phrase 'lawfully made under this title', but to the language used in a party's brief. Justice Breyer's parsing of the language of the brief suggests an inattentiveness to the distinction between instances of language 'use' and 'mention' (cf. Devitt and Sterelny 1999: 40). Legal discussions of the meaning of statutory and constitutional text require attention to the 'mention' aspect of language; in such discussions, language functions as a target of analysis rather than a tool for communication. Language-use hypotheticals also 'mention' samples of language use. In contrast, a legal argument, such as a brief, uses language to explain the meaning or content of the statutory provision, without offering (or mentioning) that paraphrase itself as legally operative. Justice Breyer ignores this distinction and in the process gives the respondents' argument a kind of quasi-legal status; his discussion provides support for Nourse's accusation that petty textualism often draws judges down a kind of argumentative garden path.

Dissenting in *Kirtsaaeng*, Justice Ginsburg recruits dictionary definitions to counter those offered by Justice Breyer, as she did in *Taniguchi* (562). She also offers dictionary definitions of words Justice Breyer did not address (such as 'made'; 563 n.4) and, without responding to his rhododendron hypothetical, presents a language-application hypothetical of her own: 'one might say that driving on the right side of the road in England is "lawful" under U.S. law, but that would be so only because U.S. law has nothing to say about the subject' (563). She does not further elaborate on this hypothetical, however, and she does not explain why it might be more germane to the case than Justice Breyer's example.

The *Kirtsaeng* opinions illustrate how the use of linguistic hypotheticals in a petty-textualist framework can generate tangential debates distinct from those prompted by dictionary definitions. The tangents that arise due to language-use hypotheticals might have several effects on opinions' readers. They might

---

[11] Specifically, Wiley argued that 'under this title' meant 'in conformance with the Copyright Act *where the Copyright Act is applicable*' and that 'the Act "is applicable" only in the United States' (*Kirtsaeng v. John Wiley & Sons, Inc.*, 568 U.S. 519, 531 (2013) (emphasis in original)).

reinforce the appropriateness of language-use or language-application hypotheticals in arguments about statutory or constitutional meaning, perhaps especially in cases involving complex statutory and regulatory systems and/or competing policy imperatives (as the Copyright Act does). They might also suggest that just about any off-the-cuff hypothetical is legitimate support for an argument and, indeed, virtually equivalent in its authority to dictionary definitions and judge-made law. Grasping (or generating) a sample sentence of English is a relatively effortless cognitive task; the immediate reward of performing the task seems often to distract the justices from the more demanding task of integrating the hypothetical demonstration back into the evaluation of a more extended argument.

The materials studied for this chapter suggest that the justices more or less consciously understand hypothetical examples as an effective way to make points about language meaning. Even more than dictionary definitions, such examples seem like neutral 'data', something like the contents of linguistic corpora. Unfortunately, the script established by these practices runs something like this: when you encounter a tricky question that has to do with the meaning of words, generate some sentences or phrases that you can present to support your point, then move on. We should resist this script; it short-circuits more patient – and necessary – reflection on how language, and hypothetical reasoning, work.

Appendix: US Supreme Court opinions citing dictionary definitions and language-use hypotheticals

OCTOBER TERMS 2011–13

The following abbreviations are used below.

CD contemporary dictionary, that is, a twenty-first-century dictionary; it designates the use of such a dictionary as a resource in the opinion
HD historical dictionary, or a dictionary published around the time the legal language at issue was enacted or ratified
LD legal dictionary, either contemporary or historical
EU [hypothetical] example of usage
EM example of misuse [of language]
RR reader reaction, a discussion of the reaction of hypothetical reasonable readers to real or invented examples of communication
AA absurd analogy, the presentation of absurd utterances to point out the fallacy or weakness of a party's or judge's analysis
BF back-and-forth, a debate between (or among) two (or more) justices regarding the appropriate understanding of usage hypotheticals

The words or phrases analysed in the opinion are, where appropriate, included in parentheses after the page number of each reference.

2011 term

CompuCredit Corp. v. Greenwood, 565 U.S. 95 (2012)
    Ginsburg, J., diss.: RR (110; 'right to sue')
Gonzalez v. Thaler, 565 U.S. 134, 156–7 (2012)
    Scalia, J., diss.: EM (156–7; 'equivalent')
Hosanna-Tabor Evangelical Lutheran Church & School v. EEOC, 565 U.S. 171 (2012)
    Alito, J., conc.: RR (198; 'minister'; similar comments at 198 n.1, 202, 203)
Perry v. New Hampshire, 565 U.S. 228, 244 (2012)
    Ginsburg, J.: RR (244)
Reynolds v. United States, 565 U.S. 432 (2012)
    Breyer, J.: EU (439–40; 'authority to specify')
    Scalia, J., diss.: BF (448–9)

Kawashima v. Holder, 565 U.S. 478 (2012)
  Thomas, J.: HD (484; 'deceit')
Mayo Collaborative Services v. Prometheus Labs., Inc., 566 U.S. 66 (2012)
  Breyer, J: RR (78; '"wherein" clauses' in patent claims)
Roberts v. Sea-Land Services, Inc., 566 U.S. 93 (2012)
  Sotomayor, J.: CD, LD (100, 101; 'award'); EM (102 n.5; 'awarded money damages')
  Ginsburg, J., conc. in part: CD, LD, BF (114; 'award'); EU, EM (115–16; 'awarded compensation', 'newly awarded compensation')
FAA v. Cooper, 566 U.S. 284 (2012)
  Alito, J.: CD, LD (294 n.4; 'actual damages', 'actual')
  Sotomayor, J., diss.: CD, HD, LD, BF (308; 'actual', 'actual damages', 'compensatory damages')
Rehberg v. Paulk, 566 U.S. 356 (2012)
  Alito, J.: AA (372 n.3)
Caraco Pharmaceutical Labs., Ltd. v. Novo Nordisk A/S, 566 U.S. 399 (2012)
  Kagan, J.: EU (424; 'not a/an')
Mohamad v. Palestinian Authority, 566 U.S. 449 (2012)
  Sotomayor, J.: HD, EU (454; 'individual')
United States v. Home Concrete & Supply, LLC, 566 U.S. 478, 482 (2012)
  Breyer, J.: HD (482; 'omit'); AA (485–6)
Hall v. United States, 566 U.S. 506 (2012)
  Sotomayor, J.: HD, LD (511–12; 'incur')
  Breyer, J., diss.: EU (531; 'incurred')
Astrue v. Caputo, 566 U.S. 541 (2012)
  Ginsburg, J.: CD, HD (551; 'child')
Taniguchi v. Kan Pacific Saipan, Ltd., 556 U.S. 560 (2012)
  Alito, J.: HD (566–8; 'interpreter')
  Ginsburg, J., diss.: HD, LD (576; 'interpreter', 'translate')
Freeman v. Quicken Loans, Inc., 566 U.S. 624 (2012)
  Scalia, J.: CD, EU (630–1, 633–4, 365; 'portion', 'percentage', 'split', 'make a charge', 'accept a charge')
Christopher v. SmithKline Beecham Corp., 567 U.S. 142 (2012)
  Alito, J.: CD (154 n.12; 'transaction', 'consummate')
  Breyer, J., diss.: EU (171, 174–5; 'sold', 'sell')
Arizona v. United States, 567 U.S. 387 (2012)
  Alito, J., conc. in part: EM (456; 'cooperate')
Nat'l Federation of Indep. Businesses v. Sebelius, 567 U.S. 519 (2012)
  Roberts, C.J.: HD (550–1 n.4; 'direct'); EM (555 n.6, 556, 558; 'active in the market', 'own sake'); RR (582 n.2)
  Ginsburg, J., conc. in part: EU, BF (607–8, 612–13; 'active in the market'); AA (616–17)
  Scalia, J., diss.: HD (649–50; 'regulate'); EM (660; 'activity'); AA (647–8, 649, 656, 658, 687–8)

2012 term

Los Angeles County Flood Control Dist. v. Nat. Res. Defense Council, Inc., 568 U.S. 78 (2013)
    Ginsburg, J.: CD, EM (82–3; 'add')
Lozman v. City of Riviera Beach, 568 U.S. 115 (2013)
    Breyer, J.: HD (120–1, 123; 'transportation', 'contrivance', 'craft'); EU (120–1; 'capable')
Johnson v. Williams, 568 U.S. 289 (2013)
    Scalia, J.: LD (307–8; 'formal language . . . preceding the announcement of . . . judgment')
Marx v. General Revenue Corp., 568 U.S. 371 (2013)
    Thomas, J.: RR (379 n.4; 'an instruction on [a] medication label to "take [it] twice a day unless otherwise directed"')
    Sotomayor, J., diss.: CD, HD (389, 390–1; 'provide', 'otherwise', 'contrary'); RR, BF (391)
Gabelli v. Securities & Exchange Comm'n, 568 U.S. 442 (2013)
    Roberts, C.J.: LD (448; 'accrue')
Kirtsaeng v. John Wiley & Sons, 568 U.S. 519 (2013)
    Breyer, J.: HD, LD (530–1; 'under'); EU, RR (531; 'any'); EU (532; 'applies')
    Ginsburg, J., diss.: HD, LD, BF (563; 'under'); HD (563 n.4; 'made'); EM (563; 'lawful')
Decker v. Northwest Environmental Defense Center, 568 U.S. 597 (2013)
    Kennedy, J.: CD (612–13; 'manufacturing', 'processing')
    Scalia, J., conc. in part: RR (624; hypothetical statutory provision)
Moncrieffe v. Holder, 569 U.S. ___ (2013)
    Alito, J., diss.: EM (slip op. 10–11; 'convicted of or for')
McQuiggin v. Perkins, 569 U.S. ___ (2013)
    Scalia, J., diss.: AA (slip op. 6)
Sebelius v. Cloer, 569 U.S. ___ (2013)
    Sotomayor, J.: EU (slip op. 6; 'filed')
Maryland v. King, 569 U.S. ___ (2013)
    Scalia, J., diss.: EM (slip op. 5–6, 10; 'identifying')
Arizona v. Inter Tribal Council of Arizona, Inc., 570 U.S. ___ (2013)
    Scalia, J.: HD (slip op. 6–7; 'accept'); EU (slip op. 6–7; 'accept and use'); AA (slip op. 7)
    Thomas, J., diss.: EU, BF (slip op. 3–4; 'accept and use')
    Alito, J., diss.: EU, BF (slip op. 7–8; 'accept and use')
Maracich v. Spears, 570 U.S. ___ (2013)
    Ginsburg, J., diss.: AA (slip op. 17)
Agency for Int'l Development v. Alliance for Open Society Int'l, 570 U.S. ___ (2013)
    Scalia, J., diss.: AA (slip op. 6)

Salinas v. Texas, 570 U.S. ___ (2013)
  Breyer, J., diss.: RR (slip op. 11; words or actions by a person in custody)
Descamps v. United States, 570 U.S. ___ (2013)
  Alito, J., diss.: EM (slip op. 4–5; 'convicted of or for')
Univ. of Texas Southwestern Med. Ctr. v. Nassar, 570 U.S. ___ (2013)
  Kennedy, J.: HD (slip op. 9–10; 'because of')
Vance v. Ball State Univ., 570 U.S. ___ (2013)
  Alito, J.: HD (slip op. 10–11; 'supervisor')
Shelby County v. Holder, 570 U.S. ___ (2013)
  Roberts, C.J.: AA (slip op. 21–2)
  Ginsburg, J., diss.: BF (slip op. 25 n.8, 33)
Adoptive Couple v. Baby Girl, 570 U.S. ___ (2013)
  Alito, J.: HD (slip op. 8, 12; 'continued', 'breakup')
  Thomas, J., conc.: HD (slip op. 4; 'commerce')
  Scalia, J., diss.: HD, BF (slip op. 1; 'continued')
  Sotomayor, J., diss.: HD (slip op. 7–8; 'breakup')
Hollingsworth v. Perry, 570 U.S. ___ (2013)
  Scalia, J.: HD (slip op. 4–5; 'obtain'); EU, EM (slip op. 8–9; 'obtained and exercised')

2013 term

United States v. Woods, 571 U.S. ___ (2013)
  Scalia, J.: EU (slip op. 14; appositive use of 'or')
Mississippi ex rel. Hood v. AU Optronics Corp., 571 U.S. ___ (2014)
  Sotomayor, J.: HD, LD (slip op. 7–8; 'plaintiff')
Burrage v. United States, 571 U.S. ___ (2014)
  Scalia, J.: HD, LD (slip op. 13–14, 6; 'contributing cause', 'results'); EU, EM (slip op. 7–8; 'resulted from')
Sandifer v. United States Steel Corp., 571 U.S. ___ (2014)
  Scalia, J.: HD (slip op. 6–7; 'clothes', 'change'); EU (slip op. 7, 14–15; 'protective clothing', 'protective clothes', 'spending'); EM (slip op. 10; 'changed clothes')
Air Wisconsin Airlines Corp. v. Hoeper, 571 U.S. ___ (2014)
  Sotomayor, J.: RR (slip op. 11 n.3, 15; 'blown up', '[u]nstable')
  Scalia, J., conc. in part, diss. in part: RR, BF (slip op. 4; 'unstable'); EU, RR (slip op. 5; 'mental [in]stability')
Fernandez v. California, 571 U.S. ___ (2014)
  Alito, J.: RR (slip op. 11, 11 n.5; 'stay out')
Lawson v. FMR LLC, 571 U.S. ___ (2014)
  Ginsburg, J.: EU (slip op. 23; 'contractor')
  Sotomayor, J., diss.: AA (slip op. 2)

Lozano v. Montoya Alvarez, 572 U.S. ___ (2014)
    Alito, J., conc.: RR (slip op. 3; 'Come straight home from school, unless one of your friends invites you to a movie')
Rosemond v. United States, 572 U.S. ___ (2014)
    Kagan, J.: RR (slip op. 17; 'knew his cohort used a firearm')
United States v. Quality Stores, Inc., 572 U.S. ___ (2014)
    Kennedy, J.: EM (slip op. 4, 9; 'severance payment', 'all')
United States v. Castleman, 572 U.S. ___ (2014)
    Sotomayor, J.: RR (slip op. 6–7; 'violence', 'domestic violence'); EM (slip op. 7; 'violence'); EM (slip op. 13, 14–15; 'use of force', 'crime of violence')
Prado Navarette v. California, 572 U.S. ___ (2014)
    Scalia, J., diss.: RR (slip op. 6; '[A truck r]an [me] off the roadway')
Paroline v. United States, 572 U.S. ___ (2014)
    Kennedy, J.: RR (slip op. 8; 'costs incurred by the victim')
EPA v. EME Homer City Generation, L.P., 572 U.S. ___ (2014)
    Scalia, J., diss.: EU (slip op. 4; 'significant'); AA (slip op. 6)
Octane Fitness, LLC v. ICON Health & Fitness, Inc., 572 U.S. ___ (2014)
    Sotomayor, J.: HD (slip op. 7; 'exceptional')
Town of Greece v. Galloway, 572 U.S. ___ (2014)
    Kennedy, J.: RR (slip op. 5–6, 13–14; 'let us pray', 'Lord of Lords', 'King of Kings')
    Kagan, J., diss.: RR (slip op. 2–3, 13, 14, 17)
Tolan v. Cotton, 572 U.S. ___ (2014)
    Per curiam: LD (slip op. 9; 'threat')
Bond v. United States, 572 U.S. ___ (2014)
    Roberts, C.J.: CD, HD (slip op. 15–16; 'weapon'); EM (slip op. 15, 16; 'chemical weapon', 'combat')
    Scalia, J., conc. in judgment: RR, BF (slip op. 5; 'chemical weapon')
Scialabba v. Cuellar de Osorio, 573 U.S. ___ (2014)
    Kagan, J.: HD (slip op. 15; 'automatic'); EU (slip op. 28 & n.15, 29; 'and', 'shall')
    Roberts, C.J., conc. in judgment: RR (slip op. 3; hypothetical statutory provision)
    Sotomayor, J., diss.: EU, BF (slip op. 9–10; 'and'); HD (slip op. 12–13; 'automatic', 'convert'); RR, BF (slip op. 20–1 & 21 n.9; hypothetical provision)
Clark v. Rameker, 573 U.S. ___ (2014)
    Sotomayor, J.: HD (slip op. 5; 'funds', 'retirement'); RR (slip op. 8; 'retirement funds'); EU (slip op. 10; 'to the extent that')
Abramski v. United States, 573 U.S. ___ (2014)
    Kagan, J.: EU, BF (slip op. 9 n.5; 'sells')
    Scalia, J., diss.: EM, BF (slip op. 4 & n.2; 'sells'); AA (slip op. 14)

Halliburton Co. v. Erica P. John Fund, 573 U.S. ___ (2014)
    Thomas, J., conc. in judgment: RR (slip op. 11; stock market prices)
Utility Air Regulatory Group v. EPA, 573 U.S. ___ (2014)
    Breyer, J., conc. in part, diss. in part: EM (slip op. 5; 'any')
Loughrin v. United States, 573 U.S. ___ (2014)
    Kagan, J.: CD, HD, EM (slip op. 11, 12; 'by means of'); BF (slip op. 14 n.8; 'by means of')
    Scalia, J., conc. in part & in judgment: CD, HD, EU, EM, BF (slip op. 2–4; 'by means of')
Riley v. California, 573 U.S. ___ (2014)
    Roberts, C.J.: AA (slip op. 16–17)
American Broadcasting Cos. v. Aereo, Inc., 573 U.S. ___ (2014)
    Breyer, J.: EU, EM (slip op. 13, 15; 'transmit', 'performance', 'to the public')
McCullen v. Coakley, 573 U.S. ___ (2014)
    Roberts, C.J.: RR (slip op. 22; 'a strained voice or a waving hand [as opposed to] a direct greeting or an outstretched arm')
    Scalia, J., conc. in judgment: RR (slip op. 4; sample statements); AA (slip op. 7)
    Alito, J., conc. in judgment: RR (slip op. 2; statements by hypothetical 'sidewalk counselor' and 'clinic employee')
NLRB v. Noel Canning, 573 U.S. ___ (2014)
    Breyer, J.: HD (slip op. 9–10, 22; 'recess', 'the', 'happen', 'vacancy')
    Scalia, J., conc. in judgment: HD, BF (slip op. 9, 11, 27; 'session', 'recess', 'happen'); EU, EM (slip op. 27, 28 n.8; 'happen'); AA (slip op. 21–2; see also 42–3); RR (slip op. 28; 'happen')

Bibliography

Aprill, E. P. (1998), 'The Law of the Word: Dictionary Shopping in the Supreme Court', 30 *Arizona State Law Journal*, 275–336.

Benesh, S. C. and J. J. Czarnecki (2009), 'The Ideology of Legal Interpretation', 29 *Washington University Journal of Law & Public Policy*, 113.

Bogdan, R. J. (2013), *Mindvaults: Sociocultural Grounds for Pretending and Imagining*, Cambridge, MA: MIT Press.

Brudney, J. J. and L. Baum (2013), 'Oasis or Mirage: The Supreme Court's Thirst for Dictionaries in the Rehnquist and Roberts Eras', 55 *William & Mary Law Review*, 483–580.

Calhoun, J. (2014), Note, 'Measuring the Fortress: Explaining Trends in Supreme Court and Circuit Court Dictionary Use', 124 *Yale Law Journal*, 484–527.

Cross, F. (2009), *The Theory and Practice of Statutory Interpretation*, Palo Alto, CA: Stanford University Press.

Cross, F. (2012), 'The Ideology of Supreme Court Opinions and Citations', 97 *Iowa Law Review*, 693.

Devitt, M. and K. Sterelny (1999), *Language and Reality: An Introduction to the Philosophy of Language*, Cambridge, MA: MIT Press.
Feltovich, P. J., M. J. Prietula and K. A. Ericsson (2006), 'Studies of Expertise from Psychological Perspectives', in K. A. Ericsson, N. Charness, P. J. Feltovich and R. R. Hoffman (eds), *The Cambridge Handbook of Expertise and Expert Performance*, Cambridge: Cambridge University Press, 41.
Gewirtz, P. (1982), 'The Jurisprudence of Hypotheticals', 32 *Journal of Legal Education*, 120.
Ginsburg, R. Bader, with M. Hartnett and W. W. Williams (2016), *My Own Words*, New York: Simon & Schuster.
Gluck, A. (2010), 'The States as Laboratories of Statutory Interpretation: Methodological Consensus and the New Modified Textualism', 119 *Yale Law Journal*, 1750.
Gries, S. Th. and B. Slocum (2017), 'Ordinary Meaning and Corpus Linguistics', 2017 *Brigham Young University Law Review*, 1417–72.
Hart, H. L. A. (1958), 'Positivism and the Separation of Law and Morals', 71 *Harvard Law Review*, 573.
Harvard Law Review (1994), 'Looking It Up: Dictionaries and Statutory Interpretation', 107 *Harvard Law Review*, 1437–54.
Lee, T. R. and S. C. Mouritsen (2018), 'Judging Ordinary Meaning', 127 *Yale Law Journal*, 788.
Mertz, E. (2007), *The Language of Law School: Learning to 'Think Like a Lawyer'*, Oxford: Oxford University Press.
Mitchell, G. (2004), 'Case Studies, Counterfactuals, and Causal Explanations', 152 *University of Pennsylvania Law Review*, 1517.
Mouritsen, S. C. (2010), 'The Dictionary Is Not a Fortress: Definitional Fallacies and a Corpus-Based Approach to Plain Meaning', 2010 *Brigham Young University Law Review*, 1915–80.
Nourse, V. (2016), *Misreading Law, Misreading Democracy*, Cambridge, MA: Harvard University Press.
Petroski, K. (2018), *Fiction and the Languages of Law: Understanding Contemporary Legal Discourse*, London: Routledge.
Scalia, Antonin (1997), *A Matter of Interpretation: Federal Courts and the Law*, Princeton, NJ: Princeton University Press.
Scalia, A. and B. A. Garner (2012), *Reading Law: The Interpretation of Legal Texts*, St. Paul, MN: Thomson West.
Schank, R. C. and R. P. Abelson (1977), *Scripts, Plans, Goals, and Understanding: An Inquiry into Human Knowledge*, Mahwah, NJ: Lawrence Erlbaum.
Schauer, F. (2008), 'A Critical Guide to Vehicles in the Park', 83 *New York University Law Review*, 1109.
Schlag, P. (1999), 'No Vehicles in the Park', 23 *Seattle University Law Review*, 381.
Slocum, B. (2015), *Ordinary Meaning: A Theory of the Most Fundamental Principle of Legal Interpretation*, Chicago: University of Chicago Press.

Stalnaker, R. C. (2014), *Context*, Oxford: Oxford University Press.
Strassfeld, R. N. (1992), 'If . . .: Counterfactuals in the Law', 60 *George Washington Law Review*, 339.
Thumma, S. A. and J. L. Kirchmeier (1999), 'The Lexicon Has Become a Fortress: The United States Supreme Court's Use of Dictionaries', 47 *Buffalo Law Review*, 227–562.
Weinstein, J. (2005), 'Against Dictionaries: Using Analogical Reasoning to Achieve a More Restrained Textualism', 30 *University of Michigan Journal of Law Reform*, 649.

Chapter 9

Showing by Fiction: Audience of Extra-legal References in Judicial Decisions

Terezie Smejkalová

1. INTRODUCTION

It is often argued that law – and judicial decisions – are not primarily addressed to the laypeople whose life they regulate but to other legal actors: bodies of the state, courts – in short, lawyers (Stevenson 2005: 108, 112; Kelsen 1945: 61; Smejkalová and Škop 2017). To be fully capable of using all that law has to offer, one has to acquire knowledge that is predominantly sign-based. Legal education is understood as a matter of learning to fully participate in legal discourse (language acquisition and interpreting legal signs) (Garret 2010: 62–3; Chen 1995). The discourse of judicial decisions (or more precisely the discourse of rationales of judicial decisions) is a matter of legal rules as well as formalised convention. While some of its content is prescribed by black-letter law, some – especially the argumentative parts – are a matter of convention, or fashion/custom.

Judicial decisions play a specific normative role even in traditional civil law systems, such as that of the Czech Republic. For this reason, many civil law scholars have shifted their attention to study this normative role and analyse various elements that contribute to it (for example, MacCormick and Summers 1997). Some of the elements which are being addressed are the references to various sources the judge uses to make his or her decision, such as laws, other judicial decisions, doctrinal legal writing or even extra-legal writing.

The legal system of the Czech Republic has a strong tradition of legal formalism stemming from the legal positivism of Kelsen and Weyr, which is in many ways still tied to the years of the communist regime the country endured. The socialist legal systems were built on the supremacy of a parliamentary 'statute' and its judicial decision-making was very formalistic (David and Brierley 1978; Lasser 1994–5; 1997–8).[1] Since the Velvet Revolution, a shift in the legal culture has been taking place. The Czech apex courts, including the new Constitutional Court, have adopted and focused on complex ways to justify decisions in hard cases. Among these, there started to be made references to doctrinal writing and,

---

[1] On characteristics of socialist legal systems see, for example, David and Brierley (1978). On comparison of style of justifications of judicial decisions in common law and civil law see Lasser (1994–5, 1997–8).

on rather rare occasions, even to extra-legal writing: literary works, such as novels or plays.

These references to extra-legal writing appear in various forms: from a mere mention of a name of a writer to lengthy quotations followed by a full reference to the source. References to these sources may of course be subtler: a hint, a phrase. But since these are much more difficult to spot (and it may sometimes be impossible to prove a hint or a phrase is such a reference at all), I will focus solely on overt references and will examine the role of these: may we dismiss them as purely rhetorical ornaments or do they have any communicative value? Is this communicative value related to a specific audience? And since they are essentially extra-legal, may their communicative value be intended for those among all the possible future readers of judicial decisions with no legal education?

Building on the specific case of referring to extra-legal literary writing, this chapter will argue that showing, referencing and using examples in law is essentially a matter of addressing an argument to a specific audience.

In consequence, and building upon Perelman and Olbrechts-Tyteca's (2008) theory of argumentation, I will argue that while a reference to a well known extra-legal source, image or symbol may in fact serve as an example or an aid in explaining complex socio-legal phenomena, a reference to a source that is not well known not only does not serve as an example but also fails to establish communion between the speaker and his or her audience, and in consequence is not persuasive.

2. COMMUNION AS AN IDEAL SITUATION OF PERSUASION

The main purpose of the rationale part of any judicial decision is to provide justification for the decision given and to persuade the reader (audience) that the decision made was the right one.

Theories of argumentation discuss various requirements that must be fulfilled for an argument to be 'correct', such as acceptability and relevance. Arguments that are built on unacceptable premises and those that are not relevant to the argumentative situation at hand do not contribute to the goal of persuading the audience (Walton 2006). Grice makes a similar point in the context of explaining the cooperative principle of conversation. Even though legal argumentation can hardly be considered a conversation guided by the whole of cooperative principle, Grice, too, points out that a contribution to a conversation must be relevant to the discussed topic. However, relevance in itself is a complex issue that carries with it a number of problems. Even Grice himself admits that relevance to a communicative situation is a matter of focus, individuality of subjects engaged in communication and other issues (Grice 1991: 22–40). However, correctness of an argument in itself does not entail that the argumentation would be persuasive.

For Perelman and Olbrechts-Tyteca persuasive argumentation is, inter alia, a matter of 'communion', i.e., an agreement of a society on shared values (Perelman and Olbrechts-Tyteca 2008: 239–41). Plantin adds that 'communion' is in fact the final phase, the goal of argumentation where those who persuade and those who are persuaded unite around a shared understanding or shared experience (Plantin 2009: 333).

Law and the language of legal communication have often been described as something specific that is not accessible to those without legal education, and there have been various attempts to bring law closer to laypeople (Mellinkoff 1963; Bhatia 1983; Cao 2007).[2] A plain, legal-text-based formalised argumentation, aiming almost at a purely syllogistic format,[3] is criticised in terms of its intelligibility to an audience with no formal legal schooling and which is therefore far from a communion between the court and such an audience. Creating a situation of shared understanding and shared experience between a court and a lay audience entails a presence of figures of communion: allusion, metaphor, rhetorical questions, illustration or examples (Perelman and Olbrechts-Tyteca 2008: 239–41). Referring to works of art, cultural symbols or fictional stories may be considered an argumentation device aiming to call upon shared knowledge and experience to create communion – an ideal situation of persuasion.[4]

Using extra-legal examples in legal argumentation may thus be considered one of the devices to help achieve communion. This is a widely accepted view: Jackson showed how each community has a stock of narratives representing the group's knowledge (Jackson 1988: 171); others believe in the importance of placing the law within a proper historical continuum (Simon-Shoshan 2013: 447, referring to Cover 1983).

But using extra-legal examples in legal argumentation may also be understood as an acknowledgment that to explain a complex legal conclusion a judge sometimes feels the need to draw on extra-legal sources. He or she understands that judicial decisions normally use a means of communication not everyone fully understands: the language of law; and that an additional argumentative step is needed to persuade (and help understand) those who do not fully comprehend this language.

What is important at this point is the notion of communication between people who do not share the same language; a communicative situation where an extra explication and showing is needed, one that needs to rely on a means of communication shared across these different languages.

---

[2] See also various attempts made within the Plain Language Campaign, the Creative Commons licensing platform and so on.
[3] Plain syllogistic decisions of the French Cour de Cassation may be quite illustrative of this extreme: they do not contain any justification but are based around stating (often in just half a page of text) that a certain situation clearly fits the conditions described in a provision of a statute, therefore leading to the one and only decision. See for example the decision of Cour de cassation Arrêt n° 1908 du 31 mars 2009 (08-88.226).
[4] Similarly, those who deal with the references to works of art in legal argumentation (Plantin 2009; Klusoňová 2015; Gadbin-George 2013) often converge on Perelman and Olbrechts-Tyteca's explication of the importance of shared social experience in any kind of communication, and – in this legal context – in argumentation.

My question here is whether references to fiction in judicial decisions may be capable of such shared communication across languages/codes. To this end, we need to approach the reference as a unit of meaning and assess its communicative value.

3. THE COMMUNICATIVE VALUE OF A REFERENCE TO FICTION

To address the issue of whether and to what extent references to fiction may be capable of bridging the legal and extra-legal worlds, we need to take into consideration at least two dimensions of a reference's meaning: the meaning of the reference to fiction itself, and the content of such reference, i.e. the content of what is being referred to. In the first dimension of meaning, our considerations are centred around interpreting the presence of a reference as a symbol. In the second dimension, we understand the reference as a hypertext, leading to an extra-legal narrative and drawing the narrative into the legal argumentation.

Acceptability of a reference and reference as a symbol

The first dimension is a matter of mere presence of a reference to something that is not a part of traditional legal argumentation but the judge has chosen to include it. May we treat it as a symbol and ask what its presence means? Does it mean anything apart from pointing to the extra-legal source? Is it fulfilling an expected role, or is it eccentric?

Acknowledgment of sources is good practice not only in academia, but also in judicial decision-making. Simply referring to the legal sources of judges' considerations is a usual and acceptable practice in justifying judicial decisions. However, the key term here is the 'legal sources'. Civil law systems recognise sources formally binding the judge in his or her decision-making. It is not surprising that extra-legal literary writing would not make it among these formally binding sources. However, in hard cases where a complex argumentation is required, interpretation of formal sources of law may require outside help (usually from past judicial decisions or doctrinal writing).

In the context of common law, Harris (1985: 209–11) empirically shows that decisions in hard cases contain more references to sources than those in simple cases.[5] Yet these findings alone are no surprise: where the decision-making requires the application of legal principles (as happens with hard cases), the need for more detailed (and therefore abundant) argumentation rises as the level of requirements for such a decision increases (Kühn 2002).

Feldman and March (1981: 171–86)[6] (albeit in respect to decision-making in businesses and corporations) claim that mere accumulation and exhibition of

---

[5] I have confirmed Harris's conclusion in my dissertation with regard to the Czech system in Smejkalová (2013b).

[6] Feldman and March's study is made with respect to businesses, although some of their findings relate to any institution making a decision.

information related to the decision functions in our present society as a sign of good decision-making. The presentation of accumulated information related to the case may then serve as a ritualistic confirmation (assurance) that those who decide do so responsibly and by taking into account all the information and sources that are available (1981: 177). I have argued elsewhere in the context of listing references to past judicial decisions (Smejkalová 2013a: 3–9) that these long lists of references may be understood in terms of their symbolic presence and may be indicative of an attempt to create an image of good and thorough decision-making. Furthermore, if Feldman and March's claims about the role of accumulation of information are valid, such references may in fact be an answer to some kind of expectation that society has of a good decision-maker. The mere presence of these lists of references to sources may have a certain symbolic value in and of itself.

Feldman and March explain this symbolic value through the nature of our society that, in their opinion, is built on a trust/faith in rational decision-making. This rational decision-making is typical of gathering as much information as possible before making a decision since our society accepts the myth of informed decision-making. And one of the elements connected to this myth is that more information leads to better decisions; it shows the proper competence of the person making the decision and at the same time legitimates his or her decisions (Harris 1985: 209).

A reference to a legal source in a rationale of a judicial decision is a matter of argumentation by which the judge shows that his or her decision is well grounded in the legal system. While just one reference to a legal norm may suffice, in a legal system that does not adhere to the doctrine of precedent, referring to just one past judicial decision does not have to be persuasive but listing five that contain, for example, the same interpretation of an applicable legal principle communicates that the decision is not isolated in the legal system but is in line with past decision-making in similar cases. Yet lists of references to sources may maintain their symbolic value in justification of decisions only when their symbolic value is established; when the message communicated by the presence of the list is understandable to both: the speaker as well as his or her audience.

However, I have suggested above that referring to extra-legal literary sources in judicial decisions is not an everyday practice in civil law jurisdictions. The trouble with extra-legal references in judicial decisions is that they have no firm standing among the legal arguments.[7] While we may theorise that the presence of a reference to an extra-legal source may be indicative of the judge's intention to link the legal issue at hand to wider non-legal realities, its capability to communicate such a message to an audience is a matter of acceptance of such an element in legal argumentation at all.

---

[7] Should we remain within the limits of the Czech legal system, the basic textbooks on legal theory often list as 'a source of law' so called 'legal appendices of extra-legal publications' (for example Harvánek et al. 2013: 237–8). While often described in terms of theocratic states where the religious writing impacts (and intermingles with) the law, the definition may encompass the literary sources we are talking about here as well.

Asking about a meaning of a presence of a reference is a matter of understanding a reference as a semantic unit in its own right, as one set within other semantic units and capable of maintaining relationships with them. The semantic level of <the reference> is not just an object (a literary work) as such but a cultural unit set within other cultural units (Eco 2009: 40).

A symbol is traditionally understood as a form that does not signify anything by itself, but rather alludes to or hints at something (Eco 1984: 144); what it hints at (its meaning) is socially, culturally and temporally conditioned, which means that it evolves. A continuously undisputed practice of referring to extra-legal literary sources in judicial decision-making may, over time, acquire a symbolic value of its own. But for any semantic unit to have a communicative value, it needs not only to be accepted as a part of the means (code) of communication, but also to be understood.

Reference as a hypertext: linking the legal and extra-legal narratives

Should we approach the references from the perspective of what exactly they refer to, our considerations shift to the extra-legal literary source itself – the work of literature, in this case – to that particular fiction, a narrative. When referring to the literary work, the court does not show it to us so that we can admire or criticise it; it does not point it out for us to comment on its quality or aesthetics. Rather, it refers to a meaning, a metaphor, something that this literary work shows. These literary works we talk about here are novels, short stories, narratives. Yet stories and narratives are hardly ever innocent. Not only do they have a message of their own (Del Mar 2013: 396) but their artistic nature makes them wide open to interpretation – a characteristic that is in legal texts often seen as unwelcome.[8] Yet even law is expected to evolve by means of interpretation.[9] However, DiMatteo (2013: 1288) points out that 'stressing narrativity [in law] is about stressing the continuity of law as well as its inherent flexibility – law is expected to be reinterpreted, to evolve, to react to social and cultural circumstances'.

Fictions, stories, narratives 'can serve as formal models, providing templates for structures we may import into our own experience' (Landy 2012: 4). If '[d]ecision-making in adjudication consists in comparing a narrative constructed from the facts of the case with the underlying narrative pattern either explicit in or underlying the conceptualized legal rule' (Del Mar 2013: 406) then showing that the underlying narrative pattern is one that is already known beyond the rigid legal structures may add extra legitimising value. Together with Del Mar we may

---

[8] For Eco (1984: 141), a work of literature is actually 'an untranslatable and unspeakable message' whose meaning cannot be separated from what it conveys. Literary works are, after all, a matter of imaginative writing. On the note that even legal texts may be considered to be examples of imaginative writing see White (1985 [1973]).

[9] See Hart's famous concept of open texture of law (Hart 2004). For a critique of this concept see, for example, Schauer (2011).

say that even in this case, in the case of a reference to an extra-legal narrative in legal reasoning, what we are dealing with is a performance that enjoys a multifaceted, multitemporal and exemplary character (Del Mar 2013: 404).

The extra-legal references in judicial decisions may be considered to play the same role in law as exemplary narratives do. Gordon recalls the *State* v. *Hundley* case (Gordon 2013: 349) dealt with by the Kansas Supreme Court; he cites a passage that concludes the finding of the facts: 'this is a textbook case of the battered wife' (Gordon 2013: 350). The court (and Gordon) treats the two words 'battered wife' as a metonymy or hypertext for a whole narrative behind it, one that is known to the reader, and thus the particular story is institutionalised as law (Gordon 2013: 350). For Gordon 'a narrative that gains an exemplary status does so because it not only tells its own story – it speaks across a range of cases broader than the exact situation from where it sprung' (Gordon 2013: 361). Although we may not straightforwardly conclude that the extra-legal reference does not become law,[10] its purpose is to link the legal considerations to extra-legal realities, ones that are usually more accessible – or deemed to be more accessible – to a possible lay reader. The phrase 'deemed to be more accessible' is crucial here.

The speaker's (i.e., the court's) intended message here is to illustrate a point: to provide an example; to prove a point; to add an argumentative value to his or her argumentation; to provide the legal system with stability across cultural shifts (Gordon 2013). But such a relationship may only be functional in legal argumentation if the extra-legal reference to a literary source is one that is truly familiar.

Familiarity is, naturally, a concept that makes no sense without a reference audience. Similarly, it makes no sense to talk about shared experience (or communion) if neither speaker nor audience knows the extra-legal literary source that is being referred to.

It follows from the above that by using the reference, the speaker – the court – believes that something would be more clearly communicated by an extra-legal element. The judge makes an assumption that the legal language is not a code he or she would share with the audience and that he or she needs to choose a different – shared – code to send the same message. The judge therefore chooses a reference to a literary work of art. We need to be aware that this is the speaker's assumption. And it is the speaker who makes yet another assumption about what the shared code actually is and that it would convey the message better.

This assumption and choice would not have been made had the speaker – the judge – not thought about who the audience of his or her decision was. Theories

---

[10] We may theorise on what happens to an extra-legal narrative when drawn into an authoritative discursive situation. On the one hand, it might be understood in terms of an attempt to ground legal considerations in wider social and cultural realities. On the other hand, we may understand it as a sort of authoritative hijacking of non-legal cultural realities, establishing them in the authoritative discourse of law and thus depriving them of their extra-legal cultural status.

of argumentation and communication as well as the more general theories of a reader (Eco 1981: 3; Clark and Carlson 1982: 344; Smejkalová and Škop 2017) teach us from different perspectives that successful communication of a message is dependent on the recipient of the message and his or her understanding, and that in order for the communication to be successful, the speaker must take the future recipient – reader – of the message into account when choosing the code. Schmid theorises that any author presumes an addressee when crafting his or her message. He understands that this presumed addressee is either a real or imagined person who might actually read the text containing the message (Schmid 2015). If the speaker errs about the shared dimensions of the code he or she is choosing, he or she may not only fail in providing the needed justification for the decision, but may also harm the argumentation (and potentially in consequence the image and legitimacy of law).

4. REFERENCE TO AN EXTRA-LEGAL SOURCE AND A FAILURE TO ESTABLISH COMMUNION

Since intelligibility is a minimum requirement for any successful communication, this means that the audience needs to understand the code. As the issue at hand is a reference to a literary work in a judicial decision, the matter of 'understanding the code' becomes more complicated and needs to be broken down into the matter of acceptance of this kind of reference in legal argumentation, and the referred-to literary work belonging to the realms of shared experience, as already mentioned above. If these two conditions are not met, the speaker's attempt to establish communion with the audience fails. Only when these conditions have been met can we ask whether the use of a particular reference has any persuasive character and whether it succeeds in creating a communion.

Depending on the shared experience and expectations regarding a reference to a work of fiction it may be persuasive and legitimising or delegitimising for the decision (and consequently the judiciary – or law – in general).

Therefore, using a reference to a literary work may fail to establish communion and harm the argumentation if

(1) it is not accepted as an argument in the given argumentative situation (it is so eccentric in justifying judicial decisions that it fails to persuade);
(2) it refers to a literary source that is not well known, which means that it fails to allude to any shared knowledge or experience, thus failing to create communion between the speaker and his or her audience.

While the first condition was discussed above and may be treated as a prerequisite for the second condition, the second condition requires more attention and will be discussed in terms of examples of overt references to literary fiction in the decisions of the Czech Constitutional Court.

5. EXAMPLES OF EXTRA-LEGAL REFERENCES IN DECISIONS OF THE CZECH CONSTITUTIONAL COURT

This chapter will now go on to analyse chosen instances where the Constitutional Court of the Czech Republic used a reference to a work of literary fiction in its majority or dissenting opinions.[11]

Example 1: illustrating the absurdity of certain situations

> By comparing the provisions of the regulation of the town of Ostrov ('a fire-fighting order') disputed by the Ministry of the Interior to the guidance issued by the very Ministry on drafting such kind of regulation we can clearly see that the wording of Art. 6/5 of the regulation in question is practically identical to the wording of Art. 6/4 of the Ministry's guidance. The Constitutional Court is thus confronted with a case in which the claimant [Ministry of the Interior] is guiding the law-making activity of the municipalities. But when the municipality follows this guidance and adjusts its regulations accordingly, the Ministry claims its contradiction with the constitutional order and with the statutes. The Ministry of the Interior creates a situation which shows that the absurd world of the novels of Franz Kafka or George Orwell, and of the plays of Samuel Beckett or Eugene Ionesco, does not have to be and is not a fiction, but it is a reality of life. (Pl. ÚS 25/06)[12]

In this decision the Constitutional Court was addressing a situation where the Ministry of the Interior issued a guidance document on how municipalities should draft their 'fire-fighting orders' and consequently claimed that an actual regulation drafted by the municipality of Ostrov in line with this guidance was unconstitutional. The Constitutional Court was baffled by the situation, thinking it absurd. To illustrate this absurdity, the Court referred to not just one extra-legal source, but several. It translated their point of 'absurdity' into a reference to the absurd worlds of the works of Franz Kafka, George Orwell, Samuel Beckett and Eugene Ionesco. Overtly, it alludes to several narratives, none of which is mentioned directly, but only through their authors. The argument they make is simple: the result would be unacceptable, because it would lead to creating a world that would be too 'absurd' or bureaucratic in the *Rechtstaat*. To better illustrate what they mean by this absurdity, they have chosen to refer to writers all of whom may be part of the Czech high school curriculum.[13] Yet anyone familiar with those

---

[11] All but one excerpt from the Constitutional Court decision used in this analysis have been translated by the author. The translation of the excerpt from decision Pl. ÚS 5/16 comes from Franz Kafka Online, <www.kafka-online.info/the-trial-page147.html> accessed 3 October 2018.

[12] Decision of the Constitutional Court of the Czech Republic of 19 September 2006 no. Pl. ÚS 25/06.

[13] The Czech Republic does not have one common high school curriculum when it comes to individual works of literary fiction. The Framework Educational Programmes do not specify authors that should be taught. For currently valid programmes see Framework Educational Programmes. Ministerstvo školství, mládeže a tělovýchovy, <www.msmt.cz/vzdelavani/skolstvi-v-cr/skolskareforma/ramcove-vzdelavaci-programy> accessed 27 March 2018. When taking into account the fact that these particular authors are known (possibly because they are part of the high school curriculum) we may also theorise that referring to such authors in a judicial decision is a matter of *argumentum ad auctoritas*. However, I am deliberately avoiding this direction of discussion to focus on other aspects of these references.

novels or plays would immediately ask whether these absurd worlds that the Court refers to are really so similar to be used in such a fashion in legal argumentation and that they in fact lack any acceptable common denominators. The decision seems to create a set, one that depicts worlds that make no sense at all. But no further explanation of these works or the nature of the absurdity of these worlds is provided by the Court.

We may argue that these worlds have nothing in common and that the claimed absurdity of these worlds rests in different dimensions. But the Court has chosen to make them seem as having a common denominator ('absurdity'). We may also argue that the tool the Court uses is the allusion not only to the absurd worlds but also to their number, as if they are saying that there is not just one author of fiction that shows the absurdity to which certain kind of interpretation of law may lead, but several of them; and that they are all showing things to society by means of literary works that created images of absurd worlds, thus revealing certain truths about human life. Since these authors might feature on the high school curriculum, even though the reader may not have read them in full, he or she will know of them and probably has the association absurd world–Beckett/Kafka/Orwell/Ionesco.[14] I suggest that this particular usage fails to establish communion with those who are in fact truly familiar with the work of the authors listed. However, we may not rule out the possibility that the mere mention of the list of depictions of certain absurdity may be capable of a certain symbolic function for those who do not have the knowledge or familiarity of the dimension of 'absurdity' involved in the worlds of the listed authors (compare the conclusions of Clark and Carlson above).[15]

> The unconditional application of the provision of § 135 of the code of civil procedure as regards the scope of application of the statute of extra-judicial rehabilitations make the first of the effects of Constitutional Court's decision I. ÚS 28/94 inapplicable (it is a more sophisticated version of a known principle contained in the well-known novel by Joseph Heller, Catch 22). (III. ÚS 150/99)[16]

Another example of the same principle as discussed above (albeit not called an 'absurd world') may be observed in another majority opinion of a decision of the Czech Constitutional Court. In the excerpt above the Court chooses to refer to Joseph Heller and his novel *Catch 22*. This decision was partially dealing with the matter of literal interpretation of the contested provisions and their teleological (purposive) interpretations. The Court argued that if the provision were applied literally and 'unconditionally', the result would be that of a Catch 22. This particular reference is used slightly more organically than the ones referred to above.

---

[14] However, my own first reaction was: this is a reduction! These worlds are not that similar in their absurdity for the Court to make this connection.

[15] On a slightly different note, we may argue that the Constitutional Court has tried to envision a comprehensive concept of absurdity, one encompassing all the dimensions of absurdity depicted by the listed works of fiction.

[16] Decision of the Constitutional Court of the Czech Republic of 20 January 2000 no III. ÚS 150/99.

The Court does not create a long list of sources but chooses to refer to just one novel, one that also features on the high school reading curriculum. This reference may also be understood as an illustration of the absurdity of a certain paradoxical situation, this time one that not only has to do with the literary work itself, but that has also been 'domesticated' as an idiom. 'It's a Catch 22' is a saying referring to the 'paradoxical situation from which an individual cannot escape because of contradictory rules',[17] so common that it has a dedicated Wikipedia page.

We may clearly understand this instance of reference to extra-legal sources as a figure of communion: the Court is using a commonplace phrase as well as a reference to the novel from which the phrase stems. Even if the audience did not know or had not read the novel itself, it is likely that they know the idiomatic phrase and understand its meaning.

Moreover, the Court does not show that the nonsensical situation that is a result of certain formalistic reading ('unconditional application') of the provision in question is not something that would be perceived as nonsensical only in terms of the law, but is a matter of widely understood principle, one that has been depicted (and ridiculed) by Joseph Heller in his novel.

Example 2: a basic principle (seemingly) taken out of an extra-legal source

> The Czech criminal procedure is traditionally not built on the principle that it would be someone's right to be subjected to a criminal procedure (Čapek, K. Povídky z druhé kapsy. Soud pana Havleny). (II. ÚS 1311/13)[18]

This instance of referring to extra-legal sources differs from the previous two in form: it resembles a typical academic reference to a source, one that would suggest that the whole content of the sentence is taken out of the bracketed source.

In this decision, the Constitutional Court dealt with a criminal case; one of its partial issues was linked to the question of whether there is a right to be subjected to criminal procedure in certain cases. When pointing out the fact that this is not the case in the Czech legal system, the court provided a nearly full-source reference to a short story by Karel Čapek, one of the best-known twentieth-century Czech writers, to support a legal claim about the basic principles of the legal system. The peculiarity of the form of this reference suggests that the legal principle itself (that 'the Czech criminal procedure is traditionally not built on the principle that it would be someone's right to be subjected to a criminal procedure') comes from a short story. If we disregard the fact that it is a rather strange conclusion, we may also hypothesise that the court attempted to use a figure of communion, trying to show that a legal principle is not something detached from non-legal realities, but in fact the theme of a short story written by someone as well-known as Čapek.

---

[17] Catch 22. Wikipedia, <https://en.wikipedia.org/wiki/Catch-22_(logic)> accessed 27 April 2018.
[18] Decision of the Constitutional Court of the Czech Republic of 30 May 2013 no II. ÚS 1311/13.

Example 3: access to law as told by Kafka

'... there are many who say the story doesn't give anyone the right to judge the doorkeeper. However he [sic] might seem to us he is still in the service of the law, so he belongs to the law, so he's beyond what man has a right to judge. In this case we can't believe the doorkeeper is the man's subordinate. Even if he has to stay at the entrance into the law his service makes him incomparably more than if he lived freely in the world. The man has come to the law for the first time and the doorkeeper is already there. He's been given his position by the law, to doubt his worth would be to doubt the law.'

'I can't say I'm in complete agreement with this view,' said K. shaking his head, 'as if you accept it you'll have to accept that everything said by the doorkeeper is true. But you've already explained very fully that that's not possible.' 'No,' said the priest, 'you don't need to accept everything as true, you only have to accept it as necessary.' 'Depressing view,' said K. 'The lie made into the rule of the world.' (Kafka, F. *Proces*. Lidové noviny, 1997, str. 169).[19] (Pl. ÚS 5/16 – dissenting opinion)

The decision of the Constitutional Court of the Czech Republic Pl. ÚS 5/16 dealt with a case of a person whose request for Czech citizenship was denied based on classified information that hinted at the possible dangers this person's presence might mean for state security. The claimant argued that it could not be in accordance with the Constitution for the decision-making to be based on information that had not been accessible to the claimant himself, since it was part of a confidential opinion given by the police. The claimant also suggested that the law this mechanism (confidential, undisclosed opinion given as evidence in court) is based on should be repealed as unconstitutional. The Court denied the claim. In one of the dissenting opinions, the judge discussed various matters that restrain individuals in accessing justice and in that context quoted a lengthy passage from Franz Kafka's *The Trial* that deals with the doorkeeper of the law. In this case, this reference is also accompanied by the full citation of the source, including the publisher and page number.

First of all, this reference is not a part of the majority opinion, which in the context of Czech decision-making means that it has practically zero normative value.[20] This fact alone means that the form and method of dissenting is not given as strictly as in the majority opinions (Kühn 2002; Smejkalová 2010), which allows for greater creativity on the part of the dissenting judges. This may be in part why the references to literary fiction appear more often in dissents (Klusoňová 2016: 162).

This reference is one of the longest references to a literary work there is within the Czech Constitutional Court case law. The long quotation itself may be understood as helpful: the dissenting judge chooses not only to refer to Kafka's trial or to a specific notion within it, but also refers to a specific image of the doorkeeper, whose job is to guard the entrance to the law. The reference here is undeniably

---

[19] Decision of the Constitutional Court of the Czech Republic of 11 October 2016 no Pl.ÚS 5/16.
[20] I use the concept of normative value here as understood by Peczenik (1997: 461–79).

different from those analysed above. We may say that it does not serve as a hypertext to a narrative placed outside the judicial decision, but through the lengthy quotation, it becomes part of the text of the decision itself.

Franz Kafka, too, belongs among the authors that would be at least mentioned in high school literature classes, but the judge has chosen not to rely on the audience to have read it, instead providing them with the quotation itself.[21]

In this particular case, the familiarity dimension ceases to be important and the reference's success as a special kind of figure of communion rests in actual understanding of the image communicated by the quoted excerpt and, naturally, the acceptability of the presence of such a lengthy extra-legal quotation in a legal text. As pointed out above, since this is a dissenting opinion, the formal rules that guide the style of justification of judicial decisions are somewhat loosened and the acceptability bar may be seen as being much lower.

> Who does have a more profound relationship to the thing, morally?
> The owner of a castle, whose family had lived there (with a brief interruption in the totalitarian times) since the 13th century generation after generation, or a warden from the time when the castle was forcibly the state's who brought his future wife to the count's bed?
> To those to whom these bits and pieces would not be enough to vividly picture those times I recommend a great novel Wirth vs. the state by a writer and barrister from Olomouc, Petr Ritter. (II. ÚS 773/07 – dissenting opinion)[22]

This particular instance of reference to fiction goes a bit further but is based on the matter of exemplarity. The judge tries to paint a picture of an understandable moral dilemma, one that would be accessible even to such a reader that cultivates a certain aversion to nobility and to returning old castles and other property to (previously) noble families (and such readers are abundant in the Czech Republic).[23] The reference is used here simply as a source of further explanation (and depiction) of this dilemma.

The author mentioned is not a well-known writer. But the argument the judge makes in this particular instance has a slightly different flavour from the previous ones. The judge's argument is based on painting a vivid picture of a complex and emotional situation and his reference to a novel (even though it is not a well-known novel) is an attempt to say that this particular emotional picture may

---

[21] A slightly distorted version of the lengthy quotation may be Constitutional Court judge Stanislav Balík's dissenting opinion in the Constitutional Court's decision no Pl. ÚS 43/13. Practically as an aside, he directly says that a full sentence taken from a fictional book is to be an inherent part of his dissenting opinion. '*Fulltextová odpověď* (srov. WERICH, Jan. Fimfárum. Praha: Albatros, 1997, s. 102) budiž nedílnou součástí tohoto odlišného stanoviska . . .' ('Let the full-text answer (cf. WERICH, Jan. Fimfárum. Prague: Albatros, 1997, p. 102) be an inherent part of this dissenting opinion . . .').

[22] Decision of the Constitutional Court of the Czech Republic of 23 August 2012 no II. ÚS 773/07.

[23] Nobility titles in the Czech Republic have been banned by law since 1918 (statute 61/1918 Sb. z. a n.) even though people from noble families are still referred to by their titles.

be also found elsewhere. This reference has the value of a hypertext: the moral dilemma the court faces in its decision-making is a moral dilemma known to society and not limited to legal considerations.

It follows from what has been said that a reference may be harmful in argumentation and fail to establish communion between the speaker and his or her audience if the argument the speaker is using is not acceptable in the argumentative situation (there is a lack of acceptance that to refer to extra-legal literature is something that can be done in law) and when the literary work referred to in the reference is not known to the audience, hence the audience fails to understand the message intended by the speaker.

While the dimension of acceptability is in essence a systemic issue (and one that may not be already fully established in the discourse of Czech judicial argumentation and may still be considered eccentric), the dimension of understanding the reference (either as a symbol carrying a message of law and legal discourse that opens up to extra-legal realities, or as a matter of knowing the narrative the reference points at) is tied to the particular audience of the judicial decision.

The chosen reference must have a communicative value in respect to the intended audience. Should it fail to achieve this quality, the communicative potential of the reference would not only be lost, but in consequence, the whole argumentation of the court would be harmed because the court failed to establish and maintain the necessary communion.

A reference may, therefore, be harmful when the judge misjudges his or her audience and any attempt to use extra-legal narratives for extra argumentative help results in:

- referring to a generally unknown narrative (book, author);
- referring to a narrative (book, author) that does not belong to an acceptable canon (but at the same time, we may theorise that referring to a narrative that belongs to a canon – 'something we had to read in high school and it was so boring' – may be harmful as well);
- an imprecise and therefore open and vague reference, since it may communicate an unintended meaning (symbols are vague and open as regards their final meaning (Eco 1984: 130) and so is imaginative writing).

6. CONCLUSION

References to extra-legal sources, such as literary fiction, are a matter of a recognised pattern. As such their main purpose is to show that the pattern is not something that would be essentially native to law only and that the judicial decision (supported, among others, by a reference to the particular work of literary fiction) belongs within the wider and accepted social and cultural space shared by the speaker and the audience.

Grounding a legal narrative into a widely understood extra-legal narrative may make law more acceptable to the audience but only on two conditions:

the reference must be an acceptable part of the legal discourse and it must be understandable/intelligible to its audience. Any metaphor, allusion or example is capable of providing this socio-cultural grounding (and has a persuasive value) only if the audience is able to make the link, since '[f]ictions . . . preach to the converted alone . . . they are powerless (by themselves) to shake our deeply held convictions' (Landy 2012: 28).

Trying to reach communion between judge and audience is a matter of understanding who that audience is, to what extent are they prepared to accept references to extra-legal sources in judicial decisions and whether or not the reference is made in an understandable manner. While showing that legal problems are capable of being illustrated by extra-legal narratives the judge chooses to communicate in a code that may be understood not only by the legally educated audience but also by laypeople. A possible lack of understanding of what the extra-legal reference should communicate may be bridged if the mere presence of such a reference carries with it a recognisable symbolic value. While it seems that we are far from being able to claim that extra-legal references in Czech judicial decisions are widely accepted as more than a curiosity, the mere presence of such argumentative devices in rationales of judicial decisions may be understood as such a symbolic step towards the opening up of the judicial discourse.

Bibliography

Bhatia, V. K. (1983), 'Simplification v. Easification – The Case of Legal Texts', 4 *Applied Linguistics*, 42–54.
Cao, D. (2007), *Translating Law*. Clevedon: Multilingual Matters.
Chen, J. (1995), 'Law as a Species of Language Acquisition', 73(3) *Washington University Law Review*, 1263–309.
Clark, H. H. and T. B. Carlson (1982), 'Hearers and Speech Acts', 58 *Language*, 332 ff.
Cover, R. M. (1983), 'The Supreme Court, 1982 Term – Foreword: Nomos and Narrative', *Faculty Scholarship Series. Paper 2705*, <www.depauw.edu/site/humanimalia/issue%2017/pdfs/The%20Supreme%20Court%201982%20Term%20--%20Foreword_%20Nomos%20and%20Narrative.pdf> accessed 1 September 2018.
David, R. and J. E. C. Brierley (1978), *Major Legal Systems in the World Today. An Introduction to the Comparative Study of Law*, London: Stevens & Sons.
Del Mar, M. (2013), 'Exemplarity and Narrativity in the Common law Tradition', 25(3) *Law and Literature*, 390–427.
DiMatteo, L. (2013), 'Contract Stories: Importance of the Contextual Approach to Law', 88 *Wash. L. Rev.*, 1287–322.
Eco, U. (1981). *The Role of the Reader: Explorations in the Semiotics of Texts*, Bloomington, IN: Indiana University Press.
Eco, U. (1984), *Semiotics and The Philosophy of Language*, Bloomington, IN: Indiana University Press.

Eco, U. (2009), *Teorie sémiotiky* (trans. Marek Sedlá ek), Praha: Argo.
Feldman, M. S. and J. G. March (1981), 'Information in Organizations as Symbol and Signal', 26(2) *Administrative Science Quarterly*, 171–86.
Gadbin-George, G. (2013), 'Literary References in United Kingdom Common Law Judgments', 14 GRAAT *Anglophone Studies Law and Literature*, 79–95, <http://www.graat.fr/4gadbin.pdf> accessed 6 September 2018.
Garret, M. L. (2010), 'Trademarks as a System of Signs: A Semiotic Look at Trademark Law', 23 *International Journal for the Semiotics of Law*, 61–75.
Gordon, R. (2013), 'Institutionalizing Exemplary Narratives: Stories as Models for and Movers of Law', 25(3) *Law and Literature*, 337–65.
Grice, P. (1991), *Studies in the Way of Words*, Cambridge, MA: Harvard University Press.
Harris, P. (1985), 'Difficult Cases and the Display of Authority', 1(1) *Journal of Law, Economics, and Organization*, 209–21.
Hart, H. L. A. (2004), *Pojem práva* (trans. Petr Fantys), Praha: Prostor.
Harvánek, J. et al. (2013), *Právní teorie*, Plzeň: Vydavatelství a nakladatelství Aleš Čeněk.
Jackson, B. (1988), *Law, Fact and Narrative Coherence*, Liverpool: Deborah Charles.
Kelsen, H. (1945), *General Theory of Law and State* (trans. Anders Wedberg), Cambridge, MA: Harvard University Press.
Klusoňová, M. (2015), 'Communitas, Communion and the Judicial Reasoning', in M. Klusoňová, M. Malaník, M. Stachoňová and M. Škop (eds), *Argumentation 2015: International Conference on Alternative Methods of Argumentation in Law*, Brno: Masaryk University, 103–20.
Klusoňová, M. (2016), 'Hnutí právo a literatura koncem 20. a na počátku 21. století', PhD thesis, Faculty of Law, Masaryk University, <https://is.muni.cz/auth/th/i6ybp/Disertace_Marketa_Klusonova.pdf> accessed 6 September 2018.
Kühn, Z. (2002), *Aplikace práva ve složitých případech. K úloze právních principů v judicature*, Praha: Karolinum.
Landy, J. (2012), *How to Do Things with Fictions*, Oxford: Oxford University Press.
Lasser, M. de S. O.-l'E. (1994–5), 'Judicial (Self-)Portraits: Judicial Discourse in the French Legal System', 104 *Yale Law Journal*, 1325–410.
Lasser, M. de S. O.-l'E. (1997–8), '"Lit. Theory" put to the Test: A Comparative Literary Analysis of American Judicial Tests and French Judicial Discourse', 111 *Harvard Law Review*, 689–770.
MacCormick, N. and R. S. Summers (eds) (1997), *Interpreting Precedents. A Comparative Study*, Aldershot: Dartmouth.
Mellinkoff, D. (1963), *The Language of the Law*, Eugene, OR: Resource Publications.
Peczenik, A. (1997), 'The Binding Force of Precedent', in N. MacCormick and R. S. Summers (eds), *Interpreting Precedents. A Comparative Study*, Aldershot: Dartmouth, 461–79.

Perelman, C. and L. Olbrechts-Tyteca (2008), *The New Rhetoric: a Treatise on Argumentation* (trans. J. Wilkinson and P. Weaver), Notre Dame, IN: University of Notre Dame Press.

Plantin, C. (2009), 'A Place for Figures of Speech in Argumentation Theory', 23 *Argumentation*, 325–37.

Schauer, F. (2011), 'On the Open Texture of Law', <https://ssrn.com/abstract=1926855> or <http://dx.doi.org/10.2139/ssrn.1926855> accessed 1 September 2018.

Schmid, W. (2015), 'Implied Reader', in P. Hühn, J. Pier, W. Schmid and J. Schönert (eds), *The Living Handbook of Narratology*, Hamburg: Hamburg University Press, <www.lhn.uni-hamburg.de/article/implied-reader> accessed 26 September 2018.

Simon-Shoshan, M. (2013), '"People Talking Without Speaking": The Semiotics of the Rabbinic Legal Exemplum as Reflected in Bavli Berakhot 11a', 25(3) *Law and Literature*, 446–65.

Smejkalová, T. (2010), 'Forma a diskurs soudního rozhodnutí', 3 *Jurisprudence*, 13–22.

Smejkalová, T. (2013a), 'Odkazy na soudní rozhodnutí a symbolická hodnota informace', 8 *Jurisprudence*, 3–9.

Smejkalová, T. (2013b), 'Soudnictví, jeho povaha a role v právním systému České republiky', PhD thesis, <https://is.muni.cz/auth/th/muz1d/Smejkalova_Soudnictvi.pdf> accessed 1 September 2018.

Smejkalová, T. and M. Škop (2017), 'A Concept of a Reader in Legislation Drafting', in M. Štěpáníková, M. Malaník, M. Hanych and M. Škop, *Argumentation 2017*. Brno: Masaryk University, 51–69.

Stevenson, D. (2005), 'To Whom is the Law Addressed', 21 *Yale Law and Policy Review*, 105–67.

Walton, D. N. (2006), *Fundamentals of Critical Argumentation*, Cambridge: Cambridge University Press.

White, J. B. (1985) [1973], *The Legal Imagination*, Chicago: University of Chicago Press.

Chapter 10

Law as a System of Topoi: Sources of Arguments v. Sources of Law

Anita Soboleva[1]

1. INTRODUCTION

The process of judges' reasoning has been investigated by many legal scholars, who have noted that it may depend not only on politics, history, morals, history, religion and scientific advances, but also on judges' ethical and aesthetical views or even their emotions (Feigenson 2010: 45–96; Sajo 2010: 354–84). If law is a 'system of legal rules', then judicial choice based on these factors should be considered as deviation from law, its violation, and should be rooted out from the judicial practice. At the same time, we can barely find any legal system which managed to avoid the influence of these factors on the application of law. In this chapter it is argued that the topical approach allows them to be encompassed as constituent parts of law. It is also argued that from the rhetorical perspective contemporary law can be understood as a system of arguments, drawn from different sources, rather than a closed system of legal rules, organised into a strict hierarchy.

2. 'SOURCES OF LAW' AS THE FIRST PILLAR OF POSITIVISM

The concept of the 'source of law' as a source from which rules derive their legal force and validity is crucial for the continental legal system and is one of its theoretical pillars. Though Hans Kelsen in as far back as 1934 drew attention to the metaphorical nature and therefore ambiguity of this expression, because it may signify many different things – 'two divergent methods for creating general norms', namely enactment and custom, 'the ultimate basis of the validity of the legal system' and, in addition, 'every legal norm, not only the general but also the individual legal norm' (Kelsen 1992: 67) – the concept of the 'source of law' in countries belonging to the Roman-Germanic legal family has for many years remained the starting point in explaining how the legal system is organised and the cornerstone of the legal dogma on which the description of different legal systems rests (David and Brierley 1978: 13–14, 94–8). While common law countries refer to 'authority',

---

[1] The publication was prepared within the framework of the Academic Fund Program at the National Research University Higher School of Economics (HSE) in 2018–19 (grant no. 18-01-0056) and of the Russian Academic Excellence Project '5–100'.

which is 'anything that a court could rely on in reaching its conclusion' (Statsky 1993: 51), and distinguish between primary authority, which includes statutes, regulations, executive orders, ordinances, treaties, court opinions and so on, and secondary authority, which includes 'any *nonlaw* that the court can rely on in reaching its conclusion', civil law countries refer to textual 'sources', which are organised in a well-defined hierarchy.

The Russian legal system belongs to the civil law tradition, similar to Germany, Italy and France. Civil law systems, as distinct from those of common law, do not recognise – at least on the level of their legal doctrine – court decisions as a valid source of law and 'rely solely on statues and other enacted law' (Maggs et al. 2015: 2). Defining the 'sources of law' as 'certain forms (statute, by-law, judicial precedent and so on), in which the legal rules are fixed and exist and which are used for the resolution of legal disputes' (Isakov 2015: 97), Russian legal scholars traditionally state that 'the main source of law in Russia, as in many European countries, are *normative legal acts*, that is, legal acts, establishing, changing or abolishing legal rules, which are aimed at regulating social relations' (Isakov 2015: 101; see also Babayev 2013: 341). A normative legal act may also be defined as 'a state act of a normative character' (Babayev 2013: 341). Being sources of law, normative legal acts have a number of characteristics, namely non-personalisation, repetition in application, formal certainty and guarantees of implementation secured by state coercion (Isakov 2015: 101).

Emphasis on the statutes and by-laws encourages continental legal scholars to focus on the predominant role of statues and acts issued by the executive within their competence and investigate the subordination of all these normative acts to each other in order to define the applicable law and the authoritative body in which the power to interpret this law is vested:

> For the civil law lawyer, – the commentators of the Russian law and legal system fairly note, – it is important to locate a given legal issue, body of law or legal institution within its proper category in an overall coherent theoretical organizational construct of law. This is far less important for the common-law lawyer, for whom organization of the law is viewed much more pragmatically, if it is thought about at all. (Maggs et al. 2015: 2)

Though judicial decisions, as stated above, are not officially recognised as a source of law in Russia (Boshno 2007: 72–8; Isakov 2015: 100), the judgements of the Constitutional Court and case law of the European Court of Human Rights (ECtHR) should be taken into consideration in judicial practice, whether the politicians, law implementers and legal academics like it or not, and the problem of their influence on the legal system has been discussed for more than twenty-five years. The discussion also includes the role of the decisions of the Supreme Court in concrete cases, the status of its so-called 'explanations' (*razjasnenija*) on matters of both substantive and procedural law, which it has the power to issue when the judicial practice in similar cases significantly varies from one court to another, the place of the 'rulings' (*postanovlenija*) of the Plenum (full bench) of the Supreme Court and, finally, the precedential character of the judgments of the Constitutional Court and the ECtHR (Maggs 2015: 25; Koroteev 2013: 5–6; Shapiro 1981: 143–50; Pomeranz and Gutbrod 2012: 4–9; Maggs 2002: 479–500).

At the same time, many scholars agree that statutes and administrative regulations 'have come to play an ever increasing role in common law systems' (Maggs et al. 2015: 2) and have reached the conclusion that two types of legal systems are moving towards each other in a globalising world. However, the dispute itself continues to spin around the sources of law and their subordination to each other, which makes this dispute positivist by nature, because all authors seem to admit that the hierarchy of authorities exist and must be strictly followed by courts in their decision-making.

As distinct from the well-established positivist approach to 'sources' or 'authorities', from which law emanates, I suggest looking at law from the rhetorical perspective. From this angle, the sources of arguments are the same for common law and civil law countries, though their frequency and especially their hierarchy is different in legal cultures and differs within the same country in different periods of its historical and political development. Later in this chapter I will adduce examples of when judges justify their choices by resorting not to authorities of higher hierarchy, but to arguments which may seem stronger to them than other arguments. They may also take into account many other considerations which lie outside the well-defined system of 'sources', routinely provided in academic works and textbooks for law students.

3. HIERARCHY OF SOURCES AS THE SECOND PILLAR OF POSITIVISM

Positivism represents law as a logically closed and consistent system, in which every case can be subsumed under a given legal rule, which, in its turn, is subordinate to other rules, built into the unified hierarchy. Legal science in countries with a civil law tradition respectfully tries to respond to challenges of legal practice by attempting to create a system which would explain the process of judicial decision-making through successive steps of logical implications, descending from upper-level rules, such as articles of constitutions, to lower-level rules, such as provisions of municipal legal acts and instructions issued by government agencies. When written rules (or provisions of 'legal normative acts') come into conflict with each other, a law-applying agent must know which rule should have a supreme force.

When the rules belong to conflicting normative acts of the same hierarchical level, the legal doctrine suggests resorting to principles *lex specialis derogat generali* and *lex posterior derogat priori*. However, it remains silent on what to do if we have a conflict of interpretations which are equally applicable. In such cases a value judgment is required. Positivism cannot answer the question of why certain judges prefer a literal interpretation, while others in similar cases resort to the purpose of the act or the intent of the drafters, or why judges in different jurisdictions using the same or similar rules in analogous cases decide them differently. For instance, the doctrine of hierarchy of sources cannot explain why different countries with similar constitutional provisions and under the same international standards resolve differently the conflicts between the right to life and the right to liberty and bodily integrity in abortion cases, between freedom of expression and the right to privacy in freedom of speech cases, between the right to secrecy of communications and concerns of state security, or between the rights of gay people to freedom of assembly and non-discrimination versus the right of believers to have their religious feelings protected.

It is clear, that the answers to these questions lie outside the realm of law understood as a 'model of rules'. Judicial decisions in the abovementioned cases cannot be considered as necessary conclusions drawn by formal logic from existing legal provisions, because they are a result of a 'balancing exercise' (as the ECtHR calls the process of weighing up the conflicting rights and interests)[2] that may have different outcomes even in countries belonging to the same legal system. In trying to decide whether one right should be protected at the expense of the other, judges put into a hierarchy different values rather than different sources of law. The same happens when a case involves a conflict of interpretations – here, again, a judicial choice becomes a value choice. The hierarchy of values can sometimes be traceable from the precedents and legal doctrines, but sometimes judges have to create it by themselves, being guided by views and propositions 'which appear to be true to all, or to most, or to the wise, and again, of the wise, either to all or to the most, or to the best known or to the most respected' (Aristotle, *Topica*, I, 1, 5 3).

In addition, as Cern et al. fairly stated, nowadays law created by the Council of Europe, the law of the European Union and the domestic law of EU Member States are united in a 'multicentric system', and 'though the hierarchy of sources of law, the issues of validity, and the hierarchy of the authorities that apply the law continue to play a crucial role', this system employs different logic, and 'within a single legal order, we deal with the occurrence of many equivalent sources of law that do not form a hierarchical system (the hierarchy of norms)' (Cern et al. 2012: 458).

Earlier, Max Rheinstein responded to the understanding of law as a closed and consistent system by saying that 'clearly such a system could never be found, and the practice of the courts, attorneys, and legislators could not take too seriously that predominance which was claimed for it' (Rheinstein 1954: 598). He calls the system, dominant in Germany, Italy and generally in Europe, 'conceptual jurisprudence' and compares it with the 'topical method', proposed by Vieweg, emphasising that 'by comparing solutions of a common problem, and of the mental ways in which the solution is found, it is possible to develop a "functional" method of comparative law', which reveals 'the necessity in legal thought to start from the problem rather than from the rule of law' (1954: 598).

---

[2] See, for example, European Court of Human Rights, *von Hannover v. Germany* (no. 2), applications nos 40660/08 and 60641/08, judgement [Grand Chamber] of 7 February 2012, § 29.

A problem-oriented approach to law fits well with the analysis of law as a system of *topoi*: if law is 'what has happened or what will happen on concrete cases' (Frank 2009: 297), then we need to shift our research interests from sources of rules to sources, from which arguments, which define what will happen in a case, are drawn.

4. TOPICS AS SOURCES OF ARGUMENTS

The word *topoi* (pl. of *topos*) in ancient Greek literally means 'places', 'seats'. In rhetoric it is used to denote places where arguments can be found. Topics (*topica*) as a system was devised by the classical rhetoricians for a pragmatic purpose: 'to help one find something to say on any given subject' (Corbett and Connors 1999: 32). In contemporary doctrine *topoi* are also interpreted as headings under which arguments can be classified (Durham 1993: xiii).

Aristotle defined the purpose of topics thus: 'to discover a method by which we shall be able to reason from generally accepted opinions about any problem set before us and shall ourselves, when sustaining an argument, avoid saying anything self-contradictory' (Aristotle, *Topica* I, 4, 100 a 18). This method, or 'line of inquiry', presupposes that we must grasp 'to how many and to what kind of objects our arguments are directed and on what bases they rest, and how we are to be well provided with these' (Aristotle, *Topica* I, 4, 101 b 10).

Cicero, in his turn, used the topical approach as a way to find arguments 'by a rational system without wandering about' (Cicero, *Topica* I, 2). He wrote:

> It is easy to find things that are hidden if the hiding place is pointed out and marked; similarly, if we wish to track down some argument we ought to know the places or topics: for that is the name given by Aristotle to the 'regions', as it were, from which arguments are drawn. (Cicero, *Topica*, I, 6–8)

The understanding of rhetorical *topica* as a methodology for problem-solving in law was suggested by Theodor Viehweg. In his view, 'legal prudence can be understood as a permanent discussion of problems', and 'problems elicit the recurring search for *topoi* that can serve as solutions' (Viehweg 1993: 89).

W. Cole Durham, Jr. shows that the topical approach may be extended even beyond the process of inventing arguments and attaining optimal solutions to legal problems. He argues, that 'Viehweg's thesis can be understood as a claim that the ideal of deductive systematization constitutes a misguided objective for the legal systems' and that if complete systematisation of law as a deductive system could ever be attained, 'the resulting mechanical jurisprudence would inevitably be inflexible and insufficiently humane', because 'questions of justice cannot be reduced to deductive algorithms that can be processed by computers' (Durham 1993: xvi). Durham agrees with Viehweg's claims that the topical mode of intellectuality 'cannot be deductively presented in its totality' (1993: xxxvii), and proceeds with the idea that legal materials in general need to be systematised in a variety of ways. He shares Viehweg's position that law does have system and structure, but notes that this structure is not axiomatic and deductive, because many legislative acts tend to be passed as ad hoc responses to current problems with minimal regard for their systematic coherence (1993: xxiv). Though Durham writes about the role of *topoi* in common law rather than in civilian systems, his remarks are useful for our concept of understanding contemporary law as a system of *topoi* in general, because judicial activism and the reliance of judges on the weight of arguments rather than on the weight of sources may be found in different jurisdictions.

Julius Stone agrees that *topoi* affect the process of good judgment and calls reasoning from *topoi* 'an open (though oriented) universe of discourse' (Stone 1964: 331). He notes that common law legal order falls short of being an axiomatic system, and that 'even when decisions are not warranted as necessary conclusions drawn by formal logic from existing legal propositions, they might nevertheless be justifiable in terms of the wider relations of law both to justice and social facts' (1964: 331). Thus, as distinct from positivist approach, rhetorical *topica* represents a kind of reasoning to which moral, social and political problems may prove more tractable. It helps to find arguments of a 'non-stringent but still trustworthy quality' (1964: 331). Such arguments are based on acceptance (by men generally, or by those most wise and illustrious – here Stone refers to Aristotle) and suggest evaluations.

The evaluative nature of *topoi* was especially important for Haïm Perelman and Lucie Olbrechts-Tyteca, who developed the classical approach by applying the notion of *topoi* (or *loci* in Latin) to 'premises of a very general nature that can serve as the bases for values and hierarchies' (Perelman and Olbrechts-Tyteca 1969: 83–4). Understood as a value, each *topos*, in their view, can be confronted with another one. To proceed with this line of argument, we can presume that any society can be characterised by the intensity of its adherence to one of these confronting values, and this adherence would influence the judicial choice.

A topical approach to the law and legal systems was also acknowledged by Joseph Esser, who suggested classifying legal orders as logically closed ('axiom-orientated') or logically open ('rhetoric- (or *topoi*-) orientated') (Esser 1956: 221). Ilmar Tammelo, commenting on Esser's treatise, notes that 'the Roman legal system and the common law legal systems *approximate* to the type of "logically open systems" whereas the Continental legal systems *approximate* to "logically closed systems" in Esser's sense' (Tammelo 1959: 187), but admits that 'rhetorical orientation' is never completely absent in any legal system. Similarly, some 'axiomatic orientation' may also be present in 'logically open' legal orders.

Petros A. Gemtos, in search of interdisciplinary cooperation between social sciences, stresses that 'the scientific status of jurisprudence is now questioned . . . because of its normative structure' (Gemtos 1989: 245) and finds new beginnings in the discussion of juristic methodological problems within the framework of the hermeneutic-topical approach. He pays tribute to Esser, who saw 'the juristic topoi as transformation canals of non-juristic values and behavioral standards into legal ones' (1989: 245), and praises *topica* exactly because 'it questions the old conception of legal order as an hierarchical system of norms which serve distinct and concrete objectives' (1989: 246).

As we can see, there is a growing dissatisfaction with the understanding of law as a hierarchical structure. I will further argue, using examples from the Russian judicial practice, that continental legal systems today are also turning into rhetoric-orientated ones and that it is possible to single out the sources of arguments (namely, *topoi*) which are the same for common law and civil law systems and that sources of law in contemporary legal systems may be considered as constituent parts of a more general system of law. Hierarchy of sources de facto does not rule the choice of the decision, but rather participates in judicial choices on equal footing with other considerations, which also constitute parts of the system of legal *topoi*.

5. HIERARCHY OF SOURCES IN RUSSIA: BETWEEN THEORY AND PRACTICE

In countries belonging to a civil law system the hierarchy of sources of law is generally the same – the serious disputes arise only with regard to the supremacy of the constitutions or the international treaties ratified by the parliaments. Leaving this question aside for a while, the hierarchy of its sources may be described as follows, starting with the higher level and then moving downward: the Constitution, statutes enacted by federal legislature, sub-statutory acts, such as presidential decrees; regulations, rules, instructions and so on, issued by the Government of the Russian Federation; legal acts issued by the ministries and other federal agencies; statutes of the subjects of federation and legal acts subordinate to them; acts of local self-government; legal acts of non-state bodies on the issues of their internal structure and activity (Maggs et al. 2015: 9–55). Then we can add such sources as decisions of the Constitutional Court, the ECtHR and the Supreme Court, although, as already stated above, their role is still under discussion.

Is this hierarchy strictly observed in practice? No. The first point of disagreement appeared with the interpretation of Part 2 of Art. 15 of the Russian Constitution: 'If an international treaty of the Russian Federation stipulates other rules than these stipulated by the statutes, the rules of the international treaty shall apply'. The Russian Constitutional Court (RCC) in the last decade has developed a doctrine of supremacy of the Constitution over international treaties and the jurisprudence of the ECtHR. Such interpretation became a result of the disagreement of the RCC with the ECtHR in three cases: *Markin*, *Anchugov and Gladkov* and *Yukos*.[3] As Maxim Timofeyev commented on the RCC decision in *Yukos*, 'it took the RCC less than two

---

[3] RCC. Case on constitutionality of the provisions of Art. 1 of the Federal Law 'On Ratification of the Convention for the Protection of Human Rights and Fundamental Freedoms and Protocols thereto', Judgment of 14 July 2015 no. 21-P/2015; ECtHR. *Markin v. Russia*, no. 30078/06, Grand Chamber judgment of 22 March 2012; RCC. *Markin (2)*. Judgment of 6 December 2013 no. 27-P; RCC. Judgment of 19 April 2016 no. 12-P/2016 in the case concerning the resolution of the question of the possibility to execute in accordance with the Constitution of the Russian Federation the Judgment of the European Court of Human Rights of 4 July 2013 in the case of *Anchugov and Gladkov v. Russia* in connection with the request of the Ministry of Justice of the Russian Federation; ECtHR. *OAO Neftyanaya KompaniyaYukos v. Russia*. Judgment of 20 September 2011; RCC. *Yukos*. Judgment of 19 January 2017.

years and only three judgements' to descend to this point (Timofeyev 2017). If in *Markin* (about parental leave for military servicemen) the RCC tried to harmonise both sources, in *Anchugov and Gladkov* (about prisoners' right to vote) this court already directly underlined the 'supremacy and supreme legal force of the Constitution of the Russian Federation in Russia's legal system (including in relation to international treaties of the Russian Federation)'.[4] In *Yukos* the RCC ruled that the respective ECtHR judgment about payment of €1,866,104,634 to the company's shareholders in respect of pecuniary damage could not be executed because it would violate the Constitution. This conclusion was based upon the argument that the statute which allowed retrospective calculation of taxes beyond the three-year term had been previously found constitutional by the RCC. De facto, the RCC formulated the position that the statute, which was found constitutional in the process of constitutional review, becomes equal in the hierarchy of sources to the Constitution itself. Constitutionality of this statute was in turn justified by appeals to the historical context of the late 1990s, characterised by uncertainty of tax legislation and judicial practice, which had had to be corrected later by the state through the introduction of special measures aimed at filling the budget in order for the government to be able to implement its social welfare policies. Thus, the RCC gave way to policy argument which overweighted both the calls to the supremacy of international law with the case law of the ECtHR and the calls to literal construction of the Tax Code. It appears that the judges of the RCC also rejected the previously widely shared view on the Constitution as 'a statute' (though the statute of the supreme force, or 'basic law'). The academic dispute mainly revolved around the questions of sovereignty of the domestic legal system and the role of the RCC as a supreme arbiter, but for us it has another important dimension: it shows how the courts can easily play with the hierarchy of sources if the decision which would follow as a strict implication from the existing sources is not the one they would like to reach.

Another example is the dispute about the supremacy and direct force of the Constitution, which is declared in Part 1 of Art. 15. The Code of Arbitrazh Procedure in its list of applicable laws to which judges must refer in the motivation part of judicial decisions (according to Art. 170 of this Code) does not mention the Constitution. It includes only 'statutes and other normative legal acts, by which the Court was guided while making its decision', though in practice the courts in commercial cases also refer to the Constitution and the interpretation of its provisions provided by the RCC. However, the ordinary courts cannot apply the Constitution directly and must refer the issue to the Constitutional Court, if they reveal the contradiction between the statutory law and the Constitutional provisions (Ryakhovskaya 2008: 127–31; Yershov 1998: 2–4). Such an approach was formulated and promoted by the RCC itself,[5] and the Supreme Court after some struggle for its own power finally had to accept this point of view.[6]

---

[4] RCC. *Anchugov and Gladkov v. Russia*. Judgment of 19 April 2016 no. 12-P/2016.
[5] RCC. *Case on interpretation of certain provisions of Articles 125, 126 and 127 of the Constitution of the Russian Federation*. Judgment of 16 June 1998 no. 19-P.
[6] See details in Sagandykov and Popov (2016: 85–90).

One more example of the illusory nature of the hierarchy of sources is the application by the administrative bodies and courts in *Shimovolos* of the statutory provisions and unpublished internal orders of the Ministry of the Interior.[7] The applicant was searched several times by police while he was travelling by train from Nizhniy Novgorod to Samara, because his name was registered in the Surveillance Database under the heading of 'Human Rights Activists'. One of the Interior Departments of Transport sent a telex to the local branches informing them that protest rallies by several opposition organisations were planned for 18 May 2007, that all possible participants travelling to Samara had to be detected and stopped, and that police had to dissuade them from going there. In trying to justify the necessity of the police measures taken, the Russian Government submitted to the ECtHR copies of these unpublished orders. These documents directed, in particular, that software databases with codenames 'Search-Highway' and 'Surveillance Control' be created and installed, and that opposition members as well as human rights activists be included in these databases, and stopped and searched whenever they travelled. The applicant claimed that on both domestic and international levels his right to privacy had been violated, and appealed the provisions of the Constitution and the European Convention on Human Rights and Fundamental Freedoms. The police and the Government, in their turn, appealed to the Administrative Offence Code, the Police Act, Operational-Search Act and unpublished orders of the Ministry, which granted them police powers to prevent terrorism and maintain public order. The appeals to constitutional and conventional values as superior in the hierarchy remained unanswered. The provision of Part 3, Art. 1 of the Constitution – 'Laws shall be officially published. Unpublished laws shall not be used. Any normative legal acts concerning human rights, freedoms and duties of man and citizen may not be used, if they are not officially published for general knowledge' – was also ignored.[8]

The judicial practice also does not have a unity of approaches towards the interrelations of codified acts and other federal laws. For example, the RCC, in its decision of 5 November 1999 no. 182-O, points out that there are no advantages of a Code compared to other laws, while in the decision of 29 June 2004 no. 13-P it admits the advantage of a codified act. The complex interaction of the Civil Code with other legislation is recognised as a problem by commentators of Russian law (Maggs et al. 2015: 400). The researchers draw attention to the inconsistencies between the Civil Code, which in its Art. 3 provides that all normative acts governing civil law relations must be adopted in accordance with this Code, and subsequent legislation which in many areas contradicts it. In the famous *TV-6* case the Higher Court of Arbitration had to decide if stockholders had the right to bring a suit for liquidation of the closed joint-stock company the Moscow Independent Broadcasting Corporation.[9] The 'On

---

[7] ECtHR. *Shimovolos v. Russia*. Application no. 30194/09, judgment of 21 June 2011.
[8] For examples of cases when the courts ignore the letter of law, violate the plain language rule and decide cases on political considerations, see also Soboleva (2013: 673–92).
[9] In February 2014 the Higher Court of Arbitration merged with the Supreme Court of the Russian Federation and ceased to exist as a separate judicial body.

Joint-Stock Companies' statute obligated them to do so, if at the end of the second financial year the value of the assets of the company was less than the amount of the minimum charter capital. At the same time, the Civil Code did not grant stockholders the right to bring suits for liquidation of the company. The Higher Court of Arbitration, as distinct from the court of cassation, ruled in favour of the plaintiff, who initiated the liquidation procedure. It said that the Civil Code established the general basis for liquidation of legal entities, while the 'On Joint-Stock Companies' statute provided for the rights and duties of stockholders in more detail. Legal scholars commented that '[t]his decision was much criticized, because its effect was to shut down the TV network, the last surviving independent television network in Russia' (Maggs et al. 2015: 404). In support of this thesis the fact was mentioned that the Presidium of the Higher Court of Arbitration, which decided the case on 11 January 2002, did not apply the amendment to the 'On Joint-Stock Companies' statute that had taken effect on 1 January 2002 and eliminated the right of stockholders to force liquidation.

Deviations from the established hierarchy of sources are routinely explained by judicial mistakes, lack of professional training of judges, the judiciary's lack of impartiality, political pressure, disputes about sovereignty, 'double standards' of international courts, deviations of some legal orders from democracy and the rule of law – that is, by reasons which legal scholars consider as falling out of the realm of law itself. Another possibility is to look at such cases from a rhetorical perspective and involve a topical approach. In this, topical, model political, pragmatic, religious, doctrinal, historical and other considerations will be included in the notion of 'law' – if not as its core element, then at least as peripheral parts of it.

The analysis of the judicial practice shows that the courts are quite selective in the choice of legal sources they use for justification of their decisions and do not feel obliged to give priority to the Constitution or international standards, if their understanding of the desirable outcome or internal feeling of the political situation so requires. This means that judicial practice becomes distant from the positivist doctrine which remains a dominant one in legal training. It allows one to argue that the Russian legal system (and probably civil law systems in general) in the contemporary world is based not on sources of law, but rather on sources of arguments, which have relatively equal force and are selected by judges according to their understanding of the appropriate decision.

6. LAW AS A SYSTEM OF *TOPOI*

It has already been proven that the interpretative techniques used by today's courts, belonging to two different legal traditions, are practically the same (Summers and Taruffo 1991: 461–510; Soboleva 2002). They employ maxims of law, text of legal statute (its literal construction, which may include discussion of ordinary meaning, terminological meaning and contextual meaning), former interpretation (precedent), legislative intent (usually searched for in *travaux préparatoires* or by comparison of different parts of the text), aim of the statute, best consequences, historical and social changes, judicial tests (criteria for case analysis developed by the courts themselves), legal doctrines and theories, social values, scientific data, social theories, statistics and common sense.[10] These sources of arguments can be represented as commonplaces (*topoi*) of legal reasoning. For *topica* as *ars inveniendi* statistics as a source of arguments in discrimination cases are as valid as literal construction is. All interpretations found as a result of the process of legal thinking are points of view that should be taken into account in order to make or justify a choice, which is always a value-choice, and the weight of arguments found in the process of legal reasoning is ruled by political, cultural, historical, religious and other considerations, which are not necessarily overtly disclosed in the administrative or judicial acts, but which are present behind the scenes. In law, the topical approach enables what is usually hidden and implicit to be dragged into the light and made explicit.

The view that the legal system includes more than just rules enacted by an authorised body is not a new one. Ronald Dworkin supplemented them with principles and policies (Dworkin 1967: 22–3). Joseph Esser included as constituent elements of a legal system legal maxims, general clauses, concepts, institutions, doctrines and the rules of the legal art or craftsmanship (Esser 1956; Rheinstein 1957: 598). All these elements can also be qualified as *topoi*.

In addition to *topoi* understood as sources of arguments, there are *topoi* understood as values. If *topoi* of the first category help to find the arguments, *topoi* of the second category rule the choice. The judges assign weight to the *topoi* of the first category on the basis of the values from the second category, thus the weight of the same arguments may be different in different jurisdictions, for different judges (as rhetors) and different audiences. In many cases politics, religion, historical background, scientific advances and other relevant considerations affect the decision-making no less than the wording of formal written texts. Thus, the system of law from the topical angle looks not like an ordered hierarchy, but rather like concentric circles, when the process of legal reasoning as a search engine starts from the letter of law and moves from the text, which forms the core of these circles, to *topoi* lying outside the text, that is from the centre to peripheral circles. Politics, morals, historical experience, religion, rule of law as peripheral circles spin around the core, which consists of the normative text and its linguistic interpretations.

We foresee at least two main points of critique of the topical approach. The first claim is that it denies any systematisation of law. But, as shown above, it also represents law as a system, though this system is not hierarchically built – it is less contingent, but still works in an orderly way. The outcome of the case is predictable, if you see the background and not only the rules. If we know that politics or religion drives the choice of judges, we can predict the decision and will not be puzzled as to why a judge has rejected a 'plain meaning rule' or made a decision ignoring the Constitution or a statute of higher hierarchy. The topical approach increases predictability, and, according to Oliver Wendell Holmes, the object of legal study is 'prediction, the prediction of the incidence of the public force through the instrumentality of the courts' (Holmes 1897: 457). Law as a

---

[10] See, for more details, Soboleva (2006: 49–63).

system of *topoi* corresponds to the understanding of law as 'systematized prediction', in which rights and duties 'are nothing but prophecies' (1897: 458).

Another claim is that the topical approach disrupts the rule of law principle and allows abuse of power by the state agencies and the courts, which will not feel restricted by any rules whatsoever. The answer to this claim is that political consideration has implicitly affected the process of legal reasoning at all times and in all countries, though to different extents (Bartels and Johnston 2015: 761–94; Hauteville 2018). Ronald Dworkin directly put forward a thesis that 'interpretation in law is essentially political' (Dworkin 1982: 274) and convincingly explained why 'reliance on political theory is not a corruption of interpretation but part of what interpretation means' (1982: 277). If the rule of law, supremacy of the Constitution, individual rights and self-restriction of government as democratic values are shared by all, by the majority or by the wisest and most powerful, then individual freedoms or right to property will be duly protected. If the government pursues other goals or people value security higher than liberty, then the supremacy of the Constitution, which proclaims priority of human rights, will not work in practice.

If the theory of 'hierarchy of sources' does not work in a significant number of cases, we need to look for another theory which would explain the judicial choice and the expectations that the general public has from the legal system and legal regulation. Topical theory of law may suggest a solution: at least, '[i]n the era of pragmatism, working out mutually acceptable solutions for specific situations of disagreement is more important than setting up formal hierarchies' (Vaypan 2014: 135).

7. CONCLUSION

If we accept the definition of law as a set of *topoi*, then we need to investigate the epideictic system of law, because the line of arguments which will be chosen by the court according to the 'topical theory of law' depends on the hierarchy of societal values. If moral, political and religious values are woven deeply into the fabric of law, their subordination to each other in the concrete society and under a concrete political regime acquires importance. If judges in different societies, using the same legal text and the same hierarchy of sources, interpret the 'letter of law' differently and arrive at different conclusions, then we can conclude that they probably share the same values, but arrange them differently in the hierarchy. The Constitution and international treaties continue to be regarded as the main texts and 'the premises of a very general nature that can serve as bases for values and hierarchies' (Perelman and Olbrechts-Tyteca 1969: 83–4), but adherence to the values proclaimed in them may differ. Consequently, the judicial decisions and interpretations become more predictable, even if they do not comply with the positivist 'hierarchy of sources'.

The value-oriented approach to *topoi* enables the topical doctrine to be used as a methodology of research of legal reasoning and decision-making in law.

To sum up, the topical approach to law and legal prudence, by dealing with 'preferable' and 'acceptable', 'less acceptable' or 'non acceptable', helps to assess and explain judicial choices of arguments based on adherence of the judges and their audience to certain values and hierarchies. We can also state with a high degree of certainty that, in addition to analytical jurisprudence, ethical jurisprudence and sociological jurisprudence we can speak of topical jurisprudence as a separate branch of legal studies.

Bibliography

Aristotle, *Topica*, in *The Basic Works of Aristotle* (1941), ed. R. McKeon, New York: Random House.

Babayev, V. K. (ed.) (2013), *Obshhaja teorija prava* [The General Theory of Law], Moscow: Urait (in Russian).

Bartels, B. L. and C. D. Johnston (2015), 'Lawyers' Perceptions of the U.S. Supreme Courts: Is the Court a "Political" Institution?', 19 *Law & Society Review*, 761–94.

Boshno, S. V. (2007), 'Precedent, zakon i doktrina (opyt sociologicheskogo issledovanija)' [Precedent, Statute and Legal Doctrine (Experience of Socio-Legal Study)], 4 *Gosudarstvo i Pravo*, 72–8 (in Russian).

Cern, K. M., P. W. Juchacz and B. Wojciechowski (2012), 'Whose Reason or Reasons Speak Through the Constitution? Introduction to the Problematics', 25(4) *International Journal for the Semiotics of Law*, 455–63.

Cicero, *Topica*, in H. M. Hubbell (trans.) (1976), *Cicero. On Invention. The Best Kind of Orator. Topics*, Loeb Classical Library Edition, Cambridge, MA: Harvard University Press.

Corbett, E. P. J. and R. J. Connors (1999), *Classical Rhetoric for the Modern Student*, New York and Oxford: Oxford University Press.

David, R. and J. E. C. Brierley (1978), *Major Legal Systems in the World Today: An Introduction to the Comparative Study of Law*, 2nd edn, New York: The Free Press.

Durham, C. W., Jr. (1993), 'Translator's Foreword', in T. Viehweg, *Topics and Law: A Contribution to Basic Research in Law*, Frankfurt am Main: Peter Lang.

Dworkin, R. (1967), 'The Model of Rules', 35(14) *University of Chicago Law Review*, 22–3.

Dworkin, R. (1982), 'Law as Interpretation', 60 *Texas Law Review*, 527–50.

Esser, J. (1956), *Grundsatz und Norm in der richterlichen Fortbildung des Privatrechts*, Tubingen: J. C. B. Mohr (Paul Siebeck).

Feigenson, N. (2010), 'Emotional Influences on Judgments of Legal Blame: How They Happen, Whether They Should, and What to Do About It', in B. H. Bornstein and R. L. Wiener (eds), *Emotion and the Law: Psychological Perspectives*, New York: Springer, 45–96.

Frank, J. (2009) [1930], *Law and the Modern Mind*, New Brunswick, NJ and London: Translation Publishers.

Gemtos P. A. (1989), 'Law and Economics: Methodological Problems in Their Interdisciplinary Cooperation', in P. Nicolacopoulos (ed.), *Greek Studies in the Philosophy and History of Science. Boston Studies in the Philosophy of Science, vol. 121*. Dordrecht: Springer.

Hauteville, J.-M. (2018), 'Why Even Germany's Federal Constitutional Court has a Politics Problem?' Handelsblatt Global, 9 November, <https://global.handelsblatt.com/politics/germany-federal-constitutional-court-judges-politics-977696> accessed 25 November 2018.

Holmes, O. W. (1897), 'The Path of the Law', 10(8) *Harvard Law Review*, 457–78.

Isakov, V. B. (ed.) (2015), *Osnovy prava: uchebnik dlja nejuridicheskih vuzov i fakul'tetov* [Basics of Law: Textbook for Non-legal Faculties], Moscow: Norma:INFRA-M (in Russian).

Kelsen, H. (1992), *Introduction to the Problems of Legal Theory* (trans. B. Paulson and S. Paulson), Oxford: Clarendon Press.

Koroteev, K. (2013), 'Are Russian Courts Capable of Creating Precedents? Overcoming Inconsistency in Case Law', 38 *Review of Central and East European Law*, 5–26.

Maggs, P. B. (2002), 'Judicial Precedent Emerges at the Supreme Court of the Russian Federation', 9(3) *Journal of East European Law*, 479–500.

Maggs, P. B., O. Schwartz, W. Burnham and G. Danilenko (2015), *Law and Legal System of the Russian Federation*, 6th edn, Huntington, NY: Juris Publishing.

Perelman, C. and L. Olbrechts-Tyteca (1969), *The New Rhetoric: A Treatise on Argumentation*, Notre Dame, IN: University of Notre Dame Press.

Pomeranz, W. and M. Gutbrod (2012), 'The Push for Precedent in Russia's Judicial System', 37(1) *Review of the Central and East European Law*, 1–30.

Rheinstein, M. (1954), 'Book Review (reviewing Theodor Viehweg, *Topik und Jurisprudenz* (1953)', 3(4) *American Journal of Comparative Law*, 597–8.

Rheinstein, M. (1957), 'Grundsatz und Norm in der richterlichen Fortbildung des Privatrechts. Tubingen: J. C. B. Mohr (Paul Siebeck). (Principle of Norm in the Judicial Development of Private Law) by Joseph Esser. Book review', 24 *University of Chicago Law Review*, 597–606.

Ryakhovskaya, T. I. (2008), 'K voprosu o roli Konstitucionnogo Suda v sfere obespecheniya pryamogo dejstviya Konstitucii Rossijskoj Federacii' [On the role of the Constitutional Court in safeguarding direct action of the Constitution of the Russian Federation], 309 *Vestnik Tomskogo gosudarstvennogo universiteta*, 127–31 (in Russian).

Sagandykov, M. S. and V. I. Popov (2016), 'The Implementation of the Principle of Direct Force of the Constitution of the Russian Federation (in the Field of Labour)', 16(1) *Bulletin of the South Ural State University*, Ser. Law, 85–90 (in Russian).

Sajo, A. (2010), 'Emotions in Constitutional Design', 8(3) *International Journal of Constitutional Law*, 354–84.

Shapiro, M. (1981), *Courts: A Comparative and Political Analysis*, Chicago: University of Chicago Press.

Soboleva, A. (2002), *Topicheskaja jurisprudencija: argumentacija i tolkovanie v prave*. [Topical jurisprudence: arguments and interpretation in law], Moscow: Dobrosvet (in Russian).

Soboleva, A. (2006), 'Topical Jurisprudence: Reconciliation of Law and Rhetoric', in A. Wagner, W. Werner and D. Cao (eds), *Interpretation, Law and the Construction of Meaning: Collected Papers on Legal Interpretation in Theory, Adjudication and Political Practice*. Heidelberg: Springer, 49–64.

Soboleva, A. (2013), 'Use and Misuse of Language in Judicial Decision-Making: Russian Experience', 26(3) *International Journal for the Semiotics of Law*, 673–92.

Statsky, W. P. (1993), *Legal Research and Writing. Some Starting Points*, 4th edn, New York: West Publishing Company.

Stone, J. (1964), *Legal System and Lawyers' Reasoning*, Stanford, CA: Stanford University Press.

Summers, R. S. and M. Taruffo (1991), 'Interpretation and Comparative Analysis', in D. N. MacCormick and R. S. Summers (eds), *Interpreting Statutes: A Comparative Study*, Aldershot: Dartmouth, 461–510.

Tammelo, I. (1959), 'On the Logical Openness of Legal Orders: A Modal Analysis of Law with Special Reference to the Logical Status of Non Liquet in International Law', 8(2) *The American Journal of Comparative Law*, 187–203.

Timofeyev, M. (2017), 'Money Makes the Court Go Round: The Russian Constitutional Court's Yukos Judgment', *Verfassungsblog on matters constitutional*, 26 January, <https://verfassungsblog.de/money-makes-the-court-go-round-the-russian-constitutional-courts-yukos-judgment> accessed 25 November 2018.

Vaypan, G. (2014), 'Acquiescence Affirmed, Its Limits Left Undefined: the Markin Judgment and the Pragmatism of the Russian Constitutional Court vis-à-vis the European Court of Human Rights', 2(3) *Russian Law Journal*, 130–40.

Viehweg, T. (1993) [1953], *Topics and Law: A Contribution to Basic Research in Law*. Frankfurt am Mein: Peter Lang.

Yershov, V. (1998), 'Pryamoe primenenie Konstitucii RF. Ot resheniya Plenuma Verhovnogo Suda RF do postanovleniya Konstitucionnogo Suda RF' [Direct application of the Constitution of the Russian Federation. From the Decision of the Plenum of the Russian Supreme Court to the Judgment of the Russian Constitutional Court], 9 *Rossijskaya yusticiya*, 2–4.

Index

Abelson, R. P., 126
Achilles, 11–12, 14
Agamben, G., 5n, 13–17, 21–2
Aguado, M. I. Peña, 87
Ando, C., 17
Ankersmit, F. R., 67
Antaki, M., 5, 10–12, 17
Aprill, E. P., 121n
Arendt, H., 10–12, 12n, 13–15, 21, 23–4
Aristotle, 14, 29, 87, 159–61
Arjona, C., 56
Atkin, Lord, 20, 21, 22

Babayev, V. K., 157
Barry, B. M., 60
Bartels, B. L., 167
Barthes, R., 15, 29–30, 32, 34, 67, 71
Baum, L., 126–7
Bauman, Z., 57, 58
Baumann, G., 51–3
Bearn, G., 89
Beckett, S., 147–8
Benesh, S. C., 120
Benhabib, S., 56n, 58
Bernardi, A., 61
Bernardini, M. G., 101n
Bhatia, V. K., 141
Bissoondath, N., 57
Bogdan, R. J., 126
Boshno, S. V., 157
Brierley, J. E. C., 139, 156
Bromberger, S., 68
Bronze, F. J., 38, 40, 42–6

Brudney, J. J., 120–1
Bubner, R., 95
Butler, J., 101–6, 103n, 106n, 108–11, 114–16

Calabresi, G., 35
Calhoun, J., 121n
Caniglia, E., 58
Cao, D., 141
Carlson, T. B., 146, 148
Carr, D., 70
Castells, M., 52
Cavarero, A., 11
Cern, K. M., 159
Cesarino, C., 107n
Chaemsaithong, K., 67
Chamberlain, E., 19–20
Charon, R., 72
Chen, J., 139
Chiassoni, P., 40
Cicero, 160
Cigarini, L., 107
Clark, H. H., 146, 148
Coke, Sir E., 2
Coleman, D. L., 57
Condello, A., 9, 14, 17, 104n
Connors, R. J., 160
Constable, M., 6n, 11
Coombe, R. J., 56
Corax, 30
Corbett, E. P. J., 160
Cover, R. M., 141
Cowan, J. K., 53
Cross, F., 120
Czarnecki, J. J., 120

David, R., 139
d'Azeglio, M., 51
de Lubac, H., 2n
De Maglie, C., 56n
de Saussure, F., 72, 87
Del Mar, M., 9, 20, 144–5
Delage, C., 5n
Dembour, M. B., 59
Deneen, P. J., 12
Derrida, J., 28, 34, 87–9, 91
Desaults-Stein, J., 6n
Devitt, M., 129
DiMatteo, L., 144
Douzinas, C., 83, 88–90
Dupieux, Q., 66
Durham, C. W., Jr, 160–1
Dworkin, R., 43, 166–7

Eco, U., 71, 144, 146, 152
Esser, J., 42–3, 161, 166

Fanciullacci, R., 104, 107, 115–16
Feigenson, N., 156
Feldman, M. S., 142, 143
Felski, R., 2n
Feltovich, P. J., 126
Ferrajoli, L., 59–60
Ferrando, S., 104
Ferrara, A., 9–10
Fikentscher, W., 42
Fischer, O., 67
Fish, S., 57f, 60
Fitzpatrick, P., 59
Forray, V., 16
Foucault, M., 14, 19, 87, 102
Frank, J., 10, 12, 160

Gadamer, H. G., 12, 16, 24, 95
Gadbin-George, G., 141n
Gagarin, M., 29, 30, 34
Garner, B. A., 120
Garret, M. L., 139
Gaudêncio, A. M., 41, 46, 97
Geertz, C., 54, 55

Gelley, A., 9–10, 15
Gemtos P. A., 161
Genette, G., 31–2, 34
Gewirtz, P., 119n
Giglioli, P. P., 53–5
Ginsburg, R. Bader, 122, 126n, 128–9
Giolo, O., 101n
Giuliani, A., 92, 94, 111–15, 112n, 115n
Gluck, A., 120
Goodrich, P., 16, 31–5, 88
Gordon, R. W., 17, 145
Gorgias, 30
Greenlee, D., 69
Grey, T. C., 40
Grice, P., 140
Gries, S. Th., 121n
Gröschner, R., 43
Guaraldo, O., 116
Gutbrod, M., 158

Habermas, J., 52
Halle, M., 68
Hamlet, 28–9, 32–3
Harris, P., 142, 143
Hart, H. L. A., 85, 127, 144n
Harvánek, J., 143n
Hauteville, J.-M., 167
Haverkamp, A., 17
Heffer, C., 68
Hegel, G. W. F., 86, 95, 102n, 116
Heidegger, M., 10, 23, 87, 93, 96
Heller, J., 148–9
Hjelmslev, L. T., 71
Hobsbawm, E. J., 51
Holmes, O. W., 166
Humphrey, M., 69

Ibbetson, D. J., 40
Ionesco, E., 147–8
Isakov, V. B., 157

Jackson, B., 93, 141
Jesus, 12, 14

Jhering, R. v., 39–40
Johnston, C. D., 167

Kafka, F., 147, 148, 150–1
Kant, I., 11–15, 23, 87, 94n
Kavanagh, T. M., 67
Kearns, T. R., 34–5, 62
Kelsen, H., 40, 112, 139, 156
Kennedy, D., 88
Kirchmeier, J. L., 121n
Klusoňová, M., 141n, 150
Koroteev, K., 158
Kriele, M., 42–3
Kristeva, J., 12
Kühn, Z., 142, 150

Landy, J., 144, 153
Langdell, C. C., 40, 84
Larenz, K., 40
Lasser, M. de S. O.-l'E., 139
Lee, T. R., 121
Leo Enos, R., 31
Leone, M., 69, 78
Lernestedt, C., 57, 60
Levinas, E., 87, 90
Libreria delle donne di Milano, 109n
Liddell, H. G., 15
Linhares, J. M., 38, 46, 84, 91–4, 96–7
Lombardi, L., 95
Lowrie, M., 9
Lüdemann, S., 9
Lyotard, J. F., 87, 89

Maalouf, A., 53
MacCormick, N., 83, 85–6, 139
MacDonald, M., 1
McLachlin, B. M., 18–22
Macmillan, Lord, 20, 22
McNeill, W. H., 51, 56n
Maffettone, S., 59
Maggs, P. B., 157–8, 162, 164–5
Manderson, D., 16, 21
Mandler, J. M., 68
March, J. G., 142, 143

Marcuse, H., 102n, 114n, 116n
Marx, K., 86, 102n
Mastromartino, F., 104
Mattozzi, A., 68
Mellinkoff, D., 141
Merry, S. E., 55, 59
Mertz, E., 127
Meyer, L.R., 10, 23–4
Miller, D., 53
Mitchell, G., 119n
Modood, T., 51, 58
Mohr, R., 56n
Monceri, F., 56
Mouritsen, C., 121
Muraro, L., 106, 107, 108, 109, 110–11
Mureinik, E., 10
Müller, M., 73

Nänny, M., 67
Neves, A. Castanheira, 38–43, 45–6, 84, 91, 94, 96, 98
Nietzsche, F., 1, 87
Nonet, P., 10
Norrie, A., 56
Nöth, W., 39, 41
Nourse, V., 127–9
Nuotio, K., 57, 61–2
Nussbaum, M., 88n

O'Connor, D. K., 12
Odysseus, 12
O'Hagan, J., 55
Olbrechts-Tyteca, L., 34, 140–1, 141n, 161, 167
Orban, C., 67
Orwell, G., 147–8
Ost, F., 38

Peczenik, A., 44, 150n
Peirce, C. S., 69
Perelman, C., 1, 34, 140–1, 141n, 161, 167
Petroski, K., 120–1, 125

Pettit, P., 38
Philipopoulous-Mihalopoulos, A., 6n
Pimont, S., 16
Plantin, C., 140–1, 141n
Plato, 12, 29–30, 30n
Pomeranz, W., 158
Popov, V. I., 163n
Popovici, A., 17
Posner, R., 40
Poulter, S., 52
Precht, J., 73
Protagoras, 30
Puchta, G. F., 40
Putz, C., 69

Radbruch, G., 38
Ranger, T. O., 51
Rattansi, A., 53
Ravaioli, P., 53–5
Rawls, J., 57
Raz, J., 52
Reale, M., 93
Remote, F., 54
Rheinstein, M., 159, 166
Riedel, M., 95
Rosen, L., 62
Rudan, P., 116
Ryakhovskaya, T. I., 163

Sagandykov, M. S., 163n
Sajo, A., 156
Sallust, 66
Sarat, A., 34–5, 62
Savigny, F. K. Von, 45
Scalia, A., 120, 122–3
Schank, R. C., 126
Schapp, 42
Schauer, F., 38, 127, 144n
Scheppele, K. L, 17
Scherrer, C. P., 52
Schlag, P., 127
Schmid, W., 146
Schulz, F., 92, 94
Scott, R., 15

Scotti, G., 60
Seibert, T. M., 87
Shakespeare, W., 1, 28
Shapiro, M., 158
Simon-Shoshan, M., 141
Simpson, A. W. B., 16–17
Škop, M., 139, 146
Slocum, B., 119, 121n
Smejkalová, T., 139, 142n, 143, 146, 150
Smith, P. C., 10–11
Soboleva, A., 164n, 165, 166n
Socrates, 12, 30
Stalnaker, R. C., 126
Statsky, W. P., 157
Sterelny, K., 129
Stern, S., 17
Stevenson, D., 139
Stone, J., 161
Strassfeld, R. N., 119n
Summers, R. S., 139, 165
Sunstein, C. R., 116n

Tamanaha, B. Z., 84
Tammelo, I., 161
Taruffo, M., 165
Taylor, C., 12
Thankerton, Lord, 22
Thumma, S. A., 121n
Timofeyev, M., 162–3
Tisias, 30
Tomlins, C., 6n
Toracca, T., 9
Truffin, B., 56
Tylor, E. B., 53–4

Umbach, M., 69
Unger, R. M., 18, 21, 23

Van Den Akker, C., 70
Vaquero, Á. Nuñez, 38, 40
Vaypan, G., 167
Viehweg, T., 95, 160
Vismann, C., 5, 16

Waldron, J., 60, 93–4
Walton, D. N., 140
Walzer, M., 57
Warrington, R. 88–90
Weber, E., 51
Weinstein, J., 121n
Welsch, W., 87–8
Wetzel, L., 67–8
White, J. B., 10–11, 15, 17, 35, 144n
Wilberforce, Lord, 20

Winter, S. L., 24
Wittgenstein, L., 10, 23, 24, 68, 87
Wolterstorff, N., 68

Yershov, V., 163
Young, I. M., 53, 58

Zamboni, C., 105, 106
Zemach, E., 68
Zerilli, L. M. G., 10

EU representative:
Easy Access System Europe
Mustamäe tee 50, 10621 Tallinn, Estonia
Gpsr.requests@easproject.com

www.ingramcontent.com/pod-product-compliance
Lightning Source LLC
Chambersburg PA
CBHW070358240426
43671CB00013BA/2558